DISCLAIMER AND COPYRIGHT

Assertion of facts and opinions expressed in this book represent the best efforts of the authors and are not intended to reflect the views, opinions, or official policies of the Loudoun County Democratic Committee or other political or campaign organizations. Although the authors have made every effort to ensure that the information in this book was correct at press time, they do not assume and hereby disclaim any liability to any party for any loss, damage, or disruption caused by errors or omissions, whether such errors or omissions result from negligence, accident, or any other cause.

Copyright © 2012 by Swing County LLC. All rights reserved. No part of this publication may be reproduced, distributed, or transmitted in any form or by any means, including photocopying, recording, or other electronic or mechanical methods, without the prior written permission of Swing County LLC, except in the case of brief quotations embodied in critical reviews and certain other noncommercial uses permitted by copyright law. For permission requests, go to www.swingcounty.com

First Edition

SWING COUNTY

WWW.SWINGCOUNTY.COM

DEDICATION

We dedicate this book to those who have left this earth during or after the Great Campaign of 2008. Their contributions to this mighty effort are truly appreciated and will not be forgotten.

Joyce McLaurin
Mukit Hossain
Dan Brigham
Tina Gulland
Judy Coughlin
Alice Flemming-Williams

TABLE OF CONTENTS

Introduction 1
Prologue 6
Swing County in a Swing State 10
The Grass Grows from the Roots 19
The Early Bird Gets the Worm 38
Primary Time 61
Those Who Know the Rules, RULE 80
The Nitty Gritty Of Inside Politics 100
Convention Combat 119
Marking Time 130
Dramatis Personae 146
And a Cast of Thousands 181
The Big Rumble 207
The Election Week Brawl 232
Celebration 243
Where Are They Now 257
Epilogue 262
Afterword 268

Introduction

"This is the true joy of life. The being used for a purpose recognized by yourself as a mighty one. The being a force of nature instead of a feverish, selfish little clod of ailments and grievances complaining that the world will not devote itself to making you happy.

"I am of the opinion that my life belongs to the whole community, and as long as I live, it is my privilege to do for it whatever I can. I want to be thoroughly used up when I die. For the harder I work, the more I live.

"Life is no brief candle to me. It is a sort of splendid torch which I've got a hold of for a moment, and I want to make it burn as brightly as possible before handing it on to future generations." —Man and Superman, George Bernard Shaw, 1903

This is the story of how a newly targeted swing county in a newly targeted swing state attempted to 'change the world' in the 2008 presidential election.

When we began, we pondered the probable audience: political junkies; Obama enthusiasts; potential volunteers; historians; or some combination of them. We started the book without nailing it down. Participants' recollections from Barack Obama's announcement in early 2007 through his Inauguration in 2009 were a powerful emotional experience for them and for the interviewers.

It really came down to this: our hope is that this book will be read by those of you who have not yet had the exhilarating experience of working for a cause that is outside the usual parameters of life—school, work, marriage, and family. We hope that this book will stimulate you to work hard with others for a cause greater than yourselves, with a vision of improving the world. With Obama, many of us had found a worthwhile cause.

In the first decade of the 21st century, the political scene changed dramatically in Loudoun County, Virginia. The population surge of young, highly educated, independent, diverse 'swing voters' forced local and statewide candidates of both parties to increase substantially their focus and campaign resources in this county. However, these efforts did not include presidential campaigns. Both sides had rated the state as a safe win for Republicans for nearly a half-century and thus 'not in play.' All that changed in 2008.

Loudoun County, Virginia, is indeed special. It is a large

county in the Washington, DC exurbs. For the last decade it has been rated in the top ten for population growth, jobs, and family income, and is populated by thousands of fierce independents. For half a century, it has been a reliable predictor of Virginia's voting outcomes, and neither the state nor county had voted Democratic in Presidential elections since Lyndon Johnson carried both in 1964.

Using Barack Obama's national website, I founded the Loudoun County for Obama (LCO) grassroots 'Group' shortly after his announcement for President on February 10, 2007. Obama insisted his national campaign empower local people throughout the nation *to organize themselves*. This turned out to be one of the major keys to our success. Members of grassroots organizations are often of different political persuasions, frequently new to politics, and usually prefer to operate outside the formal structure of a political party or campaign. Starting this organization in Loudoun County was critical, since the local Democratic Party remained uncommitted until the presidential nominee was officially chosen, 18 months later.

Marcia Carlyn discovered this LCO website just a couple of weeks after it was approved and in no time at all, she accepted my invitation to be a co-administrator of the website and the group. This was without a doubt the best decision I made during the campaign. Over the next year, the two of us did everything we could think of to expand and train our grassroots network. As we approached the Virginia primary in February 2008 (the week after 'Super Tuesday'), we were excited about our prospects. Our grassroots organization had grown to over 500 diverse, enthusiastic, creative supporters who been taught the basics, but had added their own numerous creative ideas to this business of local campaigning. We were determined to do everything possible to add to Obama's momentum by giving him a big primary win in Loudoun County. We were on our own until Obama was certain to be the Democratic nominee in June of 2008.

I am a native Californian, and soon after graduating from UCLA with an engineering degree, I moved to Virginia Beach in 1963. There I learned the political ropes, and within a year I was actively engaged in grassroots politics, primarily in opposition to the entrenched Democratic Byrd political machine (and they were experts at the game). Being denied a role within the party, I threw myself into local and state campaigns for issues and candidates, usually in a leadership role. We did have a number of successful campaigns, and although my political allies and I were frozen out of the local Democratic Party for several years, I successfully ran the

Virginia Beach 1976 Jimmy Carter campaign and consequently became a National Delegate.

Shortly after my divorce in 1978, I moved north to heavily populated Fairfax County, and within a few months, was elected as one of the Vice Chairs of the local Democratic committee. Fifteen years after that, I moved to Loudoun County, joined the Loudoun County Democratic Committee (LCDC), ran a number of campaigns, and served as the Democratic County Chair in 1999 and 2000.

By contrast, Marcia was new to Loudoun County and had never been active with the local Democratic committee. She proved to complement me perfectly with her communication and database skills, her drive, intelligence, and most of all—her enthusiasm! It was infectious, and through her, hundreds of new people caught the political bug. In most ways she was the voice of this grassroots campaign.

Marcia was born in Buffalo, NY, spent her childhood in Arlington, VA and earned degrees from the University of Wisconsin (BS), Stanford University (MS), and Michigan State University (MBA, PhD). She worked in the 1980s for the Democratic Speaker of the Michigan House of Representatives as Director of Data Processing and held other positions in the public and private sector. In 1995 she established her own business (Carlyn Consulting), which specialized in program evaluation and strategic planning to improve organizational performance. Her experience and contributions proved to be invaluable to our grassroots efforts.

In the production of this book, I was fortunate to recruit two very talented writers to join me—Ed Robisheaux and Ann Robinson. The book reflects Ed's unique voice as narrator. Unbeknownst to Marcia and me, he and his wife, Barbara, had worked on the Obama campaign directly through the national campaign and then for one of the local campaign organizations. They knocked on about a thousand doors and made over 2,000 phone calls for Obama. Neither of them had ever worked in a campaign before, nor were they ever involved with a political party. Coincidentally, Barbara spent most of her early years in Southern California within ten miles of my residence at the time. It is a small world.

Ed was born in Houston in 1947 and moved with his family to Corpus Christi, Texas in 1952. He graduated from Texas Tech University in 1968 with a BA degree in History and attended the University of Oregon from 1968-1972 where he earned a PhD in History. Ed has done research in numerous historical archives in

France and the United States.

S. Ann Robinson, Contributing Writer/Editor, wrote the Prologue, Chapter 10, the Epilogue and most of the other individual profile sketches of our featured participants. She previously had worked with me in the LCDC for seven years as a volunteer, Treasurer, and then district chair. Ann was born in Texas, graduated from The University of Texas in Austin, and arrived in Virginia after traveling throughout the U.S. and Europe with her military spouse, an army officer. She actively supported local campaigns in Loudoun with time and money for 15 years, writing and speaking not only for candidates but for progressive issues as well. Her most recent trend analyses can be found at www.shenandoahpress.org.

For two years, Ann's by-line, "S. Ann Robinson," headed *The Issue Barometer*, a monthly global corporate subscription publication, where she worked as a staff writer and research assistant. As a freelance author, Ms. Robinson publishes numerous [paid] pieces in the Shenandoah Press and nonfiction anthologies, as well as in fiction and poetry. A former business manager/comptroller, Ann also works for three area community colleges instructing career-minded adults in Workforce Development accounting courses and leading seminars on "Interpreting Financial Statements."

This book is primarily a story about how the Loudoun County for Obama group organized itself into one of the strongest grassroots organizations in the Commonwealth of Virginia, and perhaps the entire United States. We operated independently of, and without direction from, any Democratic Party organization or campaign for 18 months. The paid staffers of the State Coordinated Campaign arrived in early June 2008 and the Obama campaign staffers immediately followed; they were separate campaign organizations. At this point the role of our grassroots organization dramatically changed.

How we adapted to this new reality is an important part of our story. We describe the ups and downs of this change, along with the resulting conflicts and their resolutions. We explain how the major players and power organizations successfully combined to coordinate thousands of new volunteers who poured into the county from all parts of the nation (and the world) to turn the presidential vote in Loudoun County Blue.

This book is a collaboration, not only among the three of us, but also with 150 people who consented to oral interviews, including most of the key players. All interviews were digitally recorded and are available for libraries and historians who wish to go into the details of what happened here. Although we are disappointed that none of the Obama paid staffers participated in the interviews, those around them freely did so, and we have done our best to describe the staffers' very significant work. In the end, we believe we have drawn an accurate picture of their very capable and energetic contributions because of interviews from multiple sources.

Many thanks go to Jill Winter for copy-editing, useful suggestions, and her unflagging personal support, Deb Morbeto for all of the design, covers, website, and marketing, and Larry Roeder and Cindy Winter for production assistance. Thanks to Marcia Carlyn as well for her many contributions to this project.

Compiling this book has in itself been a unique learning experience. Interviewing and then listening to and analyzing these recorded interviews have been extremely rewarding. It allowed us to expand our understanding of what turned out to be the most exciting and historic campaign of our lifetimes.

As we listened to the interviews, we were constantly amazed and awed at the size and scope of the campaign in Loudoun County. In addition to the organizational volunteers, we found many who had volunteered in virtual isolation, motivated simply by their own conviction that they were making a difference in a decisive way. Their biographies led us to the conclusion that Loudoun County was blessed with some of the finest and most politically motivated people who participated in this historic election.

We are proud of our work in the Great Campaign of 2008, and we are proud of our President. We helped to change the world. It doesn't get better than that.

Rolland D. 'Rollie' Winter
October 2012

Book Note: We urge the readers to submit book corrections and suggestions to our website: www.swingcounty.com There you will also find the Appendix, some interviews, and pictures.

Prologue

The young father looked at her in dismay. *"Is it over? Have we missed it? I just got off work!"*

Each hand held that of a child: a boy about seven years old; a girl maybe five. They gazed at her, panting from exertion, faces crumbling in disappointment—both his and the children's.

"No," replied the older woman, *"you can still make it. He was still speaking. I had to leave early to ....."*

But before she could finish, the man swung his daughter onto his hip and began running again in the direction of a field where more than 30,000 people stood in the October sunlight pledging a covenant with Barack Obama.

The cheers and chants of the enthralled supporters reached the ears of the smiling senior as she watched the young family sprint—first past the historic Harrison House where Robert E. Lee and his generals had planned the Battle of Antietam in 1862, and then past a quarter-mile row of 4ft x 6ft McCain/Palin yard signs—so they, too, could answer: *"Yes we can!" "Yes we can!"*

Shouts of grandiose hyperbole on October 22, 2008, in Leesburg, Virginia? A "fairy tale"? Not at all. Virginia had changed the world many times before. And, even if the tens of thousands of people who gathered in that sun-drenched field in Leesburg were not in that moment thinking of history, history was nonetheless thinking of them. An easy day's journey from Jamestown, Monticello, Williamsburg, Mount Vernon, Yorktown, Philadelphia, Harpers Ferry, Bull Run, Antietam, Gettysburg, the Twin Towers Memorial, Wall Street—and only minutes away from the nation's Capitol, the Pentagon, and Arlington Cemetery—the crowd stood listening, as serenely centered as the hub of a wheel, the wheel which had so often driven the country's destiny into world-changing leadership.

There, the soul of Virginia hung in the air: *"Give me liberty or give me death"*; *"We hold these truths to be self-evident"*; *"We the People, in order to form a more perfect Union"*; *"Congress shall make no law respecting an establishment of religion, or prohibiting the free exercise thereof."* The forces that formed a Nation and held it together, while most of Europe fell prey to the tyranny of anarchy that birthed a dictator, were the voices that led the debates in the halls, councils and homes of Virginians: Patrick Henry, Thomas Jefferson, James Madison,

George Mason. All were tied to a clear and undying faith in the enduring pragmatism of George Washington.

Yes, Virginians had every right—possibly even every responsibility—to assume that their choices could again change America and change the world. But that responsibility did not lead automatically to a particular choice in this presidential election. Just as the early Virginia dynasty had hammered out the compromises to contain all the forces behind individualism, nationalism, states' rights, agrarian culture and economic progress—and just as in 1861, when Loudoun County voted first to remain with the Union, then changed its vote and joined the Confederacy (after Fort Sumter was fired upon), but then revealed its torment by providing a Union regiment—the Commonwealth and many in the County were not of one mind in 2008.

Not only were all of the earlier issues still at play in wealthy, highly educated Loudoun County, but all of the unrequited angst of the last 40 years as well: the hovering "ghosts of Vietnam" still haunting their memorial. The wilderness wandering of civil rights advocates after the death of Martin Luther King, Jr., the persistence of the Sons of the Confederacy to justify their history, the cry of strong women for their potential to be fulfilled. These yearning demands found embodied expression here in the mayor who had been a naval officer, the councilwoman who had fought in Desert Storm, the older woman who had worked with Gloria Steinem, the Vietnam veteran who had flown helicopter sorties in three tours of duty. The barbershop owner, who as a young Black man had been told he could not give haircuts to his friends, the elder African-American woman who had heard Martin Luther King's "*I Have a Dream*" speech as a girl and then been told as a woman to work 13-hour shifts on every Election Day, serving the parties of the rich and famous instead of voting. In 2006, a Leesburg councilman proposed adding Confederate flag symbols to the Town gateways.

As Loudoun County chose, so would the State and the Nation. The world waited and hoped—its thoughts no less mythic—as the Four Horses of the Apocalypse strained for release: terrorism in the name of righteousness, an unjustified war in Iraq with the specter of torture shaming a proud people, economic failure of the global markets highlighting a stark divide between rich and poor. Would pandemic catastrophe be unleashed or held in check? These anxieties met in the cafes and coffee shops of Loudoun: the colonel who served at the Pentagon on 9/11, the returning foot soldier from

Afghanistan, the Muslim family whose house had been raided without a warrant, the teacher whose home fell into foreclosure.

The heightened energy attracted the very young—an 11-year old girl who squeezed and pleaded her way through a crowd to touch the hand of Sarah Palin, and a 12-year-old boy who walked the streets with his handmade Obama flyers day after day, replacing his burned yard signs in the mornings, undaunted. And the very old—a 95-year old activist who circulated a ballot petition, promoted voter registration, and hosted a campaign postcard-writing party.

All of the campaigns met all of the forces here in Loudoun County. The outcome could not be predicted. Just as the idealism and fervent demands of the 18th century required pragmatic action and, above all, a political person who could weave the disparate parts into a whole, the decision point of 2007-2008 would be seized by the heirs of James Madison's temperament—those who "knew the ropes" and how to connect otherwise unrelated interests into a functioning body.

But in a county with only eight percent African-American voters and no university campus to bolster new voting rolls, the campaign season had begun in 2007 with low expectations by most Loudoun Democrats, fully aware that local Republican meetings often attracted many more active voters than their own.

Loudoun County, Virginia, had been conservative for 44 years. Every presidential election since 1965 had resulted in a majority vote for the Republican candidate. The county was also one of the last in the country to comply with school integration orders, and in 1968 county officials ordered the municipal pool destroyed rather than let Black children swim with white.

Yet, over a 20-month period, from February 2007 to November 2008, the grassroots "Loudoun County for Obama" community, led by Rollie Winter and Marcia Carlyn, grew from a tiny group of three to over 4,000 supporters. They hosted over 1,000 events, raised nearly $80,000 for the national campaign, and created such a tight-knit, highly functioning organization that when the paid staffers arrived from the national headquarters late in the day, they were handed a ground game that actually had a shot at winning.

What originally inspired them and their earliest recruits in 2007, even though Senator Obama polled 20 points behind Senator Hillary Clinton? How did they turn this inspiration into an energetic, creative movement long before the Virginia primary? What were the challenges of working through tensions between the various Power

Groups in the campaign? When a strong grassroots movement bubbled up to meet a roiling top-down campaign machine, everything depended on one key ability.

This is Loudoun's story.

A. Ann Robinson

Swing County in a Swing State

That's my point, Virginia. That's how this thing started. It shows you what one voice can do. One voice can change a room. And if a voice can change a room, it can change a city. And if it can change a city, it can change a state. And if it can change a state, it can change a nation. And if it can change a nation, it can change the world. Virginia, your voice can change the world tomorrow. In 21 hours if you are willing to endure some rain, if you are willing to drag that person you know is not going to vote to the polls, if you are willing to organize and volunteer in the offices, if you are willing to stand with me, if you are willing to fight with me, I know your voice will matter. So I just got one question for you, Virginia. Are you Fired Up? Are you Ready to Go? Fired Up! Ready to Go! Fired Up! Ready to Go! Fired Up! Ready to Go! Virginia, let's go change the world.—Barack Obama, Virginia, November 3, 2008

Can I have your whole mind for a few minutes?

On an early September day 2008 in the parking lot of Heritage High School on the southeast side of Leesburg, Amanda Millard laid out the stakes for about ten of us. It was a bright sunny day, and it was hot, hot, hot. John McCain had just taken the lead in the polls over Barack Obama. Amanda was a paid staffer for the combined Democratic campaign in Loudoun (called Virginia Victory 2008 or VV08 for short). The combination part comes from the three candidates running for President, U.S. Senate, and House of Representatives. Amanda came from Alexandria, Virginia, but her assigned territory was the small towns, rural suburbs, and countryside in Loudoun County. Amanda was all campaign professional all the time.

"People," Amanda said, "I've just got off the phone and was told we have to win Virginia to win the election. It's not optional anymore. We have to win this state. And to win this state we have to win Loudoun County. As Loudoun County goes, so goes Virginia." Conrad Chafee, another staffer with the VV08 Campaign, later told me that Amanda's announcement came after Sarah Palin's candidacy briefly lifted the McCain campaign ahead of the Obama campaign in the polls.

A month later, the day before the election, I was up with the sun in Philomont and had to get to the Obama field office in

Leesburg pronto. Philomont is an old town, been here since at least 1830, though nobody really knows when it was founded. Legend has it the place was named from the contraction of "Philo," meaning brotherly love, and "mont," because the village is at the foot of the Blue Ridge Mountains. In the mid 1920's, Philomont (population around 70 on a cool day) sported seven drug stores that sold patent medicine out the front doors and moonshine whiskey out the back doors. The liquor was distilled on the banks of the Beaver Dam Creek three miles southeast of the village. In America, Prohibition was on but in Philomont it was off. In Philomont in 2008, the moonshine was off but the election was on. It was going to be a hell of a day, but I didn't know it then, not at 9:30 a.m. on the morning of November 3, the day before the Great Campaign of 2008.

If you are wondering who I am, I will tell you that I'm a nobody. I am a volunteer worker for the Obama Campaign in Loudoun County, Virginia. I'm but an extra in this grand theatrical production known as the 2008 Obama Campaign. I'm a nobody, but in March 2008 I volunteered to try to Make a Difference, one of thousands of nobodies in Loudoun County who got off their sofas so that Maybe This Time, in this election, Maybe Things Could be Different.

This is not MY story; this is OUR story, the story of those who worked in the Obama Campaign in Loudoun County from 2006-2008. There were a lot of us, well over 10,000 when said and done—including a bunch of folks who came here from other Virginia counties, other states, and even other countries—in a county with a population of 300,000. We have a story to tell about how a grassroots group that started out with only two "believers" 20 months earlier became one of the keys to Barack Obama's ultimate victory. We were trying to do one hell of a thing here, and it is one hell of a tale to tell. So let's start telling it.

This morning it's breakfast. Then it's off to Leesburg, Virginia and the Obama Campaign field headquarters on Market Street adjacent to Dodona Manor, the former home of George Marshall, Chief of Staff of the United States Army in World War II and the major force behind the post-war "Marshall Plan".

Loudoun County, Virginia, was hived off Fairfax County in 1757. This place reeks of history. When the British invaded Washington during the War of 1812, twenty-two wagon loads of documents, including the Declaration of Independence and the Constitution of the United States, were hidden in the cellar of

Rokeby House 2.4 miles south of Leesburg here in Loudoun County. Charles Binns II, clerk of the circuit court of Loudoun County, built Rokeby House in 1757. It's still there. You can still see the vaulted room in the cellar where they hid the documents, though you have to make private arrangements to do it. I've seen it. I have photographs of it. You can get them too; you just have to get off your Barcalounger to get them.

James Monroe once lived near the village of Aldie in Loudoun County. Aldie is just southwest of Rokeby House and is where the Little River Turnpike, now Route 50, intersects the Little River. George Mercer built the original gristmill here in 1765. The gristmill still stands and on weekends they will mill wheat and corn for you. Three battles were fought here during the Civil War in the summer of 1863. In June of the same year, George Armstrong Custer of The Little Bighorn fame on a bet tried to jump the Little River on his horse. He didn't make it.

The "Old Red Head," Arthur Godfrey, also known as the "Warbling Banjoist of Baltimore," did his radio show from Beacon Hill outside of Leesburg in the 1950s. Godfrey built the first airport in Leesburg to accommodate his private plane and was riding high until he fired the celebrated crooner Julius La Rosa live on the air in 1953. Jack Beavers, another nobody, parks his private plane there today, and it was used from time to time in the Great Campaign of 2008. Relatives of the Godfrey family still live in Philomont not far from the Hibbs Bridge where the Beaver Dam Creek crosses the Snickersville Turnpike. Yeah, that's where all that whiskey was distilled and sold out the back doors of the drug stores in Philomont during Prohibition. They don't call them drug stores for nothing.

The day before the election, it came down to this. Virginia, which had not voted Democratic in a presidential election since 1964, was now in play and a critical swing state. If the Obama Campaign could carry Virginia, it could carry the nation. Loudoun County's thousands of volunteers for the Obama Campaign were now at the focal point of something really big. If we could swing this county, we could swing this state, and if we could swing this state, we could swing this country, and we were just naive enough to think we could do it. That's where things stood on the morning of November 3, 2008.

I drive into the parking lot at the Leesburg Obama headquarters on Market Street and find one of the few remaining parking places. It's 10 a.m., I'm right on time, and there are people everywhere. The place looks like an ant bed. I've never seen anything like it; I don't ever expect to see anything like it ever again. Newbies are everywhere being trained to canvass, knotted up in groups all over the parking lot. There are big circles of canvassers with a staging manager in the center of each group. I spot Tracy Hadden Loh, the finest phone banker I ever witnessed during the campaign, but now she's standing there canvass training like the Pied Piper of Leesburg surrounded by newcomers trying to learn in 15 minutes how to go out and Make A Difference.

I whistle in to the HQ and spot Gail Wise, a fixture in this place. I don't think I ever went into that office when I didn't see Gail Wise, a key leader in the grassroots Loudoun County for Obama movement since the first of the year. What a hero. Gail was an important figure in making that office effective. When the Obama field organizers arrived in early July and opened the Leesburg HQ, Gail realized right away that they were overloaded and needed help. She volunteered to greet Obama supporters who stopped by, recruited some Eager Beavers to help her, and handled a lot of the office logistics. The Eager Beavers were a bunch of local residents who had given their heart and souls and hundreds of volunteer hours to Hope and Change for the last several months. Today at the HQ, the joint is jumping. I mean, it's a zoo inside, crammed with people; there must be 50 of them in there, a veritable rabbit warren of activity.

I'm looking for Amanda Millard, my field organizer who got me into canvassing some five months ago. Five months ago—it seems like an eternity since I started out on this adventure after discovering MyBarackObama.com (MyBO for short), the incredible social networking website created by Chris Hughes for the national Obama campaign. More about MyBO later; we'll also say a lot more about canvassing in due time. Amanda works for one of several groups that have been active on the Democratic side in Loudoun. At times these groups were fighting like cats and dogs, but I knew nothing of it at the time. Some pretty surprising things happened here.

Amanda is nowhere to be found. So I go on the porch, and soon here she comes with her Dad right behind her. Now we're going to get some action. Amanda comes in, heads off for a room that passes for an office, and I go in the office. It's David Cannady's office. I never knew where Dad went.

"OK, I said, what do we do today?" Amanda hands me a

canvassing package, which is a list of addresses where I'm supposed to knock on doors and ask a series of questions.

One look at the canvassing package and I look at Amanda and say, "You can't give me this! I can't believe this! I can't do this!" And she says, "Why not?" And I say, "Because yesterday I was running that Canvass Staging Operation out of Rosemeade Street in Leesburg and I sent two canvassers into this same complex and the property manager of the place grabbed them and told them to get out or she would call the police and have them thrown in jail! And she said if anyone else came into this place, they were going to jail too. Amanda, you must be kidding!" And she said, "Well, go and give it one more try."

I can't believe it. I think, it's a kamikaze mission, and I don't want to spend election night in jail. I want to watch the election results on television.

I head out of Amanda's "office" and a few feet away there's a kid standing there who looks positively lost. One look at him and I know he's wandered in from the street, and he really is lost. He has that look about him that he's come to volunteer to do something, but nobody has taken him under his wing yet. and he's clueless. Later, I learned he wasn't a kid. He was 26 years old, and he was in the Navy. Like any good sailor, he needs a Sea Daddy.

So I go up to him and say, "Hi, you looking to volunteer for the campaign?" And he says, "Yes." "OK, well, I'm going to do some canvassing, you wanna come with me and learn how to do it?" And he says, "Yes, I would like that." "Good, I'll show you how to do it, then tomorrow you can show someone else how to do it," and he says "Great." So I say, "OK, I got a canvassing package here, and we have to sign it out, and then we'll be outta here."

We sign the package out, and then we're off to the car. My car. On the right, Tracy Hadden Loh is still holding forth. Unbelievable. She's sitting on the balcony of the porch. "We don't know whether this is going to work," she says. "Nobody has ever attempted a Get Out The Vote operation on this scale before. It's either going to flop or be a big success, but we don't know which." I'm thinking, this scene is like something out of Fellini's movie *8½*. All those nuns lined up. Marching, marching, marching. I wave at Tracy. She doesn't wave back. She's totally into what she's doing.

We get in the car, and I introduce myself, "My name is Ed, what's your name?" "James." And I said, "James, have you ever done this kind of thing before?" "No, I never have." So I said, "James, why are you doing it now?" And he said, "I'm doing it for my kids."

It was what we in the campaign called a "Golly Gee Moment". We'd all had them. Someone would say something about why they were out in the street campaigning, and then everyone in earshot would lean back and think, "Golly Gee!" We were never prepared for these moments when they happened, and they didn't happen very often, but they did happen. Such moments hadn't occurred in my previous campaigns, which was why it was so startling in this one. Moments like this popped everything into focus. It reminded us of why we were doing this. It reminded us why we were fed up and why we wanted things to be different This Time.

"James, we're not going to do a normal canvass this morning," I said. "We've been given a property complex to canvass where I sent people yesterday. It's a gated community and everything inside is private property. Yesterday the property manager threatened to call the police and have our people thrown in jail. She said anyone else coming in there from the campaign would have trespassing charges filed against him or her. So I told our people to get out of there. Most canvassing isn't like that. This one will be really tough. We can't get caught. We're looking at the coppers and the maybe slammer if we're caught."

There's dead silence in the car for a while, and then James said, "I've got an idea." I asked, "What's your idea?" He said, "Well, suppose we go in there and ask for the sales manager. I'm getting out of the Navy in about six months, and we can tell the sales manager that we were just driving by, saw the place, and decided to check it out. You know, they might think differently about us if they think we're looking to buy."

I think about this for a while and then say, "James, that sounds pretty good to me. Let's give it a try." So we arrive in the parking lot and we strip all campaign stickers, buttons, hats, everything off us that could give us away as working for the Obama campaign. We get out of the car and head for the main office, where a lady comes up and asks if she can help us. And I said we'd like to see the sales manager because we were interested in maybe buying a unit in the complex. The lady says we must mean the property manager because the property manager does all the sales. I'm thinking, "No, not the property manager! That's the one who threatened to put our people in jail," but now there's no way out. So here comes the property manager. I say with a straight face, "My name is Ed and this is my friend James and we were driving by and saw this place from the road and it looked interesting. James here is getting out of the Navy in about six months, and he's looking for a place to buy."

So the property manager launches into her act—talking talking talking—showering James with literature, and then says, "I've got a demonstrator unit I'd like to show you if you have time." And James with a straight face says, "Well, I don't know if Ed here has the time to see a demonstrator unit. Ed, do you have time?" And I said, "Well, we're here so we might as well take a look." Off we go to see the demonstrator unit.

When we walked in, I clearly remember looking down at the carpet on the floor and thinking to myself, "White white white is the color of our carpet." This, of course, is a line right out of Mel Brooks' movie *The Producers*. The property manager begins showing the place to James. I mean, he's going to be the buyer of this $400,000 place when he's out of the Navy with no income, probably on a liar loan, but then this whole bit is just a scam so we can get into the property and canvass it. The whole scenario is yet another improbable thing in a campaign that itself is wholly improbable, except this one we are living out in real time. Perception is reality.

Suddenly James lifts his arm and points at the carpet. He then tells the property manager that the color of the carpet isn't good because he has two small children. "Can we change the carpet to a different color?" And she says, "No problem. We'll rip that carpet out and put whatever color of carpet you want." Then James points at the wall and says, "Can we change the paint on these walls? My kids are going to be hard on them." She says something to the effect that we'll paint the walls whatever color you want.

This canvass had clearly "gone circus." When a canvass goes circus, there's no telling what will happen next or where it will end up. In fact, this canvass had gone beyond circus—it had gone carnival, which is bigger and wilder than a circus. And believe me, at this point I had knocked on over a thousand doors in this campaign. I know what a canvass circus and carnival look like. Wild stuff can happen. Moreover, when a canvass goes circus the last person to know is the canvasser himself. That's just the way it is. Often you don't know the thing has gone circus until you've left the door and had some time to sort out all the stuff that happened. This time, what would happen next was utterly unpredictable.

Back at the door I'm thinking, what in the hell is going on here? How did this happen? I'm supposed to be teaching him how to canvass, and now he's teaching me. I'm the guy that's knocked a thousand doors and made 2,000 phone calls for Obama, but now I am a student to a teacher who's never done any of this before.

In retrospect, here's another understanding of this happening. In this campaign, stuff bubbled up from the bottom. In this campaign totally unpredictable things happened because of the unique inspirations of "we the people." Volunteers routinely came up with their own solutions to problems. With no one telling us what to do, we figured things out ourselves. And this freedom empowered us. Read this paragraph again. It's the essence of what happened here in Loudoun County. James came to an understanding of what needed to be done, and he did it. It was "we the people" in action.

Meanwhile, I'm wondering, "How in the world did I end up talking to a property manager in a gated community on the southeast side of Leesburg, Virginia discussing a $400,000 property we have no intention of buying when all we really wanted to do was to help the Obama campaign win this election?" And somehow I'm caught up in a surreal drama with jail on the one side and a canvass for no pay on the other. Call it what you want, for me it's another Golly Gee Moment, and like all Golly Gee Moments, it came out of nowhere.

At this point, the property manager thinks she has a mark because James has asked so many questions. She was living proof that the propensity of human beings for self-delusion is literally without limit. "I can tell you are really interested in this place," she says. "I have another demonstrator unit I'd like to show you." James asks me if I have time to see it too. "Well, we're here," I say, "we might as well."

So we go to the next demonstrator unit. Inside the second demonstrator it's the same carnival as the first, except this time James wants to change the plumbing fixtures in the bathroom. Can you imagine that? He's not happy with the gold plated plumbing fixtures. I couldn't believe it. "I'm not a gold plated kind of guy," he says, and I'm all but busting a gut trying not to break out laughing. I mean, right now I've got some serious personal control problems here.

"No problem," says the property manager, "We'll put whatever you want in there." This just isn't real. Tell me this is not real.

Finally the property manager says, "James, why don't you take some time and tour the property. We have a nice facility here. You can see the recreation room, the pool, the landscaping, the buildings, everything." And James says, "Do we have time to do that?" And I said, "Well, sounds OK to me."

So now we've managed to get an invitation to walk the grounds of a gated community to do our secret canvass. It is what we wanted to do all along, and it is as improbable an event as anything else in this improbable campaign. And we've done it with a creative 26-year-old young man who has never canvassed a door in his life and may never do so again. It's a bubble up from the bottom moment if ever there was one.

We walked back to the car for canvassing packages, put them down our coats, and we canvassed every unit in the joint. We canvassed the hell out of that place. We knocked every door on that walk list. Yes, every one of them. When we finished, we drove back to Amanda's office to have lunch. I said to her with pride, "You are not going to believe what we just did." I told her the story, and she said, "Ed, I can't believe you did that." And I said, "Amanda, I didn't do it, WE did it." It was in miniature the story of this campaign.

Right there, you can see the type of grassroots energy and creativity that was the key to Making It Happen in Loudoun County. A young man who had never canvassed a door in his life taught someone who had knocked a thousand doors how to 'Make It Happen'. We saw this kind of thing time and time again—native energy sparking creative imagination to solve practical problems. The history of this campaign was never about ME, but always about US. Nobody did it; WE did it.

This is our history. It's the story of Rollie Winter, the story of Marcia Carlyn, and the tale of the Bus Lady, the Shoe Lady, the Teamster Brothers, the Post Card Ladies, the Brit Lady, the Cookie Lady, the Brick Lady, the Muffin Lady, the Button Lady and many more. It's Joyce McLaurin's inspirational biography. It's about Hope and Change, the inspiration that This Time Things Can Be Different, the belief that We Are a Better People Than This; it's the story of thousands of Nobodies who came out to Make A Difference and who really Wanted to Make a Difference This Time. It is how an improbable grassroots campaign started in 2006 with one person and grew into thousands to take to the Loudoun streets to Make It Happen. It's a barn-burner of a story. It's how we tried to flip a county to flip a state to flip a nation. It's the story of a swing county in a swing state and what happened here. It's the story of our experiences, our hopes, our dreams, and why some of us even quit our jobs to do it. We think we have one great story to tell. And now we're going to tell it.

The Grass Grows from the Roots

But here's what I understand, that as long as all of us are together, as long as we are all committed, then there's nothing we can't do. That's why we started off this campaign saying, "Yes We Can!".... If you're willing to work for it, if you're willing to roll up your sleeves, if you're willing to lock arms, and march, and talk to your friends, talk to your neighbors, make a phone call, do some organizing, yes do some community organizing, then I promise you, we will win Virginia! We will win this general election and you and I together, we will change the country and change the world. God bless you and God bless the United States of America—Barack Obama, Virginia, November 1, 2008

I was up at the crack of dawn to get ready for a visit with Rollie Winter, the person who has the best overall perspective on what happened here during the campaign. Oh, and his name is pronounced Raleigh, as in Sir Walter ... He started all this craziness here in Loudoun County, and by that I mean the Obama campaign in Loudoun. It was an amazing thing because what happened here may have national implications. We executed a game plan that convinced a previous long-time Republican county to vote Democratic, and the question is: How did we do it?

So I picked up my things and this time headed out east on the Snickersville Turnpike. It's beautiful weather outside and almost everything imaginable is in bloom, and the sun on the old stone walls always makes for a picturesque view, so the drive was pretty spectacular.

The route from Philomont down the Snickersville Turnpike is a trip back into "Old Virginny." If you want to understand the Turnpike, the first thing you need to do is forget about the notion that "Snickersville" has anything to do with candy bars. That stuff is for tourists. If you're looking for candy, I suggest you go into the Philomont General Store, where you can find all the candy you want, some of it homemade, and lots of it pretty good. If you're looking for a bar, I suggest you go down to Middleburg, and there you can sit in the chair at the Red Fox Inn where Elizabeth Taylor used to drink way too much back when she was married to John Warner. Do go to Middleburg at Christmas time when you can see the annual parade of the foxhounds down Main Street.

I'm driving driving driving down the Turnpike trying to figure out how Loudoun County managed to get over 2000 people walking the streets and making calls for Obama on some days in October 2008 heading into the election. How did they turn out those crowds? And how did they find and motivate thousands of Loudoun residents before the National Obama organization had even opened its first Loudoun County field office in July 2008? It has to take one good organization to pull that off. Already I've figured out it's going to take more than a single conversation with Rollie Winter. I'm going to have to talk to him a whole lot of times and also with a whole lot of other folks. The thing here was just too big for one person to explain, and no one person can know the whole story.

Just past Mountville, I left the Turnpike and bore left on Lime Kiln Road. If you're lucky you can see the sheep behind the southeast stone wall on the right. Sheep are like sheeple, except they have far more admirable qualities and are much easier to manage. When I was young, I thought that the difference between sheep and sheeple was that sheeple didn't stink, but that was before I knocked on a thousand doors in the Obama campaign. Today I have, shall we say, a much more pedestrian view of the universe.

I'll tell you just a little more about this route into Leesburg, but I really need to get on soon with the primary story. Lime Kiln Road dead ends in the east on the Old Carolina Road, now Route 15, and renamed the James Monroe Highway. Turn left and you'll immediately pass by the Little Oatlands and Oatlands Plantations on the right—the latter being the most visited tourist attraction in Loudoun County. Rollie and his wife, Jill, have lived there or the other in a rented bungalow away from the crowds since moving to the county back in 1992. After Oatlands, go another six miles, and you reach Leesburg, the county seat. This stretch of the Old Carolina Road from Oatlands to the outskirts of Leesburg explodes in red-purple every spring when the redbud understory trees reawaken from their winter sleep—about the time the cherry trees bloom at the tidal basin in DC. Splendorific!

In fact, this road is a major part of the Journey through Hallowed Ground, a designated national scenic highway from Gettysburg to Charlottesville. According to the late historian C. Vann Woodward, this touring route has 'soaked up more of the blood, sweat, and tears of American history than any other part of the country.'

As you approach Leesburg you'll notice you don't see all those signs shilling for the Rotarians, Ruritans, the Lions Club and so forth. Of all these, I never figured out the Lions Club. I've spoken at a number of Lions Club meetings, and I've never seen a lion at any one of them.

You don't see those signs entering Leesburg because they had a big dust up here back in 2006. It seems as though the Sons of the Confederacy decided it would be a real good idea to post a Confederate battle flag on gateway roads going into Leesburg. "Heritage, not hate" they said, but that's not the way African Americans saw and see it. They thought it was Not A Very Good Idea, and they weren't the only ones to see it that way. 'The Wah' was fought largely to keep African Americans working in slavery, and seeing that battle flag when you enter town just reminds folks that the South was prepared to fight to keep some people in bondage down at places like Oatlands.

In a more modern context, the hate-mongers who chose lynching, cross burning and voter intimidation since 'The Wah', have also chosen to adopt Confederate flag symbols. The flag is sometimes used in a modern context to mean "We don't want YOU here! Stay out!" Even if that is not the intention, it is still the message received. Leesburg did well to deny this mixed message. To avoid discrimination charges against any one group, the city of Leesburg took down all organizational signs leading into the city.

Kelly Burk, who at the time was on the Leesburg Town Council, was one of those who fought this thing and said it was "not appropriate." And her side won, God bless her. I'll tell you about Kelly Burk. After strongly supporting Hillary in 2007, she became a good, solid Obama volunteer in 2008. She has the distinction of being the only known Obama volunteer in the 2008 campaign to have canvassed a naked man at the door. Yup. Kelly went out canvassing one day and had a nudist show up at the door, and the only thing he had on was his alarm clock. How about that? You can't make up stuff this good. Later I asked Kelly, "What did you do?" And Kelly said, "I tried to act as if nothing had happened." Well, excuse me; it seems as if "nothing" was exactly what did happen!

Now we're way ahead of ourselves, and we need to get back on the straight road because we must tell our story, and I am meeting Rollie at 10:00 a.m. Rollie, as it turns out, has a varied and full political activist background. But first I want to know what makes him tick. When he tells me his parents were from Nebraska, my head spins 360 degrees as I am reminded of that great line from the movie *"The Unforgiven,"* where English Bob tells Little Bill that he'd heard he was dead. And Little Bill says, "I heard that one myself, Bob. Hell, I even thought I was dead till I found out it was just I was in Nebraska." Fortunately, Rollie was born in California. And let me quickly add that Rollie doesn't share these feelings. In fact, he and his family were in Nebraska for Christmas.

His parents married in Nebraska and left that very same night for Southern California, settling in an orange grove owned by his Dad's dad in Whittier, not too far from Los Angeles. At an early age, Rollie found he liked to be a part of groups—groups with a common cause—a score or more of them. To put it plainly, he was a 'joiner' and got his jollies working with and through people in organizations. He studied how to make groups work and soon discovered parliamentary procedure—nothing complicated—just using the basic techniques of talking about one subject at a time, taking turns, not speaking until recognized, and so on. Much later he was to become a lay expert on the subject, which served him well in many subsequent organizations. He also learned at a young age that he really liked to run things—especially his way.

Rollie was fortunate to be selected an Evans Scholar, a scholarship program overseen by the Western Golf Association, attended UCLA, and majored in Engineering from 1956 to 1961. He was totally apolitical during the bland Eisenhower years. At 21, he registered as an Independent in California and voted for Richard Nixon, his one and only Republican vote in a lifetime of politics. But give him a break; he and Nixon were both born in Whittier. Before leaving for Virginia, Rollie did cast his California gubernatorial vote for Pat Brown, Jerry's dad, over Nixon.

He ignored his engineering degree and started a career in the computer business, and in 1963, he and wife hooked it to Falls Church in the Old Dominion. During the drive from California to Virginia, Rollie stopped in Nebraska to visit his maternal grandparents at the farm. He had a chat with Grandpa Harms about politics and asked him why he was a Democrat, one of very few in that Red state. His grandfather's take on it was, among other things, that Democrats generally believed the government had an obligation to help the poor and middle-class. Republicans helped rich people. Grandpa believed in Franklin Roosevelt and loved Harry Truman. Rollie finally decided he really was a Democrat.

Nine months later, Rollie's company transferred him to their new Norfolk office in southeast Virginia. He took up residence in the old Princess Anne County, now Virginia Beach. The first known settler in that area of Virginia was Adam Thoroughgood in 1622. He came over from England at age 18 as an indentured servant, a 50-cent phrase to describe a term-limited slave. They earned their freedom by working for a specified number of years, often seven.

Thoroughgood did something pretty amazing for a former indentured servant. By 1629 he had shed his servitude and a few years later became a Delegate to the Virginia House of Burgesses. When Virginia was split up into eight counties in 1637, he managed to get his prior home of Norfolk, England, into the name of the New Norfolk County. Over the years, this land was divided and re-divided into smaller and smaller parcels. However, on January 1, 1963 (eight months before Rollie arrived), the small resort city along the Atlantic Ocean called Virginia Beach merged with the surrounding Princess Anne County and created a new, much larger Virginia Beach.

When you talk about Virginia Beach, like Loudoun County, it's all about change. Just before the merger, Princess Anne County had begun its rapid growth as a bedroom community for the other Tidewater localities, primarily Norfolk. In fact, for a number of years it was the fastest growing county in the country. We'll see that same theme resurface again in Fairfax County, and then again in Loudoun County. Growth seemed to follow Rollie around like a puppy.

When Rollie arrived in the early 1960's, the local government in Virginia Beach was run by Sydney Kellam and his cronies, called 'The Organization', which was part of the larger 'Byrd Organization' that had controlled state politics for the previous 40 years. Harry Flood Byrd, first a Governor and then a long-time Senator, established a series of relationships with local officials in virtually every rural county in Virginia. In the 60's, they still called themselves 'Democrats', but it was of the Southern variety. There were pockets of resistance to their control—mostly in South East and Northern Virginia. It was this monolithic domination of local and state government that motivated Rollie to get into politics.

But it wasn't only the control thing; it was what they supported. The Byrd Organization used its virtual monopoly over political power in the state to fight integration and the African American vote, primarily through a poll tax. Fewer than 10% of theoretically eligible African American voters were voting in those days, which helped the Organization anoint future Governors, Senators, Congressmen, Judges, and a host of local elected officials, as well as the Democratic Committees. Most elections in Virginia were landslides because a most of the electorate had given up on the system. And that's not all. The state opposed liquor by the drink, kept stores closed on Sunday ('Blue Laws'), supported miscegenation, and refused to issue state bonds to build infrastructure, including roads. It was a 'pay as you go' economic system.

All of this nonsense was in place when Rollie arrived in Virginia in 1963. He bought a home in the old Princess Anne County area in its first large, low-cost development called Aragona Village. Within a few months, he filed as one of four plaintiffs in a one-man, one-vote lawsuit against the City of Virginia Beach that went all the way to the Supreme Court. He was the only witness for the plaintiffs, with Henry Howell as the pro-bono attorney. Henry, a self-styled liberal populist, went on to be elected Lt. Governor of Virginia in 1971, sandwiched between failed attempts to become Governor.

A couple of years after the suit was filed, Rollie unsuccessfully ran as an Independent for City Council in Virginia Beach, with integration of the public schools as a major plank in his platform. Yep, the schools were still segregated. Later, he helped organize and lead two groups in two other local elections, one of which successfully elected a bi-partisan slate of City Council members.

In the late sixties, he started a company called 'Voter Services of Virginia,' the first business in the Commonwealth that computerized the voter registration lists in the six cities of the Tidewater area. Early statewide clients included Henry Howell, Lt. Governor 'Sarge' Reynolds, Senator Bill Soong, and a number of local candidates. Republicans effectively put him out of business after copying his list.

In 1976, a good friend of his, Jim Gibbs, ran Jimmy Carter's statewide primary campaign from Rollie's personal residence for eight months. Rollie led a majority of Virginia Beach state delegates to the Virginia Democratic Convention that for the first time in fifty years was not comprised 100% of Byrd supported delegates! He was also elected a Jimmy Carter National Delegate to the Democratic National Convention in NYC. A decade later, the city turned Republican and has been voting that way since.

In 1978, Rollie took a new software job in Fairfax County and shortly relocating, was elected Vice Chair of Information for the Fairfax Democrats and managed their voter lists. Within a year, he was doing the same for other Northern Virginia localities, and eventually ran the whole state program. He remembers one evening, well after midnight, when former Lt. Governor Don Beyer joined him at the computer center to see how the system worked and how labels and lists were selected and printed. That was during Don's introduction to political campaigns, in Ira Lechner's challenge to Republican Frank Wolf in Wolf's first re-election effort to Congress. It was a close election, with Wolf hanging on with a 53% win. It's never been close again. Frank Wolf is still in Congress after 30 years.

In 1993, Loudoun County was the next and last stop for Rollie. He immediately joined the Loudoun County Democratic Committee (LCDC) and has served in a variety of positions since then, including district chair, Vice-Chair and Chair. He also managed a half-dozen campaigns and once ran for House of Delegates.

I just had to ask him: Why Obama? How the H E double L did he figure Obama had a chance of carrying Virginia? A young, inexperienced, African American man with an extremely strange name? Sounded foreign to me—maybe even Muslim! And in Virginia? Could Rollie see into the future?

His reply: "The SPEECH!" The 2004 convention speech had blown him away. And the response to it was incredible—in and outside of the convention. Secondly, Rollie had always liked 'smart' candidates. Although he respected Hillary greatly, he felt strongly that there was no way she could carry Virginia. Rollie had too many moderate Democratic and Independent friends who had expressed their very vehement, unfavorable opinion of the Clintons. And finally, Rollie had read Obama's books. They were the clincher. He was particularly impressed with Obama's approach to problem solving—putting the best available minds of differing opinions in the room, listening and asking questions, and striving for consensus. For him, Obama was the real deal.

"But how did you figure that an African American man could be elected in Virginia? That doesn't seem likely." "Not a problem," he said. "We have already crossed that line. In 1989 Doug Wilder was elected as the first African American Governor of Virginia, following a stint as Lt. Governor. Virginia had already shown that it could elect an African American if the circumstances were right." I asked, "When did you get started?" He said, "Late 2006. I knew that the earlier I began, the more significant I could become in the campaign. The key to success in presidential politics is to pick your horse early but pick the right horse."

So Rollie got started. First he went on the Internet and searched for any early campaign efforts for Obama. He found a "Draft Obama" site and signed up. He knew that before reaching out to other members on the local Democratic committee (LCDC), he had to notify their Chair, Thom Beres, about his plans. He showed me the email he sent him: "I've decided to get involved with the 'draft Obama' organization. It's fun to pick your horse at the beginning of the race—when you don't even know how fast he/she really is. To that end, I would like to have you post my interest in Obama in the LCDC Newsletter asking anyone interested in Obama at this stage of the game to contact me. Of course, if you do it for me/Obama, you would do it for any of the other candidates (which I encourage you to do). The more folks working on a Democratic campaign means the more support for the eventual Democratic candidate in 2008!"

Thom sent him a positive response, so Rollie was off and running. And after Thom's time as party Chair at the end of 2007, Thom became an important part of the Obama campaign in Loudoun County and statewide.

The next thing on Rollie's agenda in January 2007 was to contact Eileen Bartels, one of the most dedicated, hardworking Democrats in Loudoun County. She had been in charge of running the LCDC headquarters the previous five years or so and was expecting to do the same in 2007. She never felt it worthwhile to open the office this time of year because of inactivity, but didn't have any objections if someone else wanted to do so. Rollie then contacted Thom Beres again and got his OK. Rollie later recruited several others to help him keep the office open 3-4 hours a day throughout the next few months.

The LCDC Headquarters was strategically located in the center of historic Leesburg, at the intersection of King and Market streets in a second-story walk-up. Across from the office on King Street is the Leesburg Restaurant where the gang writing this book has spent many a Friday lunch discussing our progress or lack thereof. Owner Robin Peacemaker runs this family restaurant and takes good care of us. As you head towards that main intersection from the restaurant, you need to look around because if you have good eyes you can see the bullet holes left by Elijah White's Partisan 35th battalion of Virginia cavalry which are still there from that shootout with the Maryland Cavalry in September, 1862. Nearby you'll see a statue of a Confederate soldier standing in the square of the Loudoun County Courthouse. What you need to do is look at the statue's eyes. He's looking at the neon sign across King Street at Payne's Biker Bar right in front of him. The neon sign on the Bar says, "Better off here than across the street." The sign is really saying that across the street behind the Confederate soldier is the County Jail. I can't argue with that. On any given day you're definitely better off drinking in a bar than being in the Loudoun County Jail.

Back on point, Rollie then launched into the very early days of the Obama campaign in Loudoun in 2007. He started going to the office several hours a week, putting out signs, and interacting with the community. As an example, one day in February, he came into the office, retrieved the phone messages, and found one from Linda Grant. She and her husband John lived out in Lovettsville, one of Loudoun County's rural towns, and wanted to help Democrats and the Obama campaign. They became very helpful throughout the campaign. And, as you will learn later, daughter Kathryn became a very important full-time paid staffer in the election machinery.

Within a couple of weeks of Obama's announcement, Rollie discovered MyBO and that changed everything. It set off a chain reaction of major events destined to affect everything in the Obama campaign in Loudoun County. MyBO is what the volunteers and staffers in the Obama campaign called the website my.barackobama.com. The story of MyBO goes back to a man by the name of Chris Hughes.

Chris Hughes, along with Mark Zuckerberg and others developed Facebook in 2004. Zuckerberg was the lead developer. The site was an instant hit, attracted 10 million users by 2008. Nothing like this had ever happened before.

In the fall of 2006, Chris Hughes received an email from Reggie Love, personal aide to Barack Obama and a recent graduate of Duke University. Senator Obama understood the potential of online social networking, and he wanted a Facebook page. Chris Hughes was the Facebook customer representative who handled the contact. Jim Brayton, Obama's Internet director, liked the idea, and Love set up the Senator's profile on Facebook. It wasn't long before they realized how helpful this type of social networking would be for an Obama presidential campaign.

A few weeks before Obama's official announcement in January 2007, Love arranged a meeting between Brayton and Hughes in Union Station in Washington DC. The Obama campaign had realized the incredible potential of organizing supporters online. Brayton decided to hire Hughes on the spot, realizing Hughes had the creativity and skills to create a powerful organizing tool for the campaign. Hughes accepted and told a stunned Mark Zuckerberg he was leaving Facebook to supervise the creation of a social networking site for the Obama campaign. Later, Hughes said he would never have left Facebook for anyone but Barack Obama.

On February 10, 2007, Obama declared his intention to run for the presidency and MyBO, went live. Less than two weeks after the announcement, Rollie found MyBO, signed up, and created the group "Loudoun County for Obama," dubbed "LCO." He immediately recognized its organizing potential to create a local grassroots effort. Anyone in the world could find the group on the Internet and connect with other Obama supporters in the area with this easy-to-use MyBO website. Better yet, anyone living in Loudoun County who joined LCO was then a prime prospect to help grow the local organization. Only a few of those who joined used their real names, but as administrator of the group, Rollie could send messages to all the new members and ask them to "friend him" and thus obtain their real names and email addresses. Powerful information. I could see Rollie's eyes brighten up as he started to tell me about this fantastic tool.

"Rollie, you sound like this was your Holy Grail moment!"

"It was! It was! I can't describe to you the sense of frustration I felt in the 2000 and 2004 presidential elections with the lack of support I experienced from the state and national presidential campaigns. It was really lame. As usual, they had rightly kissed Virginia off as a Red State, but why not give us a hand? Presidential years are party building years. Why not consider the long term? But they simply weren't interested in helping local party organizations that way.

"Nevertheless, I would optimistically begin by calling my way through the state campaign office, and then the national office, searching for an enlightened decision maker. I hoped to find someone who would agree to send us the names and contact information of people in Loudoun County who had contacted them directly. I wanted to recruit those interested to help us locally and plug them into our Get Out The Vote (GOTV) efforts and perhaps turn them into local party supporters.

"At first I could not understand their reluctance to share names with those of us on the ground who wanted to help their candidate. They weren't here. There wasn't anyone else going to do the grunt work. However, after many years in this business, I now understand it. The people in charge of national campaigns want to use potential volunteers and donors for their own purposes—to solicit money from them and perhaps to get them to volunteer in undecided swing states, which certainly didn't include Virginia. We were deep RED! They also wanted to control the message to their supporters. For all they knew, we could have been flakes and potentially cause them some real problems by misusing their list. I can understand that position, but I sure don't agree with it. I was thinking more long-term."

"Did the Gore and Kerry campaigns ever send you anything?"

"We got *nada* from the Gore campaign, but persistence paid off with the Kerry campaign. They finally did send us a few hundred names that arrived in a batch three days before the election. We sure had to scramble to make use of them. As far as I know, they didn't send names to any other locality in Virginia.

"So, yes, MyBO was our 'Holy Grail' of community organizing. It was an extremely helpful way to build a group of Obama grassroots supporters. It would be operating outside of the local Democratic committee and the paid staff that might eventually come on the scene. And there was talk that Virginia may be in play in 2008. Although we received suggested events and activities from the national campaign folks, it was never mandated.

"The lack of cooperation from the Gore and Kerry campaigns exemplifies a type of conflict that frequently occurs in political campaigns. In those two elections, the conflict was simply between the local Democratic committee running the local campaign for President and the national campaign organization, which is not a part of the Democratic Party at any level. In Swing States, it gets much more complicated because there are thousands of separate organizations across the country competing for resources. Voting outcomes can be substantially affected by how well these conflicts are resolved. In this book we refer to these competing organizations as 'Power Groups.' Later I will point out some of the conflicts that arose between these groups as they competed for authority and resources during the 2008 campaign here in Loudoun County."

"What made you think Virginia might be in play that election year?"

"Just after Obama's announcement, the Virginia State Democrats were getting ready to host their annual JJ (Jefferson-Jackson) Dinner in Richmond. As usual, it was scheduled at a downtown hotel, and they had been expecting about 1,200 for the dinner, with a bunch of hoot-em-up parties and receptions before and after the main event. I have gone to a number of them over the years. Virginia usually attracted important political figures as the main dinner speaker, and I remember meeting Evan Bayh, Andrew Cuomo, and Bill Bradley among others.

"About a week before the dinner, it was suddenly announced that Obama was going to attend this event and would be the main speaker! That resulted in a mad rush for tickets. Amy McLaughlin, the Executive Director of the Democratic Party at the time, saw the opportunity to turn this into a spectacular event and booked the Convention Center for a sit-down dinner for 4,000 people, the largest in Virginia's history. And the ticket price was over a hundred bucks! It was oversubscribed. By the way, Amy got her political start right here in Loudoun County in the late nineties while I was the local Democratic Chair. She's now working at the DNC—a bright, capable, political operative."

"Were you able to get a ticket?"

"Yes I did. Actually I already had one for me and one for my buddy, Jean Garneau, a long-time personal friend of mine who lives in Fairfax. Although he normally voted Republican, Jean and I often attended state events together. Loudoun County had previously secured a couple of tables so we were all set. We had a terrific time at the event. To be in the same room with Obama and see him in action was inspiring. That night, when he introduced him, Tim Kaine announced his support for Obama, the first governor to do so outside of Illinois. Afterwards I was able to shake Obama's hand, telling him I had connected with the 'Draft Obama' folks, and he thanked me for that."

Rollie's handshaking experience comes from a lot of years in politics; he knows how to do it even when competing with 4,000 people who all want to touch The Man. In fact Rollie has sort of made a hobby of shaking hands with the guest speakers in his political life. The key to his success is to spot the rope line and case out in advance how the guest of honor is entering and exiting the speaking area. Then either before or after the event, you make a beeline for the rope line. A common rookie mistake is to go for the candidate directly. Everyone does that, resulting in a twenty to fifty-deep throng of people, all trying to get close enough to take his picture or shake his hand. The further from the stage, the fewer the people. Get positioned on the rope line even if it is out of sight from the stage, and let the celebrity come to YOU! Have a felt tip pen ready, and your ticket handy, and you can often get a prize souvenir for the event!

In 2005, Tim Kaine narrowly carried Loudoun County for Governor, and in 2006, the state went for US Senator Jim Webb over incumbent George Allen in a spectacular upset. With a 50.1% win, Loudoun County contributed just over 1,000 votes in the narrow statewide 10,000-vote victory for Webb. And if you remember your history, that win gave control of the U.S. Senate to the Democrats by two votes (51-49), denying VP Dick Cheney the opportunity to cast tie breaking votes on partisan issues.

In 2007, Loudoun Democrats were gearing up for a ton of local races that were scheduled for November. In these months before the Board of Supervisors and other local races, Rollie understood that it was extremely important for our grassroots volunteers to tread carefully so that none of the candidates would feel that the Obama effort diverted resources (people and money) from their own campaigns. Despite their efforts, some complaints were heard from those candidates—mostly because the new Obama recruits didn't especially want to work in the local Democratic campaigns. Some of our candidates had difficulty understanding that many of the LCO volunteers simply didn't consider themselves Democrats!

So I asked Rollie why in the world he started so early in the Obama campaign! "I had three major reasons for starting so early: I wanted to lead the effort, expand the Democratic base, and be ready for the early Virginia presidential primary in 2008.

"I like to be in charge and I've learned that if you want to play a leading role in a presidential election, you have to pick your candidate early. And of course, you have to pick the right one. I understand 'early' is a subjective term, and these campaigns have started earlier and earlier as the primaries are moved up on the calendar. You also have to consider the span of control. I picked the county level. Because of my contacts in Fairfax County, however, I could just as easily have picked a larger area, say a Congressional District or all of Northern Virginia. With the aid of the Internet, if you have the contacts and credibility, you can make it happen.

In Virginia's off-year elections (no statewide candidates), despite the many candidates, we have the lowest voter turnouts and fewest volunteers. Few join the Democrats in off years. New activists usually work only for the particular candidate that drew them into his or her campaign. It's quite different in presidential election years. These years are party-building years. New volunteers pour into these campaigns; several join the Party, and then stick around after the election is over. Rollie realized that starting the Obama effort early would expand the party-building opportunity by several months. LCO was successful in recruiting a number of the newly found Obama supporters into the local Democratic Party in mid to late 2007, many of whom also supported the local candidates.

Rollie also realized that the date for the Virginia presidential primary in 2008 was unusually early, just one week after Super Tuesday. Since LCO had to run a relatively quiet campaign until the local elections were over in November 2007, there would be only two months left to get ready for the primary with the holidays right smack dab in the middle of that period. Obama's early start in Loudoun County proved to be a substantial factor in the primary outcome.

Now back to early 2007 and the beginnings of LCO. A day or two after Rollie registered LCO with MyBO, he received notification that "Your group, Loudoun County for Obama, has been successfully created. Your group is pending a site administrator's approval. You will receive an email confirmation when it has been approved." The final approval followed about two weeks later. And he soon learned that when you build an online MyBO group, they will come. Come they did—LCO began attracting interested members. Rollie was hopeful he would find volunteers and new leaders among them. Two people he did not know joined the very first week. One of them was Lindsey Brooks.

Probably the most used feature of MyBO was "event posting." Anyone could post them, specifying their contact information and the what, where and when. These events then became visible for those searching for activities in their area. Lindsey responded to Obama's national campaign appeal that all groups in the country schedule a campaign kickoff event on Saturday, March 24. Rollie wasn't ready for that, but Lindsey Brooks was. She posted an event for that Saturday called "Old Town Leesburg Kickoff Event" which Rollie signed up to attend. This was exactly what he was looking for—an opportunity to meet new people and recruit additional organizers for LCO.

When talking with Lindsey, he learned that she had created a MyBO group for Loudoun County, named "Loudoun Families for Obama." It was an offshoot of a new national site with the same theme started by a friend of hers, Ruthi David, who lived in Fairfax County. We write more about Ruthi later, but for now, I'll tell you this. She was the very first person to walk in and volunteer for the first campaign office in the country for Obama—in DC. It was devoted to fundraising. They asked her to form her own MyBO group, "Families for Obama," to use for fundraising.

At the time Rollie met Lindsey, she was helping Ruthi with a $1,000 per person fundraiser in Middleburg here in Loudoun, hosted by Sheila Johnson (co-founder of the cable network Black Entertainment Television 'BET') and featuring Barack himself! But Rollie was not interested in fundraising directly. He was interested in creating a local organization for the ground game in Loudoun, and wanted to be recognized by the Obama people as the GOTO guy in Loudoun County.

Rollie wanted to get together with Lindsey to see how best they could work together to mobilize Loudoun County for Obama. Because of busy schedules, it didn't happen, but while these discussions were underway, Marcia Carlyn discovered MyBO and LCO. Marcia didn't sign up for LCO right away, but after looking at the other available groups in the area, decided to follow up with Rollie by phone. In their first conversation, Marcia let him know that she had an out of town commitment that weekend and couldn't attend Lindsey's party, but wanted to get together on her return. With the arrival of Marcia Carlyn our story takes a sharp turn in the road, and we'll get to that soon.

"Lindsey's local party was a success," Rollie said, "with about a dozen people showing up, generating a lot of initial enthusiasm. The national campaign had sent suggestions to Lindsey for hosting the party, including the video of Obama's announcement speech in Springfield, IL. There was to be a live connection to the Internet to watch Obama give us a live pep talk, but we had difficulty making that connection."

Rollie only knew one person there, a very active Loudoun County Democratic Committee officer, Vice Chair Ellen Heald. Another woman living in Leesburg was there who had started another MyBO group in Loudoun County called "Leesburg for Obama." Like Lindsey, she soon joined the LCO group and became very active for a couple of months, then disappeared, and never resurfaced. We never did learn why she dropped out. Other MyBO groups popped up from Loudoun from time to time that had varying degree of usefulness, but LCO was always the dominant group in Loudoun.

For now, though, this is getting entirely too granular, and I'm out of here. I'll talk to Rollie again and Marcia Carlyn later, but I have to go to Bluemont to see the old Snickersville train station, take some photos and recharge my batteries. This stuff gets heavy after a while, and you just need to get away from it.

To get to Bluemont you take the Old Colonial Highway, now Route 7, for 15 miles out of Leesburg heading west towards Winchester in the Shenandoah Valley. Bluemont has an interesting history. Early Virginians called the place Pun'kin Town because it was located way in the backwoods. Settlement by white people dates from the 1730s but it was the Snicker family who eventually gave their name to the place. As early as the 1740s, Henry Snicker settled the area and the gap in the Blue Ridge Mountains here connecting to the Shenandoah Valley took the name Snicker's Gap. Old Indian trails led the way. Go west from Bluemont 'til you cross the Snicker's Gap and you're in the Shenandoah Valley.

Pun'kin Town didn't get an official name until the post office opened an office in the village in 1807 and christened the place "Snicker's Gap," probably named after William or Edwin Snicker. In September 1864, John Singleton Mosby's Partisan Rangers literally caught the 8th New York Cavalry asleep in the town, then named Snickersville, and gave them a thorough spanking. The Yankee cavalry never knew what hit them until it was too late.

What really made Bluemont famous was the arrival of the Washington and Old Dominion Railroad in 1900. Innkeepers had established resorts in the Blue Ridge because in the summertime the temperature was cooler than in the former swamp known as Washington, DC. Wealthy people would summer in the Blue Ridge because of the cooler climate. So in 1900 the town raised the money and persuaded the old Southern Railroad to lay track from Round Hill, which connected to DC, to Bluemont. Then the Southern leased the track to the Washington and Old Dominion Railroad.

The railroad arrived July 4, 1900, and it soon attracted lots of tourists. Some came from Washington just for the day. Others spent the entire summer in the resorts. By 1911 there were four trains a day coming and going from Bluemont. Alas, nothing lasts forever. By 1939 the automobile had killed the railroad, and train service to Bluemont ceased. The spread of modern electrical air conditioning after the Second World War ended the need to go to the mountains to get cool air in the summer. That wasn't all bad. There now is a popular bike and walking trail that runs from Alexandria, Virginia all the way to Bluemont using the train's old railbed.

A few days later I'm back at Rust Library in Leesburg to talk to Marcia Carlyn. It doesn't take long to realize this is one very special person. Marcia Carlyn was born in Buffalo, New York and raised in Arlington, Virginia. She earned a B.S. degree in Mathematics at the University of Wisconsin, Madison in 1966. She went on for an M.A. in Mathematics Education at Stanford University and later took a PhD in Social and Philosophical Foundations (with a minor in Statistics and Research Design) at Michigan State University. In 1987 she earned an MBA in Finance at Michigan State. That's more degrees than there are varieties of peanuts grown in Virginia.

One thing I learned from Marcia, though, is that she never mentioned her academic degrees during the Obama campaign or any other political campaign. She said she learned to stay mum on that subject in the early 1980's when she worked for the Speaker of the Michigan House of Representatives as Director of Data Processing. On her first day of work, she unpacked her nameplate (Marcia Carlyn, PhD) and proudly placed it on her desk as she had in her previous university job. Much to her surprise, when the Speaker walked in to welcome her, he snatched up the nameplate and told her to deep-six it—he never wanted to see it again. As he explained, "A PhD is a kiss of death in the political world you're now in. People will think you're an airy head academic and you'll lose all credibility." She followed his advice and never mentioned her degrees in any of her political ventures from that point on. She sums it up this way: "Academic degrees can be very helpful in learning valuable skills and broadening one's understanding of the world, but they can easily set you apart from others. That's not what you want in a grassroots campaign!"

Like Rollie and a whole bunch of other supporters, Marcia heard Obama's address to the Democratic National Convention back in 2004, was deeply moved, and vowed that if Obama were ever to run for president, she would do whatever she could to support him. She had volunteered for many Democrats over the years and had even been a precinct delegate for George McGovern, but she had never before had such a strong reaction to a potential candidate. On February 10, 2007, she was thrilled to hear Barack Obama announce his candidacy before a crowd of 15,000 at the Old State Capitol building in Springfield, Illinois. Although it was a bitter cold day in Springfield, his televised speech warmed her heart as well as the hearts of a lot of other Americans.

By mid-March, Marcia had heard about MyBO and began looking to see what kind of organizing was happening in Loudoun County. She found the three groups online and wanted to figure out which was the best organized. When she called the administrator for Loudoun County for Obama, she reached a guy by the name of Rollie Winter and they connected immediately. Rollie suggested she attend a fundraising event for Kelly Burk in Leesburg the following Saturday where he could introduce her to the LCDC leadership who were sure to attend. Kelly was running for the Board of Supervisors.

In addition to looking forward to meeting Rollie in person, Marcia was there on a mission—to learn what kind of databases were available to identify potential Obama voters. Rollie introduced her to Thom Beres and told her of the databases that were available, including the newly released Voter Activation Network (VAN) which had basic information about all the registered voters in Virginia and their likely political affiliation (thanks to a lot of hard work by the National Democratic Party and the Democratic Party of Virginia). However, because Marcia wanted to register new voters, she decided the best plan was to start with U.S. Census data.

Rollie scheduled a meeting with Lindsey and Marcia the following week to decide where they go from here. They met at the Democratic Headquarters in Leesburg. Rich Culbert was at the office when everyone arrived. He had been recently hired by the State Democratic Party to help Loudoun County elect those running for state office. Rollie invited him to listen in, and as a result he understood from the beginning that finding early Obama enthusiasts could actually help his recruiting efforts in 2007.

Rollie said the meeting went well but Lindsey informed them she would only be helping in Loudoun from time to time, concentrating her energy on the Families for Obama groups. Marcia was interested in pursuing the use of Census data. Rollie was going to work on organization development. He agreed to put together another meeting with a larger group in a couple of weeks.

Marcia then waded knee deep in data. You see, Loudoun County isn't like a big or even medium-size city where you can easily identify large areas of potential Obama voters; rather, such areas are scattered around the county. Census data would allow LCO to identify specific areas in the county (census blocks and block groups) where voter registration efforts could be aimed to reach targeted populations. Maps could then be drawn up to direct volunteers to go door-to-door in the most promising neighborhoods and register new voters in a more efficient way.

Marcia contacted the National Obama campaign in early April 2007 to find out which demographic variables they recommended. Luke Peterson, the Data Manager for the national campaign, explained that his group was rolling census information into all their modeling and analysis, using a broad range of census variables to varying degrees depending on the purpose of a particular model. Although he didn't identify their highest priority demographic variables as she had hoped, his response was very encouraging. He said in his email, "Given that we're running a new type of campaign here and really trying to let folks in the field participate and innovate—any research of this type that you pursue there in Loudoun County would likely be helpful to our Loudoun County efforts if not eventually to the national program. We are going to rely on a lot of our knowledgeable friends like you to try to determine what courses of action might yield the best results."

Encouraged to use her own judgment, Marcia proposed and Rollie agreed to use the following demographics to identify the highest priority neighborhoods in Loudoun County for registering new voters—race (African Americans and Hispanics), age (18-29), and renter-occupied households. Their reasoning was based on a couple of recent national polls showing that 88% of African Americans, 73% of Hispanics, and 61% of 18-29 year-olds said they voted Democratic. Marcia then proceeded to download and analyze census data, identify neighborhood blocks with the highest concentration of these demographics, and create maps (using Google Maps) showing which blocks to canvass. The maps proved to be very helpful to folks who volunteered to help with LCO's voter registration drives.

During the spring of 2007, Rollie and Marcia spent a lot of time laying the groundwork and focusing on how to build an effective grassroots organization, the likes of which had never before been seen in Loudoun. They were grateful they had the national campaign's blessing to try out many things on their own without having to follow a centralized playbook. This freedom to experiment to find creative ways to recruit and inspire volunteers played a major role in the outcomes of the primary and presidential elections in Loudoun County and Virginia as a whole.

The Early Bird Gets the Worm

"The early bird catcheth the worm."—John Ray, *A collection of English proverbs (1670)*

Now I am going to tell you all about the fine art of finding worms. I am back on the pony again riding to the Rust Library in Leesburg to talk to Marcia Carlyn to get more pieces of the puzzle of what happened here in Loudoun County in 2007 in preparation for the 2008 presidential election. I have to figure out all this stuff about building a group, early organizing, email lists, and rolodexes and why all that's important.

This time we're going down the Turnpike in the direction of Mountville but we're turning left on Watermill Road right at the Hibbs Bridge crossing the Beaver Dam Creek. This is where they distilled all that whiskey back in the 1920s. Yes, I turned left years ago, but this time I'm now turning left on the road. It takes about a half an hour to get to Rust, and when I go rolling in Marcia is already there. Marcia is important to the story because she's one of the two people who actually set in motion the Great Grassroots Campaign of 2008.

By late spring of 2007, Marcia and Rollie definitely understood the major challenges they faced in Loudoun County. Like Virginia, the place had not voted for a Democrat since Lyndon Johnson in 1964, 43 years ago. George W. Bush, whom Molly Ivins called "The Boy President," carried Loudoun easily in 2004, with John Kerry getting only 44% of the vote. To win in 2008, Barack Obama would need to get a whole lot more votes than Kerry did, taking into account that Loudoun was one of the fastest growing counties in the nation (consistently ranked among the top five counties in growth).

In the first chapter I introduced you to the combined Democratic campaign, VV08. Dan Chavez, the Regional Field Organizer for VV08 assigned to Loudoun County, told me it was his opinion that a flip this big was as rare as finding a horned toad in Alaska. What's weird about that is that the horned toad really isn't a toad at all, but maybe we will tell that story some night in the bar at the Red Fox Inn in Middleburg. In all honesty, to set the record straight, there was once a horned toad in Wasilla, but she's gone now.

Part of Dan's perspective came from his father, who has run regional Democratic presidential campaigns for many years. The challenge for Democrats in Virginia was daunting.

VV08 was a big deal in this county for the 2008 election, and I will spend a lot of time later telling you about them as well as the Obama Campaign For Change (CFC) and the other Power Groups in town. Here's something else you probably don't know. The national Obama website, MyBO, wasn't only for organizing groups like LCO, it also empowered individuals directly to canvass, make calls, or raise money. Barbara and I didn't start to make calls until early 2008, but we were examples of those who did that. Others started much sooner. We didn't know anything about LCO at the time. Robyn Hyman, and Carolyn Ronis also worked directly for the national campaign. Robin made over a thousand calls before finding and joining LCO. I don't have a clue how many people in Loudoun County supported Obama this way. Could have been 10, Could have been 100.

There was one other special category of volunteers. They were the people who created their own campaigns, independent of all organized efforts. They were the bloggers, like Juan Perez, or the McDermotts who started about the time Rollie and Marcia formed Loudoun County for Obama. Ali McDermott and her two sons, Darby and Bobby, became impatient to begin campaigning, so they created and photocopied their own distribution literature and went door-to-door for Obama in Loudoun's large South Riding development in Loudoun County. A few months later, they joined LCO, and continued working non-stop for Obama for the duration. Quite a story here, folks, and we'll tell you all about it at the right time. And there were the few who called the national campaign and asked what state needed their help and then went there and did it, like Daniel Dennison and Larry Roeder. It took a village to win an election. We'll be writing more about these heroic people in later chapters.

Marcia and Rollie had to come up with a plan to turn the county blue, and the execution of that plan wasn't going to be easy. It required organizing a mass of mostly brand new volunteers, who in turn would motivate a lot of usual non-voters, a task about as easy as herding cats.

To win in Loudoun County, Democrats had to turn out a high percentage of their voters who liked Barack Obama. That, however, would not be enough. They also had to register a LOT of new Democratic voters to increase the base enough to outnumber the Republicans. Obama and his people knew that from the git go. Git all you got, git more, and you git the election. But how do you actually do this? You do it four ways.

You start by getting Rollie to fire up his Rolodex, work the phones and emails, and drum up volunteers for the campaign. The challenge here was that it was April 2007, 10 months before the Democratic primary and 19 months before Election Day, and there was plenty of talk going on about Hillary Clinton. A lot of women around here felt it was waaaay past time to crash that glass ceiling! So most of the Democratic base wasn't yet on board for Obama, and many didn't even know who he was. Still, you do what you can do.

Second, as I mentioned in the last chapter, Marcia had few potential databases she could employ to track down possible Democratic voters. Marcia wanted to find unregistered voters who would be more likely than the typical Loudoun resident to vote for Obama. Census data looked promising at this stage of the grassroots campaign, so Marcia rolled up her sleeves and learned how to order, download, and analyze the huge data files available from the U.S. Census Bureau. Now you get Marcia to download census data and identify neighborhoods where the demographics were most likely to produce Obama voters.

Third, you train as many volunteers as possible about Virginia's voter registration requirements and you send them out to canvass Marcia's targeted neighborhoods with a bundle of registration forms.

And fourth, to keep track of the Obama supporters, Marcia and Rollie created and maintained an Excel spreadsheet dubbed the "Big List". Marcia volunteered to be in charge of the database. The Big List was used to record whatever information was available on each supporter, including first name, last name, email address, home phone, cell phone, home address, general location within the county, whether the person had joined LCO and/or whether they had volunteered, and some coded notes she used for keeping track of individual interests and other relevant information. Supporters who provided this information were assured that it would never be shared with anyone except the local Obama campaign. The Big List proved to be critically important throughout the grassroots campaign.

Marcia updated the spreadsheet with Rollie's input and after every LCO event (not a trivial task) and was able to analyze the data in ways that were very helpful to the campaign. For example, she could quickly identify from the codes those supporters who lived in a certain area of the county or who were interested in a particular activity (such as voter registration). Their email addresses could then be copied and pasted into a special email message aimed at that group. Because the Big List gave them this type of flexibility in their communications and because a whole lot of these interested prospects were not interested in joining the MyBO list, Marcia and Rollie decided to use the Big List rather than MyBO for their email messages. MyBO, however, was a key factor in their success because it was an excellent social networking tool that LCO used in a variety of ways. For example, MyBO was especially helpful in announcing upcoming LCO activities to a broad population and in finding new supporters.

Before we get into the canvassing, I need to expand a bit on some challenging aspects of Loudoun County.

From a political point of view, an especially relevant characteristic of Loudoun County is that it has a much smaller African American population than many other counties in Virginia and in the country as a whole. Basically, Loudoun is an affluent place with a large white population. In 2007, 72% of Loudoun's total population (272,000) was white. Less than 8% of the population was African American and less than 10% was Hispanic. Loudoun County was unique in another important way—it had the highest median household income ($107,207) of counties exceeding 250,000 in populations in 2007! These demographics explain a great deal about why Loudoun had been leaning Republican for decades and why it would be so challenging for an African American presidential candidate to carry the day in this particular county.

Loudoun County has no large urban center with a concentration of Democratic voters. In addition, there are no central university campuses here. The handful of colleges and satellite campuses scattered around Loudoun have mostly commuter students mainlining on Republican notions fed to them by their parents who grew up eating Republican myths and still believing them. One of these colleges in particular, the fast-growing Patrick Henry College, specialized in producing Republican activists. At one point in the Bush years, there were more interns in the White House from this college than from any other college in the country. They were committed. The kids aren't off on their own yet to learn to think for themselves and find out how we got into the current mess we're in, where high-cost student loans have turned a lot of our college grads into a new generation of indentured servants. Of course we here in Virginia know all about indentured servants because they came over to the Jamestown colony in the 1600s.

Further, just in case you are living in Wyoming, Utah, or Outer Mongolia, an indentured servant is someone who must work off his or her debt with his or her own labor. In the good old days this was usually seven years, but under Republican rules, it may take 20-30 years for current students to be truly free of this awful burden. The rules were actually better in the 17th century than in the 21st. This was one of the reasons we were out to change things. Republicans had wrecked the economy as they were on their way out the door and enslaved our youth to Big Finance, and we wanted to stop it and stop it now.

Right from the beginning, Marcia started contacting folks at Obama's campaign headquarters in Chicago, some regional directors (paid campaign staffers in charge of multiple states), and leaders of other MyBO groups to ask for help. Her persistence paid off and demonstrated some key differences between Marcia and Rollie. Rollie knew—or thought he did—that trying to reach someone with authority at a national campaign office would be a complete waste of time. Loudoun County for Obama was just one of thousands of local campaign efforts in the country that were seeking help. The national campaign couldn't possibly give us any kind of quality time and assistance. It seemed hopeless to him to even try. So much for Rollie's thinking—Marcia was undeterred from her priorities by his somewhat dour, pessimistic thinking on this point.

It's really an understatement to call Marcia Carlyn "persistent" when she's pursuing a cause that's dear to her heart. She is relentless and just doesn't give up. In this case, it only took her a few weeks to identify some key players in the Obama organization on the Obama website, contact them by email, follow up with a phone call if she could get their number, explain how important Loudoun County would be to Obama's ultimate victory, and achieve results. Also working to her favor was that we were one of the first MyBO groups to start using the new system. They were grateful for her feedback.

Although she never received a direct response from David Axelrod or David Plouffe (not surprisingly), she found that nearly all the other high-level folks she contacted in the national campaign during those early months were very helpful, including Trista Allen (Southern Field Director), Temo Figueroa (National Field Director),

Luke Peterson (National Data Manager), Chris Hughes (Director of Online Organizing), Meaghan Burdick (Director of Grassroots Fundraising), and Nikki Sutton (Southeast Field Director and Online Organizer). It's extremely unlikely that any other grassroots organization in the country interacted with so many of these important national campaign operatives.

For example, Marcia learned from Temo Figueroa in April that the campaign would be printing brochures and other literature for the June 9th Walk for Change (Obama's kickoff grassroots National Canvass Day in 2007), enabling LCO to put in a large order as soon as the materials became available. Her biggest success, however, was convincing Trista Allen to send her a terrific head shot photo of Obama along with written permission to use this photo and the campaign's rising sun logo on the materials the group planned to create themselves (flyers, posters, door hangers, etc.) to help win Loudoun County. The photo and the logo were used throughout the campaign, but they were critical in the spring of 2007. Here's why—Marcia and Rollie discovered early on that a lot of the folks they were targeting didn't have a clue who "Barack Obama" was and they didn't care to find out. Then Marcia had an inspiration. Why not show them his picture? Why not indeed? As soon as she showed them his photo, most of them grinned and said something like, "Oh that guy, oh yeah, I've seen him on TV." And once that happened, they wanted to know more and often decided to register to vote and get on LCO's email list. From that point on, LCO used that wonderful head shot of Barack Obama and the rising sun logo on all their materials during door-to-door canvassing, and at every community event.

While Marcia was going after help from the national Obama campaign, Rollie was shaking the bushes and setting up the next LCO meeting with a wider audience. They needed a place to hold the meeting, and Marcia mentioned to Rollie that KD Kidder had joined MyBO. Rollie knew KD well from earlier campaigns and other associations. She, along with her husband, Neil Steinberg, offered their place of business in Leesburg named Photoworks, for this first real meeting of LCO in late April. The location was handy—just a block from the LCDC headquarters and right above the corner vintner. Yes, I told you it was handy. Along with KD came her mom, an extraordinary woman whom I will glorify later in this story. KD offered a number of important resources throughout the campaign. She had a large email list of her progressive and political friends. Most of those on her list were PALs, members of the Loudoun

County Progressive Action League, an outgrowth of the Dean and the Kucinich campaign organizations of the same name—a liberal group of earnest, dedicated, committed activists. Loudoun isn't entirely conservative!

About a dozen showed up at the LCO meeting at Photoworks. One of them was Jan Hyland. She had signed up at MyBO as 'Jan from Leesburg.' Rollie had a hunch about her that proved right. It was the same Jan who was a headquarters' staffer for Lt. Governor Don Beyer for several years when he was active in Virginia politics. Initially she actually took care of his kids, but by the time Don was in his third statewide campaign as he ran for Governor, she was number two or three in his inner circle—running what was called 'Virginians for Beyer.' Rollie ran the Loudoun campaign for him under that banner, and thus worked closely with Jan for several months. They had become good friends. Jan did not live in Loudoun at that time.

One of the first items on the agenda for that first meeting was to develop a Mission Statement for LCO. After a lot of discussion, Jan volunteered to put together a draft and run it by Marcia and Rollie before presenting it to the group at its next meeting. It was modified a bit, presented and adopted at the June meeting. The full statement is in the Appendix, but here it is in summary form:

"Our Mission is to establish a campaign organization to identify Obama supporters in Loudoun County and turn them out in the Virginia Democratic primary to be held on February 12, 2008. To accomplish this, we will: hold social and visibility events, register voters, conduct voter outreach and voter persuasion, work with local Dems, encourage MyBO use, encourage contributions to the Obama campaign, and HAVE FUN!"

This all led to a real burst of activity in June and the months following.

Obama's first big coordinated group event was the Walk for Change, a national outreach and voter registration drive scheduled for Saturday, June 9th. This would be LCO's first major canvassing event as well, and the core team was excited and also a bit anxious about how it would turn out. Their decision was to focus on a few neighborhoods in the towns of Leesburg and Purcellville based on the census data Marcia had analyzed. The Obama campaign opened up the floodgates for this event, providing the MyBO groups with glossy printed handouts and other literature. The national campaign also provided detailed instructions on how to conduct the Walk for Change, some of which LCO accepted and some of which they did not. For example, the campaign wanted the Loudoun volunteers to ask for donations when they knocked on doors, but Marcia and others thought it way too early to be asking for money in conservative Loudoun County, so they did it a different way.

In addition to handing out information on Barack Obama, volunteers carried voter registration forms and tally sheets. The tally sheets were developed by LCO and included a 1-to-5 "Obamater rating" for volunteers to record how strongly each potential voter supported Obama. The ratings ranged from 5 = "hot" (strong supporter) to 1 = "cold" (no support). LCO later had to reverse the order to match the national campaign's coding system. Either way, the tally sheets worked well and helped LCO collect the names and email addresses of people who liked Obama or were leaning his way. From the beginning, Marcia was fanatical about collecting email addresses! She felt it was the most practical way to stay in touch with a growing list of supporters in Loudoun. It took some practice, however, for the LCO volunteers to figure out the best way to get folks to willingly hand over their email addresses. I'll fill you in later on what they learned.

One of the earliest forays into the canvassing was in selected areas of the Town of Purcellville, located in the county. The first weekend that Rollie did some canvassing he joined Toni Rader and they paired up to take on one of the targeted neighborhoods. Toni turned out to be one of the early stalwarts of LCO.

In the Great Campaign of 2008, Toni Rader did it all. She started early, phone banked, canvassed, hosted post card writing parties—Toni Rader was everywhere, all over the turf. She was a tireless volunteer for the Obama Campaign, worked with Marcia Carlyn from early on, and was a fixture in the Purcellville area throughout the campaign. Just about everyone knew Toni Rader because she was so active in so many different activities. Early in the campaign, Toni ordered a pair of tennis shoes emblazoned with the words "Obama 2008" on the sides. She wore the shoes whenever she canvassed or did other Obama events. The shoes became so famous the Smithsonian Museum has requested she donate the shoes to the museum. The shoes are headed to immortality in the Smithsonian. So is Toni Rader.

Although most of LCO's volunteers had never canvassed before, the Walk for Change turned out to be a big success—they knocked on hundreds of doors, found a few volunteers, and left literature where no one answered the door. The results also showed that LCO's strategy for picking neighborhoods was a good one—an analysis of the Obamater ratings found that 25% of the people contacted said they supported or were leaning toward Obama and only 4% said they would be voting Republican.

To celebrate LCO's Walk for Change and kick off the local campaign in style, Rollie and Jill Winter threw a big party for all the volunteers after the event. It was free for the walkers and ten bucks for other attendees. It was a barbecue at their home at Little Oatlands—a thank you for all who participated in the Walk for Change. Rollie also invited a lot of his Democratic friends; folks he knew were interested in Obama's campaign. Over 50 supporters attended the party and contributed $620 to the Obama campaign. A local neighbor contributed most of the food and drinks.

This get-together (the first of many lively parties LCO organized during the campaign) also had another purpose. Rollie and Marcia believed that politics was about people, and if people were having fun, they would come back and wouldn't mind the work of canvassing, phone banking, and other political activities. He learned through the years group activities help build relationships among volunteers and often lifelong friendships emerge. Working for the grassroots Obama campaign in Loudoun became for many something quite different from anything they had ever experienced. It enabled them to transcend the humdrum of daily life of work, television, and the tedium of repetition. The campaign became fun because it was different, because people could make new friends, be creative, do new things, and look forward to doing even more interesting things down the road.

On a completely different, but related, subject, Rollie inherited a ticket to the "Take Back America Conference" in Washington, DC scheduled on June 18–20. With only two days to pass it along, he turned to his list of liberal activists and up popped Ann Robinson's name. Perfect. She loves this stuff and will write about it afterwards—can't keep her from it! So, sure 'nuf, Ann leaped off her davenport and trekked into "The City," already fired up and ready to go. All the Democratic presidential candidates would be there, along with every major progressive player in the Democratic Party—Nancy Pelosi, Howard Dean, Jessie Jackson... Man oh woman, what a treat! Three thousand registrants coming from every state in the union and three days of workshops and networking!

Ann initially supported Bill Richardson, and in 2004 had supported John Edwards. When Obama came on the stage to address the 3,000 people in attendance at the TBA Conference, he had "cheerleaders" positioned in the room. To Ann, this meant that Obama already had a ground game, and that was impressive. This early, who else had a ground game? Plus, Obama had opposed the Iraq War from the beginning, not after everyone else opposed it, and that staked his claim as a leader. An instant opponent of that misadventure herself, Ann sat on the front row with her granddaughter's Fischer Price toy digital camera to take pictures and write notes. And she managed to get Obama's first hug at the rope line!

Later, when a former Clinton administration official introduced Hillary Clinton, and the crowd booed, well, Ann knew something was up. Clinton went on to explain she would finish the original Clinton agenda from the 1990s. But the crowd wasn't at all interested in yesterday; they wanted to hear about tomorrow. Hillary offered little of tomorrow.

The spiritual leader of the conference was Dennis Kucinich, but the attendees wouldn't vote for him—they knew he couldn't win a presidential contest. So, Obama won the straw poll of the attendees at the Conference. It was a hint of what was to come. The group included many enthusiastic young male bloggers, projected Kucinich's worldview onto Obama. This would set the stage for later disappointment. (You can read Ann's full report of this "unofficial Democratic primary" in the Appendix "www.swingcounty.com".)

The really big surprise for Ann came on June 21, the next day, when she unfolded The Washington Post, eager to read the report of this event and saw instead a full front page and another full inside page article about "Hillaryland." The Clintons appeared to have prepared the press to block out adverse coverage from the conference. It was hard for her to believe what they missed. Realizing just how powerful Hillary was and would be with the "gatekeepers" of the election cycle, amazed even Ann, who thought she had seen and heard it all, or at least enough not to be so shocked. Anyhoo, someone you'd think would be an automatic and passionate Hillary supporter joined the Loudoun Obama effort, thanks to Rollie's "Rolodex." Later Ann would have one dark day after the New Hampshire primary, wavering with millions of other women, "How can we let this moment pass for the Women's Movement?" But, she rallied and wrote a strong support statement for Rollie to circulate, favoring a steady push for Obama and eventually serving as an Obama delegate to the local District convention in 2008.

In June of 2007, Loudoun County for Obama also began the planning to participate in the petition drive to get Obama's name on the Virginia Democratic primary ballot. The primary was scheduled for February 12, 2008, a week after Super Tuesday. To set the stage, let me tell you something you may not know—Virginia has the most difficult primary entry requirements of any state in the entire nation (as most of the Republican candidates recently found out here in 2012)! Each presidential candidate had to submit petitions to the State Board of Elections by December 14, 2007, containing signatures of over 12,000 legitimate registered voters who supported putting the candidate's name on the ballot; there had to be a minimum of 400 signatures from each of Virginia's 11 Congressional Districts (CD). This was not a trivial task. We can thank the old Byrd organization for this onerous requirement. Control, control, control. That was their game.

Kevin Wolf headed up the statewide petition drive for the Obama campaign. One of Kevin's law partners was Jeffery Berman, who was Obama's National Delegate Director, recruited him for the job. Kevin's goal was 20,000 signatures before the December deadline to showcase Obama's strength and to compensate for the inevitable ineligible people signing the petitions. Kevin asked Rollie to represent the 10th CD (Congressional District) which he agreed to do. Rollie then recruited Marcia and other LCO volunteers to help reach Kevin's lofty petition goals.

According to conventional wisdom in the summer of 2007, the entire petition drive seemed almost silly. Super Tuesday was scheduled a week before the Virginia primary, and most folks in the political arena thought the Virginia primary would be irrelevant because the race would be settled by then. The smart money said Hillary Clinton would emerge as the clear winner on Super Tuesday, and Virginia's primary would amount to a coronation. The smart money lost.

Undaunted by this doom-and-gloom forecast, Kevin Wolf organized one helluva petition drive for Obama in Virginia. He started very early recruiting top-notch coordinators for each Congressional District, arranged for them to get stacks of petitions, and held weekly conference calls where the coordinators or their designated representative would check in. The weekly conference calls were used to answer questions, discuss issues that arose that week, and report the total number of signatures gathered in each CD to date. The petition drive kicked off in late June 2007 and lasted for several months.

As it turned out, the drive served an important secondary function for the Loudoun County for Obama group. It gave the group a plausible reason to approach strangers on the street and at public events (county fairs, local festivals, art shows, farmer's markets, etc.) and strike up a dialog with them about Barack Obama. Any registered voter in Virginia could sign the petition; you didn't need to be a Democrat and you didn't have to support Obama. To get people's attention, Marcia and some supporters created large posters that featured the head shot photo of Obama and the rising sun logo that the national campaign had previously given them permission to use. The poster strategy worked well, and LCO volunteers found that most of the people they approached agreed to sign the petition. The LCO volunteers also carried voter registration forms and tally sheets to collect the names and email addresses of people who liked Obama or were leaning his way. The petition drive gave the group many opportunities to recruit new supporters, register voters, and spread the word about Barack Obama.

Marcia Carlyn believed two things were powering the Loudoun campaign: (1) Barack Obama, an amazing person and candidate with the ability to touch people emotionally and inspire them with his vision for America; and (2) a first-of-its-kind grassroots group in Loudoun County that truly believed Barack's philosophy that ordinary people can do extraordinary things if they're inspired. Marcia knew, however, that you needed more than an inspiring person or issue to keep folks engaged. Every campaign has its ups and downs and some campaigns (like this one) are very long. People are unique; they have different personalities, and they're interested in different things. It was important to offer a variety of activities since not everyone likes to knock on strangers' doors, make cold calls, or ask for donations. It's so much easier if you can "catch the spark" in these others and encourage them to come up with creative ideas of their own. Their face will light up when they hit on something that inspires them. Since Marcia felt so strongly about this, she took the time to keep track of people's interests on the Big List, especially each of those who said they wanted to help.

Needless to say, there were no 'shoulds' for LCO volunteers. No one said, "You should phone bank" or "You should canvass" or "You should do this, or you should do that." If you make people feel guilty or push them out of their comfort zone, they'll most likely quit. After all, they aren't getting paid to do this. Many potential volunteers are like cats and cannot be herded. Knowing that, Marcia made a point of trying to personally answer every person who responded to one of the emails she sent to folks on the Big List. It took a lot of time but as she explains it, "My primary role was to be a communications hub, a 'human router' and a personal cheerleader for our supporters." She believed this two-way communication was a critical factor in LCO's ultimate success. Bottom line—people like to be appreciated and respected. It's the key to keeping them engaged. This was the whole philosophy of the Loudoun County for Obama grassroots organization, and it worked!

After the Walk for Change ended in June 2007, the grassroots organization received something of a jolt when they learned there would be no more glossy handouts and other printed literature from campaign headquarters. Instead, the MyBO groups were encouraged to download handouts on specific topics or create their own materials. The campaign was nice about it, and Trista Allen explained it all to Marcia Carlyn. The national Obama campaign had decided to devote nearly all its resources to the Iowa caucus because if the campaign didn't win it or come real close, the Obama campaign would be finished. It would be all over, there would be no tomorrow. And then there was the critical New Hampshire primary. Virginia's primary, she explained, was way down the pike—it even was after Super Tuesday. The campaign would shut down if Obama lost in Iowa so that's why everything had to be focused on the earlier primaries as they did not have unlimited resources.

Loudoun County for Obama got the message loud and clear—they were on their own. As it turned out, that was not a major problem. The enthusiasm in the grassroots organization was high, LCO had been given permission to use the terrific head shot photo of Barack Obama and the rising sun logo, and volunteers were finding creative ways to make their own materials to compensate for the loss of national support. Glossy literature was nice, but personal contact was nicer. It was the ultimate strength of the local movement. The group was becoming good at motivating people from within, and their volunteers found innovative solutions to the problems that emerged. This was a big part of the story of the grassroots campaign. Regardless of the difficulties, they made it work because native ingenuity and enthusiasm propelled them onward.

However, despite their high hopes and ingenuity, the

grassroots campaign made only moderate progress in the spring, summer and fall of 2007. Loudoun County for Obama was rounding up more Obama supporters and volunteers, but the pace was slower than Rollie and Marcia had hoped. It was simply so early in the presidential campaign that few people were tuned in to the election. Everyone on the Big List was invited to attend LCDC meetings, to LCO's monthly gatherings that were often held at a local restaurant, to join other volunteers at local events, to register voters (including fairs and festivals), and to gather signatures for the petition drive. Door-to-door canvassing events were also held in neighborhoods identified with census data, and the group learned which grocery store chains would allow them to set up a table outside an entrance to register voters, collect signatures, and recruit more supporters.

Another major reason that things were slower in 2007 than anticipated was because LCO was being careful not to interfere with campaigns for the 2007 November state and local elections. Rollie was especially sensitive in this regard and was very careful to not compete with the candidates. He expected to recruit many LCDC members and volunteers after these local elections were over in November.

And finally, another reason for the moderate progress in 2007 was because the grassroots organization was learning by trial and error what worked and what fell flat. The area was loaded to the gills with a highly educated population who worked mostly at commuter jobs in Washington, DC or Fairfax County. LCO volunteers soon learned that this kind of person is not home most of the time, and they're usually exhausted when they get home from work after a grueling commute. Then it's dinner with the kids and off to bed to do it again the next day. On weekends, they're taking the kids to soccer matches, swimming pools, birthday parties and all manner of things. With this lifestyle, people aren't home a lot. They don't answer their phones very often, and they're frequently not home to speak with canvassers. However, they almost all have email addresses, they read their email, and sometimes even answer it. By getting email addresses, Rollie and Marcia would have a means to communicate with this peripatetic group.

But many of these folks didn't want to give over their email addresses to a stranger. They were justifiably afraid of being put on spam mailing lists. As the LCO volunteers began canvassing and talking to folks at various events, they ran right up against this wall of reluctance to surrender email addresses.

By trial and error, Marcia began testing different ways to solve this problem. Eventually, after numerous false starts and unsuccessful attempts, she found a phrase that worked. As soon as she had talked with a person for a few moments and determined that they were a strong Obama supporter or leaned his way, she would give them a broad smile and ask, "Would you like us to keep you in the loop on our local Obama activities? All we need is your email address." She would then hand them a pen and a tally sheet on a clipboard and ask them to print their name and email address as clearly as possible. If they hesitated, she assured them that their email address would be kept confidential and would never be shared with other groups (a promise that LCO kept throughout the campaign and continues to keep). That's the phrase that worked and that's the phrase that led to a significant increase of information gathering by the grassroots campaign. The Big List was starting to take off!

During 2007, Marcia and Rollie also became much more adept at using MyBO and posting LCO events on the group's MyBO page. And although they were successful at growing the Big List, they continued to experiment with different ways to get the maximum benefit from the emails they were sending out. Marcia handled most of the emails, contacting folks on the Big List every couple of weeks to keep them updated on the national campaign and upcoming LCO activities. The intent was to keep them interested and create a sense of community. Her emails often included a summary of the latest campaign news and fun announcements, such as when Barack or Michelle would be appearing on a talk show.

With each email, Marcia tried to improve upon the last effort. In talking to supporters, she learned that the subject line of the email was more important than she had thought. Folks recommended that she mention Obama in the subject line if at all possible. Some even said they would delete an email without reading it if the subject line didn't attract their attention. She also learned from one of our volunteers, Diane Greene, how to make the emails crisper, more succinct, and to use **bold type** to highlight key points. This made sense. Most people in Loudoun County didn't have a lot of free time, so the emails had to be as short as possible. Bolded text helped to convey the message to the "glancers" (folks who were really rushed). Another important thing was to have the critical information prominently displayed so that recipients could see it right away and know whom to contact without having to search through the entire email. This was to have big implications in January 2008 when the lid blew off the Big List and things got wild and crazy.

A surprising thing happened during the summer of 2007—LCO volunteers were encountering a lot of folks who expressed distrust in Hillary Clinton. Actually the concern was more often with the ex-president. Quite a few people told canvassers they would gladly sign the Obama petition because they didn't like or trust Hillary Clinton. While gathering signatures in Old Historic Leesburg, Marcia Carlyn encountered several people who noticed her Obama poster from across the street, waited for traffic to clear, and crossed over to sign the petition, all the while announcing they did not want Hillary Clinton to be the Democratic nominee. This was not an unusual occurrence.

Although LCO's success was slower than desired in the summer of 2007, it was much faster than Hillary's or any of the other candidates' campaigns in Loudoun County. The Big List was growing, and even more importantly, LCO was finding the Eager Beavers. These super volunteers are always very important for a campaign.

The competition was practically invisible. Robert Latham, and later, Dan Moldover, headed up the Hillary for President campaign in Loudoun County, and were making little progress in spite of their diligent efforts. The Hillary campaign had pointed to Super Tuesday on February 5, 2008, fully expecting that Hillary would be selected the Democratic nominee by that time. The Virginia primary on February 12 would not be in play.

As a result, Robert and Dan couldn't get any resources for Loudoun County from their national campaign team even though it was headquartered just down the road in Arlington, Virginia. There was no canvassing in Loudoun by the Hillary campaign, and what phone banking was done was out of this national headquarters, about an hour's drive from Loudoun County. And the volunteers who made their way there phoned into the more important, early states. The Hillary campaign had concluded that Virginia was not going to be relevant in the Democratic primaries. Their thinking would later prove to be totally incorrect.

Obama on the other hand had empowered all of the states, like Virginia, through MyBO. Then they used their paid staffers in the key early states. They counted on folks like us in LCO to fill the gap. That resulted in scores of people working like crazy in 2007 to get ready for the Virginia primary; Hillary only had a few well-intended, but inexperienced, operatives to help her in Loudoun County.

The Obama campaign offered additional assistance to the MyBO groups that proved to be very helpful to LCO. Here's how things unfolded. On September 22, 2007, the campaign invited all the MyBO group administrators to participate in a conference call with Campaign Manager David Plouffe to get a preview of what to expect in the months ahead and to hear about a contest the campaign was holding. He announced that the groups that got the largest number of supporters to donate by September 30th would get a chance to have a personal conversation with Barack.

Now this sounded like fun! Rollie and Marcia immediately created a fundraising page on LCO's MyBO site and set a goal to raise $1,000 by the deadline. Marcia then sent emails to everyone on the Big List explaining the contest and urging supporters to donate through the LCO website. By that time the Big List included the 38 active members who had officially joined LCO on the website and another 190 supporters they had identified in the county. It turns out LCO almost won that contest! LCO raised $950 that week and came in #2 in the number of dollars raised and #3 in the number of donations among all the mid-sized Obama groups in the country (those with 30 to 84 members). The group that came in first (Young Lawyers for Obama) had a national membership base, so Marcia and Rollie felt LCO did really well in their first fundraising effort. Interestingly, they later learned they had raised even more money. It turned out many of their donors had hit the wrong "donate" button on LCO's confusing fundraising page, and LCO hadn't received any credit for their donations. They had actually raised nearly $2,000.

A few weeks later in October, Chris Hughes of the national campaign invited supporters to join a Grassroots Finance Committee and participate in several conference calls in which fundraising experts answered questions and provided advice on how individuals could raise funds for the campaign. Marcia joined the calls and learned a lot about effective fundraising strategies. However, instead of following the recommendation of the national campaign to raise funds on a personal fundraising page, she thought a much better approach would be to direct Loudoun supporters to the fundraising page on LCO's MyBO site. Rollie agreed with her decision. Their strategy paid off and by the election in 2008, LCO had raised nearly $80,000 for Barack Obama!

In mid-November 2007, the campaign offered another type of valuable training. Luke Peterson began a series of sessions via conference call to encourage MyBO groups to use the campaign's

Build the Hope (BTH) database. These were all the people who had signed up to volunteer on the national Obama site, but may not have joined a local group. Marcia heard about the training from Jane Van Ostern, a woman living in Richmond who had been very active in the petition drive and recently been appointed as a Virginia State Grassroots Co-Director after the petitions had been submitted. Kevin Wolf was no longer to be active in a state-coordinating role. Needless to say, Marcia jumped at the chance to participate in the training sessions, access information on Obama supporters in Loudoun County, and potentially expand LCO's Big List. She searched the BTH database for Obama supporters with Loudoun zip codes and then added registered voter data and phone numbers from the VAN database. LCO volunteers then called the prospects to confirm their interest and most of them were added to the Big List.

This unprecedented cooperation was achieved primarily because of Marcia's strong relationship with those with the juice at the Chicago headquarters and because the national campaign had no boots on the ground anywhere in Virginia. They had to rely on local organizations like LCO to get out the Obama vote for the primary. The BTH database was available only for a short period of time—a few weeks—but it paid off. We had a surge of new people to contact and people in place to process them. We later learned that access to the BTH database was ended because of perceived abuse in other parts of the country. However, they understood that LCO did not abuse the privilege and made good use of it while they had access. When you think on it, it was really amazing that the national campaign was even willing to try to do this. That was Marcia in action—a force to be reckoned with.

Given that the Hillary campaign was headquartered in Virginia, it was especially surprising that her campaign had to do a last-minute scramble to get her name on the primary ballot. Because her Virginia campaign had no local or state organizational networks worthy of the name, the Hillary for President Campaign ended up placing public ads for contractors to conduct a statewide petition drive to collect enough signatures to get her name on the ballot. They advertised they would pay one buck per name for those willing to circulate the petitions. By the time they started, Loudoun County for Obama had a head start of several months, thanks in large part to Kevin Wolf's administrative abilities, the weekly conference calls, and the CD representatives he had recruited.

One day in late November, 2007, well after the Obama

petition effort had ended in Loudoun County and all petitions submitted to Richmond, Rollie went into the LCDC headquarters and found a woman there he did not recognize. Turned out she was the person in charge of the petitions for Hillary Clinton in the 10th CD—Rollie's counterpart. She was there hoping to find canvassers to help them finish their petitioning, and they would be paid. Rollie offered to sign one for her, but indicated that other than Dan Moldover and Robert Latham, he really couldn't suggest anyone who would be interested in the effort. It was a last minute scramble, but they were finally able to put Hillary's name on the Virginia ballot.

While working on this book, one of the few people Rollie interviewed who supported Hillary was Chris Urban, a fellow who volunteered for LCDC back in 2000. A former Republican, he had by then seen the light. Turns out he was a big Bill Clinton fan and felt that Hillary deserved a shot at the presidency. He went to the headquarters in Arlington pre-primary and made phone calls. He never was told anything about the Loudoun volunteer effort; he never knew they existed. He was awed by the huge cavernous headquarters they had rented in Arlington, and then disappointed about how few volunteers showed up to work. Later he and his family went to a big Virginia rally for Clinton just before the primary and because of his volunteer status, were able to get down close and meet her. Chris had his family with him including his baby girl, who Hillary put into her arms. Politicians love babies! That became a photo op which was recorded by the press and later shown on the Katie Couric show!

After the very disappointing Virginia primary results, Chris decided he had to do a lot more than just make a few phone calls, so he started going to Pennsylvania for door-to door work. After one day of canvassing he was told that a well-known congressman was going to be in the area and wanted to know if where he had been would be good for him to visit. Chris encouraged it. Turned out it was actually Hillary who came to town, and she canvassed the same homes Chris had visited. He wished he had stayed to see it. Chris proved there was local support in Loudoun for Hillary; just hard to find.

As the days started to turn cooler, LCO volunteers had an increasing number of community events from which to choose. Fall days in Loudoun County are like a fine wine, rich in texture, full of body and wonderful to experience. Fall fairs and festivals abound in many villages and towns and the relief from the dog days of summer puts everyone in a good mood. Every day is like another explosion of joy. The Lucketts Fair kicks it all off in late August, soon followed by the Bluemont Fair, the Aldie Fair, and finally the mother of all fairs, the Waterford Fair. Marcia's emails encouraged supporters to attend these events wearing an Obama T-shirt or hat (the campaign had told LCO how to get a 15% discount on Obama merchandise). The fairs and festivals offered wonderful opportunities to meander around and register voters, collect signatures for the petition drive, and recruit more supporters.

Leesburg's Annual Halloween Parade, the longest running parade of its kind east of the Mississippi, topped off all these events. LCO volunteers came out in force to help the Democrats decorate their float and join the parade through Old Historic Leesburg, holding up Obama signs, and giving out candy to the kids. Governor Tim Kaine walked with them and a good time was had by all! A week later, many Obama supporters volunteered to help out at the polls for the state and local elections on November 6th, which turned out to be a turning point for LCO. Democrats did well in the election, and after a week or two off many of them were ready to turn their minds to presidential politics. Also, the Democratic debates were heating up and Barack Obama gave a helluva speech at the Iowa Democrats' Jefferson-Jackson (JJ) dinner on November 10th that helped him narrow the gap with Hillary Clinton.

A little later in the month, the six-month petition drive to put Obama's name on the ballot in Virginia was completed. Over the last several months, Rollie's crew in Loudoun County had secured about a thousand signatures, over the minimum quota of 400, but not as many as they wanted. Almost all of the signatures were obtained in Loudoun County by LCO volunteers despite the fact Loudoun comprised only about 40% of the 10th CD population. The campaign had shared with Rollie early in the petition drive the names and contact information of about 125 supporters who lived in the 10th CD but not in Loudoun County. He had sent three broadcast emails to them that netted 10 to 15 positive responses. He invited them to training sessions and sent them complete instructions along with blank petition forms. After following up with them numerous times, only one or two did any real work on the project. Very disappointing. Altogether, they may have collected about 100 names. But Loudoun covered their butts.

November 28th, Obama supporters submitted 20,000 names (nearly twice the number required) to the State Board of Elections.

Rollie drove to Richmond and joined 50 other people attending the outdoor publicity event prior to actually submitting the names at the Board of Elections. Kevin Wolf introduced Charley Kelly to the Obama supporters, the head guy at Governor Tim Kaine's Political Action Committee (PAC). A few moments later, Governor Kaine, the first governor in the country to endorse Obama, proudly announced that Senator Obama was the first candidate to qualify for Virginia's presidential primary. The petition drive had been a resounding success!

A couple of days later, the Democratic National Committee (DNC) convened a meeting at the Sheraton Hotel in Tysons Corner in Fairfax County, Virginia. This was a big event because all eight Democratic candidates running for president would be speaking. Before the event, rumors spread that Hillary's campaign wanted to flood the meeting room with her supporters as a show of strength. However, the Hillary campaign simply didn't have the local organizations that could mobilize enough volunteers to pull it off. The Obama campaign did; they also had Rollie Winter who knew how such things worked. He alerted the LCO folks to arrive very early to be at the front of the line. He also had identified and passed on to them exactly where to line up inside the building for the event. Turned out the room was jam packed, and there was only room for about two hundred observers of the 1,000 or so wanting in. They did have an overflow room with a TV feed, but it just wasn't the same. It was another example of how organizational experience and knowledge could lead to success. And by the way, Rollie was the very first in that line!

The day before and that morning, Rollie had worked the Obama table, alongside tables for the other candidates. The action was mostly around the Obama and Clinton outposts. The morning of the speeches, Jane Van Ostern found Rollie, introduced herself, and took him aside to let him know that leaders in the petitioning effort were to meet in a basement conference room right after Obama's speech. And be sure not to tell anyone about it except Marcia. Obama wanted to thank them for the job they had so successfully accomplished. WOW.

Twenty of them collected up in the room as directed and waited patiently. Just before Obama arrived, Kevin Wolf had them arrange themselves against a wall for pictures and to expedite a personal handshake from the candidate. Rollie was wearing his red pants and white "Vote Democratic" suspenders. Quite a sight as later pictures showed. After making a few thank-you remarks, he went down the line, and as soon as he passed Rollie, Rollie broke the line, reached over, tapped him on his shoulder to get his attention, and told him that today was the birthday of the volunteer he was just about to reach in the line. Kevin Wolf snapped that picture just as he tapped, and later told him if he had done that after Obama was elected President, the Secret Service would have had him on the floor in seconds. No touchee Presidentee without him making the first move to do so!

Marcia had thought to bring with her a couple of props to show Barack—a poster and a handheld sign. He signed the poster for her, and after he finished and was about to walk out the door, Rollie was able to retrieve the sign from Marcia and had him autograph that as well. They of course were thrilled with their new souvenirs. What a wonderful day for them.

Just after this event in early December, Loudoun County for Obama also had some really good luck. Franco Luz told Rollie that LCO could use his real estate office as a home for phone banking on weekends and evenings. This was a big surprise to Rollie because he thought Franco was a Hillary supporter. His offer was a major breakthrough since the grassroots group had tried unsuccessfully for months to find a central place to gather. Every campaign needs an office, even if it's only available part-time. Franco's office was perfect. It was centrally located in downtown Leesburg, with several rooms for callers to use and a large conference room on the second floor. Since it was a real estate office, there were several landlines that could be used by folks who didn't have cell phones. Franco and his office was a godsend, and he occasionally joined the group to work the phone banks and go out canvassing for Obama.

At LCO's first phone bank event, volunteers used a script and call list furnished by the national campaign to call voters in South Carolina. The purpose was to tell them that the Obama/Oprah rally had been moved to the University of South Carolina's football stadium because so many people wanted to attend. A week later, they called Democrats in Loudoun County to identify folks who liked Barack Obama. This time, Marcia created the call list using the VAN database, and she worked with other phone bankers to develop a suggested phone script. This was the start of the Eager Beavers, the gung-ho Obama fans who made Franco's office their second home and worked their tails off for nearly a year.

There's one more story to tell right now, and it's all about

Mike Turner. Mike had joined LCDC shortly after retiring from the Air Force in 2005. He became schooled in precinct operations and served as the precinct ops chair for the LCDC for a couple of years soon after joining. That's not an easy job. He earned his political stripes quickly and decided he had what it took to be a Congressman. In December of 2007, Mike Turner announced a run for the House of Representatives from the 10th CD. He first had to seek the Democratic nomination against Judy Feder, who had challenged incumbent Frank Wolf (no relation to Kevin Wolf) in 2006, gaining 41% of the vote, doing the best of all Democratic challengers since 1982. Judy Feder was from Fairfax, the largest jurisdiction in the 10th CD, and was strongly supported by Fairfax County Democrats as well as by Hillary Clinton supporters throughout the 10th CD.

Her strong support from the Hillary activists came about because at Mike's announcement for the seat in December, he endorsed Barack Obama! He was believed to be the first Democratic challenger for Congress in the country to have done so. This was an unprecedented act of political courage, but in some quarters, was believed to be foolhardy. At that time, Hillary was significantly leading Obama in the polls, especially in Fairfax. There were a lot more Democrats in Fairfax than in any of the other 10th CD localities, and it would be the Democrats choosing the nominee in a Democratic primary. Mike was well aware that he would likely have a tough time winning the June 2008 primary against a repeat challenger. We later learned that Judy Feder also rooted for Obama, but she was quiet about it. I believe most of the Feder supporters assumed she was for Hilary. I'll finish up the rest of Mike's story at the right time.

The Loudoun volunteers were excited as the year drew to a close. By the end of 2007, LCO's efforts were beginning pay off and a growth spurt had begun. The Virginia presidential primary was just a scant two months away. Starting from a small group of a dozen supporters in early April 2007, the Big List had now grown to 345 Loudoun residents who supported Barack Obama or were leaning his way. Nine months of grassroots organizing had resulted in nine new Obama supporters per week on average. This was far more progress than any of the other campaigns had made at that time.

Then it happened. It hit everybody full force in early January. From then until the Virginia primary on February 12th, all hell broke loose in Loudoun County!

Primary Time

"There are two primary choices in life: to accept conditions as they exist, or accept the responsibility for changing them."—Denis Waitley

As January 2008 opened, the eyes of those interested in politics were focused on January 3rd, the day of the Iowa caucus. Since 1972, Iowa has been the first state in the nation to evaluate presidential candidates of both parties. A surprisingly good showing in that year helped to promote McGovern's eventual nomination. And ever since Jimmy Carter got the huge boost to his campaign from his upset win in 1976, the Iowa caucus has progressively taken on a greater importance. Carter was the first presidential candidate to spend most of his early resources, both time and money, in Iowa. You remember Jimmy Carter, don't you? He was the peanut guy. Grew and sold a lot of peanuts. His brother Billy was into beer, and once came by Rollie's house for one. Hey, I'm not making this stuff up. It really happened. Most serious candidates since Carter have campaigned hard in Iowa in the belief that a win or a good showing would give their candidacy early momentum and national attention. Not so true for Republicans, but certainly true for Democrats.

For the Obama campaign, it was going to be a "Come to Jesus Moment." If the campaign came close or won in Iowa, it would prove that white voters would actually vote for an African American running for president. Obama could then go on to New Hampshire with momentum, the next test in the campaign. If Obama lost badly in Iowa, it would probably be the end of the Obama candidacy. At the time, the Hillary Clinton campaign was expected to get the nomination, despite her weakness in Iowa. Losing there wouldn't hurt her all that much. But Edwards was all in. He had to win or he was sourdough toast. However, a lot of observers thought that a second place finish for Hillary wouldn't hurt her campaign badly. A win by Obama would propel him from nowhere to competitive status, while a loss by Hillary would be survivable according to the Chattering Crowd of journalists. This was the conventional wisdom and it was probably correct. We'll never know about the other outcomes because Obama won more decisively than expected. Exceeding expectations is always extremely significant, especially to journalists.

Not to worry. On January 3, 2008, Obama shocked the political world by winning the Iowa caucus with 38% of the vote. As if that wasn't sensational enough, Hillary Clinton did not come in second—she came in third with 29% of the vote. John Edwards edged her out with 30%. One important consequence of the Iowa win was that African Americans around the country realized for the first time ever that a significant number of Caucasians would vote for an African American for president. And Daniel Dennison was there, taking no prisoners, but taking lots of notes. Daniel not only knows what happened here in Loudoun in the immediate days leading up to the Virginia primary, but also he has something to compare it to.

Just after Iowa, the first primary (not a caucus) was on the schedule for January 8th. An Obama win in New Hampshire might well have made the deal "signed, sealed, and delivered," to quote from Stevie Wonder's popular song that boomed out at Obama campaign rallies. Hillary Clinton won the primary with 39% of the vote, exceeding expectations. Obama was nipping at her heels with 36%, and Edwards trailed in third place with 17%. For the Obama campaign, it was a disappointing loss but not a fatal one. Edwards threw in the towel, and it looked like his withdrawal would help Obama more than Clinton. The race was now considered nearly a dead heat between Obama and Clinton.

Next up was the Nevada caucus on January 19th that resulted in another split decision. Hillary won the popular vote with 51% of the votes cast, but Obama gathered in more National Delegates. Thanks to Jeffery Berman for making that happen. He was the smart guy in the room. (Remember, he was one of Kevin Wolf's law partners.) This was another early sign that Berman had mastered the caucus and primary delegate selection process as Obama's National Delegate Director. The end result of Nevada was that the race still remained very very close. Next up was South Carolina. I'll tell you about that shortly.

While all this primary activity was going on, an interesting guest showed up at the LCDC meeting on January 24, just before the South Carolina primary. He was Joe Montano, one of three hired guns paid by the Democratic National Committee and assigned to the Democratic Party of Virginia a year earlier. His role was to report to the DNC and the state party about the on-ground strengths and weaknesses in the Northern Virginia counties and cities. DNC Chair Howard Dean, who was firmly committed to a 50-state strategy, spearheaded this initiative. Some recent state Democratic victories had moved Virginia to purple status, meaning the state could go either Democratic or Republican. If true, Virginia, as a Swing State, would be in for one helluva ride in 2008. The Obama strategists would be making the final call to fight it out in Virginia.

These Democratic victories began with Tim Kaine becoming Governor in 2005, Jim Webb winning the Senate in 2006, and Loudoun County electing a majority to the local Board of Supervisors in 2007. Joe Montano's job was to assess what was happening politically in his assigned localities and report back to the State Party on a weekly basis. He said he always gave a good report on Loudoun County because of the strong organization of the Loudoun County Democratic Committee and the Loudoun County for Obama grassroots movement.

One thing state party experts knew for sure—it was critical that Virginia keep the nomination process civil. They were careful, as were the leaders of the local Clinton campaign, to stress that both candidates were very capable, and the most important outcome was a Democratic win in November. No bridges burned, but there may have been a little charring. Joe told us that when reporting to the big shots, he always stressed that Loudoun was being very careful to keep the tensions well in check, unlike many of the other localities. And in fact, Loudoun was often cited as an example of handling these issues with sensitivity and understanding.

One of the best things about the grassroots movement in Loudoun County was the amazing people who got involved. In the weeks before the primary and throughout the rest of the campaign, there were a whole lot of smart, dedicated campaigners doing a whole lot of interesting things to help Barack Obama become our next president. Credit to Marcia and Rollie for finding these amazing supporters, but more credit to those they found for the countless hours they gave and the leadership they provided throughout the campaign. Many folks deserve to be introduced here, but if I were to do so the book would be longer than *War and Peace*. They are in no particular order except for the first.

I start with Ali McDermott and her two sons, because they were the first known Obama campaigners in Loudoun County, even before LCO was up and running. The family sat around the dining room table soon after Obama's announcement and discussed all the candidates at length. Each in turn said who they supported and why. After serious discussion and votes cast, it was unanimous! They all enthusiastically supported Obama. Darby decided that Obama was the best candidate for him. His primary motivating factor was that Obama would improve the international reputation of the United States in the world. Also, he profoundly did not want the United States to be seen as a racist country, and he felt Obama could best counter that. So the decision was made, and their family campaign started. Watch out, South Riding, the McDermotts were coming! Oh, did I forget to tell you? Darby was 12. And Bobby was 8!

They created, and then copied, their own literature. Ali contacted her local political friends to recruit her own cadre of Obama supporters. But it was the family who took their literature door-to-door and to businesses when they went shopping or out to eat. They knocked on well over a thousand doors before the primary. They were totally committed.

It got better. When Bobby went to school, he discussed the campaign with fellow students and tried to get them to persuade their parents to vote for Obama. Bobby always wore Obama buttons and stickers in school. About once a week his school teachers and principal told him to take the buttons and stickers off. Bobby told them NO, it was his civil right to wear them. The buttons and stickers stayed put. Coming out of the mouth of an 8-year-old, this was one of the most astonishing things since the invention of canned beer. Bobby had the courage of his convictions that enabled him to stand up to authority when he knew he was right, a very rare trait in an 8-year-old. Nothing intimidated this young man; no fake gun for him. Bobby McDermott was a true hero in the Great Campaign of 2008, and he did it 'his way', to paraphrase Frank Sinatra.

Darby also wore Obama stickers and buttons to school and caught unrelenting grief for doing it. He was repeatedly told to take them off, that they were a "distraction." Interestingly, most of the criticism came from his history teacher, who was a known Republican. Darby felt that if he had worn Sarah Palin buttons and stickers, nothing would have been said.

South Riding is in the Dulles district and was the fastest growing planned community in Loudoun County at the time, and close to Dulles Airport. Mostly town houses—thousands of them. The Dulles district chair was new to the job, and didn't have many active Democrats in the South Riding community. When Rollie was putting together the people for Election Day coverage, Ali agreed to take on the responsibility of finding precinct captains for the Dulles precincts, six in all, and keep him apprised of the scheduling. That took a bit of convincing. She previously had some unpleasant experiences with local political activists in Fairfax who started to go around her as she identified the people who were willing to help Democrats. That didn't set well with her at all. Rollie had no such plans and fully understood that the people she identified were her people. She would be the conduit to them unless she asked for help.

Darby was one of the most active volunteers in the entire campaign, often employing unconventional strategies. To Democrats, he pitched Obama as the candidate to support. With a few Republicans, he used a different approach. Virginia has an open primary, meaning anyone can vote in either the Republican or Democratic primaries. There was and is no party registration in Virginia. When voters come into the voting area, they are asked if they want a Democratic or Republican ballot. Darby found that Republicans didn't like Obama and thought any Republican could beat him. This, Darby stressed, was a good reason for Republicans to cross over and vote for Obama in the Democratic primary. By nominating Obama, Republicans could help select a Democrat that Republicans could defeat in the general election. Note that the Democratic Party in Loudoun did not encourage this practice—Darby thought it up all by himself!

How successful was he? We'll never know. He got more than a few Republicans to vote for Obama for sure. Kevin Turner, a precinct election official working for the Electoral Board at one of the South Riding precincts later observed that during the voting, a few people he knew as Republicans came in and requested the Democratic ballot. So Darby's strategy may have been more effective than anyone thought. (Of course there is also the likelihood that many of the moderate Republicans switched because they just didn't like McCain or felt McCain was a lock and they couldn't stand the thought of having another Clinton in the White House.)

The more poignant story of the McDermott effort came when Darby visited a farm house just outside of South Riding. That development was plopped down smack dab in the middle of farmland, and outside the edge of the development, were the few remaining farmers. Darby decided to visit one such home. The couple had to have been in their late eighties, and they were quite intrigued with this young man at their door pushing for his candidate. They invited him in and they had a long serious talk. The man did most of the talking. This was old-school Virginia. After Darby made his pitch, the old man said, "Son, I gotta tell you. I'm a Republican, and been votin that way my whole life. But I'm real impressed that yer here campaigning for your guy. But I have a piece of advice for you. You need to switch candidates." "Why is that, Sir?" "No Black man is ever goen to be elected president of these here United States. Yer wasting yer time. You seem to be a nice young man, and that's my advice."

Darby then pulled out the voting for Obama strategy to insure a November win for Republicans. The farmer said he and his wife would think on it, and Darby skedaddled. I'll finish the story later.

Now I have to tell you about Gail Wise, who got started with LCO relatively late in the game. She had served as the press secretary for the American Bar Association and once worked on Birch Bayh's communications team. Gail had a wealth of expertise. Rollie had first interacted with Gail back in 2004 when she was a strong Edwards's supporter. She then helped some in the Gore/Edwards campaign, and Rollie had put her name in his Rolodex.

Rollie contacted her early in 2007 about supporting Obama, and although she really liked him, still leaned Edwards. With Edward's withdrawal in January and the grassroots campaign taking off, Marcia was becoming waaaay over-loaded, and she jumped higher than a startled rabbit at Gail's offer to help. The two of them worked closely together from that point on, with Gail handling much of the administration for the grassroots campaign. In the weeks leading up to the primary, Gail spent endless hours mobilizing volunteers for specific activities, writing phone scripts and other informational pieces, managing the phone bank, following up with voters who requested additional information, coordinating housing for out-of-state volunteers, and assisting with the Get Out The Vote (GOTV) efforts and logistics for the Virginia primary. She was indefatigable and worked even harder after the primary—more on that later.

Bernard Hill was an early Eager Beaver. He was born in New York City in the late 1940s before the family moved to South Carolina in the 1950s. He attended Allen College in South Carolina on the unlikely combination of a dual scholarship in football and choir. The football coach and the choir director worked out a deal—Bernard could play football if it didn't interfere with the choir, and he could sing in the choir if it didn't interfere with his football! How he pulled that off I'll never know. He took his degree and became a legal assistant working in the state of Maryland for many years.

By 2007, Bernard was living in Loudoun County and had just

lost his wife of many years. He became depressed and despondent, doing little other than watching television all day. His daughter was determined to get him involved in something to move him beyond his loss. She told him to go on the Internet, go to MyBO, find something he would like to do, and then do it. She said she would pester him until he did it.

So Bernard went to the MyBO website and was promptly turned off by everything he saw—phone banking, canvassing, and data entry. None of this appealed to Bernard. But because he knew his daughter would be after him if he didn't even try, Bernard decided to fake it. He found Franco's office and poked his head in, intending to fake phone calls for an hour and then leave.

Only he didn't fake the calls. Instead, when he entered the office the electricity in the place was palpable. Bernard had never seen such energy and enthusiasm among a group of volunteers. He sat himself down and began making real phone calls. Before the night was done he became determined to return the next night. Before long he couldn't wait to get down to that office to make calls. Then he started going door-to-door, canvassing for the election. The grassroots campaign hooked Bernard Hill like a fish that had taken some sweet bait. The end result would be an amazing journey for a once angry Black boy from South Carolina. Is this a great country or what?

Patti Maslinoff was driving home on King Street from her psychiatrist's office one day when she spotted the newly placed Obama signs in front of Franco's place. What a coincidence. The major topic they had discussed at her session was whether or not she had the courage and fortitude to once again get actively involved in a community effort, and in particular, the Obama campaign. This was an extremely difficult decision for her. Let me tell you why.

As a child, she grew up in a very liberal, Jewish, activist family on Long Island, NY. Civil rights were their main cause, and we are talking about the 60's. Long story short, they stood apart in their 99% white neighborhood. Tension ran high enough that a group of neighbors circulated a petition asking that they move. It was because her family was actively supporting integration, while many of their neighbors were strongly opposed. It was thought that if they could get rid of her parents, then the possibility of African Americans trying to move into their neighborhood would be substantially reduced.

I'll talk more about Patti later, but for now, I'll just tell you the reason why Patti's stop at the headquarters was so significant for her that day. In her last years at college, she began to have severe bouts of depression. Later she was also diagnosed with obsessive-compulsive disorder. This combination of illnesses substantially affected her ability to interact with others. Since the time of her diagnosis, she had had many ups and downs—mostly downs. For her, the Obama campaign became the instrument for her return to group activism after a very long hiatus. Patti decided to take the plunge and stop by the LCO office that day, and, much to her own surprise, she soon became the famous Button Lady of the grassroots campaign.

Now I'll go back to the South Carolina primary. When Daniel Dennison joined the LCO, he added a totally new skill set to the Loudoun County for Obama grassroots campaign. It is important to note that most of Daniel's experience was working closely with national campaign staffs, helping with specific local and state campaign organizations. He took a few weeks off from work and dived right in by going to the top organizers in a state and saying, "Give me a job." They would then assign him to a locality, and he would swoop in like any other paid staffer and do the deed.

He first was involved in 2000 with the Gore campaign. He also was a volunteer organizer in the John Kerry campaign, running an operation that sent hundreds of busloads of volunteers into the battleground states of Iowa and Wisconsin. At the same time, he helped with fundraising. He and family lived in Chicago when he learned first-hand about the Cook County Democratic Machine and what a real political campaign looks like. Some organizations may do it better than Chicago's Democratic machine, but not many. He cut his teeth as an Obama volunteer organizer in the Iowa caucus, and he already knew some of the political operators from previous campaigns. Yes ma'am, Daniel Dennison knows a thing or two about presidential ground game politics in swing states. Marcia and Rollie never had that kind of experience.

With family in Northern Virginia, Daniel and his wife moved to Leesburg in 2006. He was following the 2008 presidential race closely and decided early on that his guy was Obama. He didn't know about LCO at the time. But he did know Iowa was important and trucked out there to help. Immediately after the Nevada caucus, he stopped by LCO's campaign headquarters in Leesburg, checked it out, worked the phones a bit, but then headed out to South Carolina to help the Obama campaign there. That boy just couldn't wait.

In Greenville, he worked a very poor neighborhood and was constantly eyed by street people until one day one of them asked what he was doing there. He replied that he was working for the Obama campaign. That changed everything. People in the neighborhood no longer viewed this big white guy with suspicion. He was one of them.

Late at night after the polls closed for South Carolina's primary on January 26th, Daniel Dennison and some union organizers were studying election returns and they were stunned by what they saw. It wasn't just that Obama won the primary by beating Hillary Clinton 2-1, 55% to 26%, and blowing out John Edwards in his own backyard by 3-1, it was how Obama did it. This involves another yarn.

The one thing the greybeards taught political organizers was that young people, poor people, and minorities don't vote in nearly the proportion of the rest of the population. Routinely, new organizers became determined to change this, invested a lot of time on the ground trying to alter the voting pattern, but they almost always failed. They wasted a lot of time in well-intended efforts that did not succeed. But this time, things were different.

As Daniel and others scanned the demographics of the South Carolina primary, they were shocked. Young people, poor people and minorities had turned out in historically unprecedented numbers. Daniel later said his "jaw hit the ground" when he saw those numbers and so did those of the union organizers. Nobody had ever seen anything like this in a presidential election in his or her lifetime. It was then that he realized something really big and truly unprecedented was coming down. Obama had altered the voting demographics. Obama had changed the traditional voting pool by expanding it to include groups that historically didn't vote in large numbers. Obama could win.

Daniel left South Carolina elated and hustled back to Loudoun County to help prepare for the Virginia primary two weeks later on February 12th. It appeared that the Democratic nomination was still closer than a tick on a deer. But up to then, Hillary was generally regarded as the favorite, despite recent polls showing Obama with a slight lead when Daniel showed up. Maybe the pollsters had learned that Daniel had come to town!

When Daniel returned from South Carolina, even this veteran of Chicago politics was surprised by what he saw. He had never seen a grassroots organization put together an operation as sophisticated as LCO had done. Their Big List and Eager Beaver List were political gold. The grassroots organization had now identified nearly 2,000 Loudoun voters who supported or leaned toward Obama. The Big List was growing by leaps and bounds. With no one on the ground helping from the national campaign, the grassroots movement in Loudoun County was relentlessly advancing Obama's candidacy with a multitude of locally organized events. There were debate-watching parties, primary-watching parties, free Obama yard signs and bumper stickers, and invitations to promote Obama at rallies (including the Martin Luther King march in Leesburg). LCO's communication systems were in full gear—LCO had created a terrific flyer for supporters to distribute ("8 Reasons to Vote for Barack Obama"), upcoming events were posted on MyBO, emails were going out every 2-3 days, the phone bankers were calling folks like crazy, other volunteers were phoning from home using call sheets Marcia sent them, census data was being used to create street sheets for the canvassers, Rollie was recruiting more supporters through personal phone calls and emails, the Eager Beavers were coming up with new ideas every day, and more and more volunteers were joining LCO activities to advance the cause. The Great Grassroots Campaign was on the march.

Feeling the positive energy when he entered the LCO office, Daniel Dennison made an offer that took the group by surprise: "I can help you Get Out The Vote for the primary." Daniel was incredibly skilled at GOTV efforts and, after a short get-to-know-you meeting, he was given free rein to do what he thought was needed to get out the vote. He knew how to do it; he'd done it all in Chicago, Iowa, and South Carolina. No training required, folks; he was hell on wheels, knew what to do, and did it.

Daniel brought order out of chaos at the office. Rollie was no help there at all—he was locked up in his basement, the king of precincts. Daniel had been in the office just a couple of days before an Obama staffer, Chris Lewis, showed up. He had recently been assigned to Virginia, and more specifically, to Northern Virginia to get the lay of the land. Rollie came to a planning meeting and Chris quickly realized that Daniel and Marcia had everything under control at the office. Chris did provide an updated call list from the national Obama campaign files. Turned out they didn't need it. They already had every name on his list in the Big List, plus a whole lot of others. Rollie went back to his basement to get the polls covered. The national Obama GOTV strategy did not include this activity.

Daniel then was briefed by Marcia about LCO's data collection. He was especially interested in how they were using the Big List and the VAN for phoning and canvassing. He taught the core team of Eager Beavers all about GOTV tactics, and he even convinced a friend who lived in another region to spend a week in Leesburg entering data round the clock. As Daniel explained to the group, "During the days leading up to the primary, more and more Obama supporters will be coming here to help the campaign. We absolutely need to be ready for them. We'll be prepared with phone scripts and street sheets for canvassing, and we'll train them before they start, but we may have more people than we expect so we'll need to find other things for them to do. No one should be told there's nothing for them to do!"

Marcia later told Rollie she lost sleep over this last point. If they really did get an avalanche of volunteers, what could these folks be given to do if all the call sheets and street sheets had been given out? The answer turned out to be a "honk and wave" visibility campaign. Volunteers would stand at key traffic location spots in Loudoun and wave poster signs showing Barack Obama (that same head shot photo) and the words VOTE TUESDAY. On primary day, the posters would say VOTE TODAY. Steve Ames analyzed the entire county and identified the best spots for a visibility campaign of this type (busy streets, shopping centers, etc.). He also contacted the Sheriff's Office to get their advice, since it was certainly possible that Obama volunteers might experience some harassment. Everyone liked the poster sign idea, so the LCO team bought a lot of foam board and rubber cement. Ted Carvis (Marcia's husband) cut 100 sheets of 20" x 30" foam board in half (not an easy task), and Marcia printed off hundreds of color copies of Obama's smiling face, the rising sun logo, and the messages to be displayed.

About a dozen folks volunteered to make the poster signs, and the poster party turned out to be great fun. Everyone sat around the big conference table in Franco's office doing a lot of cutting and pasting. They talked about the campaign and anything else that came to mind, all managing to tolerate the unexpectedly strong aroma of rubber cement. They were on a Glue High. The group ended up assembling 200 15" x 20" poster signs which turned out to be a great hit during the GOTV campaign. Daniel had been absolutely right about throngs of supporters showing up at headquarters. All 200 poster signs were handed out that week along with guidelines for the participants. Most of the poster signs were returned and recycled, and most were used again in November or before. All in all, Steve's "honk and wave" visibility campaign was a huge success. Parents participated with their kids, teenagers waved signs with their friends, and volunteers gave thumbs up to friendly honkers. There was no serious harassment, reporters wrote stories about the participants, and a good time was had by all!

Steve Ames showed everyone that he was a capable leader and subsequently played several important roles with LCO and the campaign. He will pop up often in the following chapters, so pay attention. Steve Ames was born in Painesville, Ohio, took a dual major degree at Hiram College in economics and psychology, and then moved to Virginia in 1980 and to Loudoun County in 1988. His introduction to politics came at the age of four when his mother took him to a John F. Kennedy rally in 1960. His father was an Ohio Political Committeeman, what in Virginia is called a precinct captain. He personally got involved in politics for the first time in January 2008 in the Obama Campaign. Like many he was impressed by Obama's keynote speech at the 2004 Democratic Convention and became a true believer. Like others, Steve discovered the Loudoun County for Obama Group on the MyBO web site. He began volunteering for the campaign by phone banking at Franco's after the Iowa Caucuses. And from that point on, Steve was indispensable to the campaign. Steve Ames is by nature very entrepreneurial and initiated many creative projects, including creating a variety of color-coded charts showing the best places in Loudoun County to set up voter registration tables and stage other "honk and wave" events. Throughout the campaign, he was a driving force behind many of LCO's grassroots projects.

Now, a little background about what happened on Super Tuesday, February 5th, a week before the Virginia primary. To the surprise of many, Barack Obama managed to fight Hillary Clinton to a draw in the 24 primaries and caucuses that were held that day. She won 46% of the popular vote; he won 45%. She won 847 delegates to the Democratic National Convention; he won 834. That's closer than leaves on a cabbage head. This was not supposed to happen. The Clinton campaign had assumed that Super Tuesday would decide the nomination in her favor, and the race would be over. However, the voters refused to anoint Hillary in a coronation in those Democratic primaries. Worse yet, Clinton had done little organizing in the states still to come. Obama, on the other hand, had expected and planned for a long race against Hillary. It looked like the battle was on, and in Virginia, only one combatant had taken the field.

The surprising outcome on Super Tuesday meant that the Virginia primary suddenly became extremely important. Virginia had not been a factor in the Democratic presidential nomination in many years. Nobody alive seemed to remember the last time Virginia was in play at primary time. Now it was on the top burner, scheduled for February 12th, along with DC and Maryland. The Mid-Atlantic Primaries, they called them.

If there was one thing in this world Daniel Dennison understood, it was 'touches.' A 'touch' is campaign slang for reaching out to a voter to contact him or her. A touch can be done with a literature drop, phone call, or a door knock to speak with the voter in person. A touch does not mean a successful contact; it means a physical effort to make the contact.

The short-term goal was to do as many touches as possible in Loudoun County on the weekend before the primary election on Tuesday, the 12th. A full year of ongoing preparation allowed the group to kick into high gear quickly. The volunteers had identified a huge number of Obama supporters. The task was to remind them several times to vote. Daniel Dennison plunged into directing the effort.

In the last three days before the Virginia primary, Loudoun County for Obama managed to touch every identified prospective Obama voter five times. FIVE TIMES! Daniel, who is in a position to know, regarded this as a remarkable accomplishment for a grassroots operation using only volunteers and with no help from paid professionals. But of course, Daniel was serving as our GOTV staff surrogate.

Loudoun County for Obama was ready for the big day. By February 12, 2008, LCO had identified over 2,500 Obama supporters in Loudoun County. Since more than one supporter was included in most email addresses and telephone numbers that had been collected, the outreach likely much greater.

Where was Rollie, when all of this was going on? He was down in his basement working the phones and emails, putting together poll worker and driver schedules for Election Day. Precinct Operations. That's Rollie's bag. And he's good at it.

He started by attempting to recruit a district coordinator for each of the 8 magisterial districts in Loudoun County. He found five of them, but then ran out of talent and came up three short so handled three of the districts himself. The district coordinator was to recruit and manage precinct captains in their districts. Altogether there were 62 precincts to be covered on Election Day. He knew it would be impossible to cover all the precincts from 5:30 a.m. to 7:00 p.m. So he decided to schedule the busy times (7-9, 11-1, and 4-7) in 50 of the largest precincts. Now that's still a lot of poll-person hours!

Every precinct required a poll opener to take signs and material to the poll and a poll closer to pick up the signs and leftover material. Delivery of the material to the openers had to be scheduled and executed. When the morning shift finished, they were instructed to leave the materials in a plastic bag next to the Obama sign. Poll workers coming later in the day would go to the sign and use the supplies found in the bag. Since many of these volunteers were new, they had to be trained. Altogether, he was looking for over a thousand volunteer-hours for poll coverage and drivers on primary day—no small task!

Instructions for the poll worker were included with the material, with a request to snag future supporters while greeting voters: "Please ask the friendlies as they leave if they would like to be added to the local OBAMA and Dem email lists to get into the loop. Collect the indicated information on the tally sheet on the clipboard. If they are real friendly, ask if they would like to volunteer and if yes, put a "V" somewhere on the line with their name."

Drivers were scheduled to circulate through the polls and note whether the poll was covered, give encouragement to the poll workers who were on the job, make sure materials were well stocked, and keep Headquarters informed as to status and any unresolved problems. Two or three drivers were assigned to work out of the headquarters to take call-ins for rides to the polls, solve material shortages, and help with problems that arose. The poll worker schedules were consolidated in ruled tablets, one for each district. Each of these tablets was divided into their precincts, and each precinct page included poll opener, closer, and poll workers with their assigned hours and contact information.

Since there were little to no ground operations planned for any of the other Democratic candidates, the Obama campaign was able to use the LCDC office for their Headquarters on primary day, with the promise of helping all those who might call or drop in, no matter whom they supported. Signs for Clinton and Obama were displayed at the front door, as they had been throughout the campaign. Rollie recruited Juan Perez and his wife, Maureen (Mo) Jules, to help him on Election Day. He had already decided to use

Tina Gulland, who, in the previous week, had agreed to come to the LCDC office on primary day and manage the drivers. Tina took the day off from the Washington Post as the Director of their radio and TV projects, to give us a hand—a very busy and capable lady indeed. She was a welcome addition to our grassroots organization and Election Day supervision.

Let me take a few lines to tell you a little more about Juan Perez, and his wife Mo. They became a big part of the LCO story, I'll introduce them here. Juan Carlos Perez was born in San Juan, Puerto Rico, and the son of Cuban refugees who fled Cuba in 1967. At the age of four he moved with his family to Miami, Florida. He received his degree from the University of Florida in Gainesville, Florida. He went to school with his wife Maureen (usually called Mo), who was also active in the 2008 presidential campaign. She earned a degree in engineering with a specialty in Computer Science from the University of North Florida in Jacksonville, Florida. There they started a company to post student résumés on the Internet, using what was then a new medium. America Online took notice of the two, hired them on the spot, and they moved to Fairfax County in 2005 and then relocated to Loudoun County. In those days America Online was headquartered here in Loudoun County.

The campaign of 2008 was the first campaign they ever participated in. They did a lot for the grassroots campaign of Rollie Winter and Marcia Carlyn. They phone banked, canvassed, travelled with the group to Chambersburg, Pennsylvania, and worked out of the local offices—they did almost everything and did it on a big scale. These two were major players in the 2008 campaign.

National polls the week before the Virginia primary had shown a remarkable surge for Obama, with a lead of nearly 15%. Few believed that Virginia could possibly do that well. Hillary was just too well entrenched. Rollie and Marcia, and most of the LCO leadership, were optimistic. However, the weather forecast was not good and would certainly suppress the vote. Since the large bulk of Obama voters were those who normally don't vote in large numbers—the young, the old, the African Americans—many thought Hillary would somehow pull it out as she did in New Hampshire, where the last poll had shown Obama ahead by 10 points, and he lost by three.

Marcia, Daniel, Gail, and Steve were ready for the Get Out The Vote phoning and visibility activities. Rollie, Juan, Mo, and Tina were ready for precinct operations. The acting district chairs had lined up the precinct captains, with the McDermotts handling the six

South Riding precincts. 50 precinct bags had been filled with materials and they, along with Obama signs, had been delivered to the openers, who in most cases, were also planning to take some of the first shift for an hour or two at the polls. After nearly a year of preparation, we were ready to take our case to the actual voters.

Late on election eve, the LCO leaders received a very supportive email message from Chris Lewis, the regional director from the Obama campaign who had been sent to oversee primary efforts in Northern Virginia. Here's what Chris told us: "Awesome work everyone! I just got off a conference call with our statewide staff and everyone is ready to go tomorrow. You should be really proud of what you have accomplished out in Loudoun, basically on your own. I am confident that your work is going to bring us a victory tomorrow."

Election Day was here! Rollie set his alarm for 4:00 a.m. and was off by 4:30 with his computer and vital papers. It was only a 15 minute drive to the LCDC Headquarters in downtown Leesburg, and the roads were nearly empty. He dressed warmly as it could get pretty chilly in the office. It was below freezing, with threatening gray skies, but fortunately no precipitation as yet. He passed right by Franco's office and saw they were not yet open for business. They were not expected until about the time the polls opened at 6:00 a.m.

The Headquarters team was in business by 4:45 a.m. But they soon discovered they had a major problem. Rollie had not gone over Tina's responsibilities for managing the drivers in nearly enough detail. Drivers were expected to show up soon to get their backup supplies and the polling places they were to monitor. There was a map on the wall showing the poll locations with their addresses. They had divided the polls up for the eight drivers with those precinct names and addresses. GPS wasn't in general use; only one or two of them had it. The big problem they faced was that the drivers didn't know the precinct locations and the best route to take between them, particularly if they didn't live in the area.

When the first driver showed up, the problem was immediately exposed. Juan Perez, the computer guru, said he could use Google and create maps and directions for the drivers and print them right then; not a problem; piece of cake. Shortly thereafter the second driver arrived. Maps not ready. Wanted to do a different route than what Juan had been working on, and Juan aimed to please—and in about 30 minutes the first driver was out the door and on his way. By then there were six more drivers waiting for instructions. One of them decided to go buy some coffee and donuts for the crew. Tina entered into the discussion and made sure they had all of the materials they were supposed to have. One of the drivers looked over his list of precincts and decided that he didn't need to wait for a map and took off. Juan produced his next map thereafter, and then had a paper jam. It was nearly 9:00 a.m. before they were all on their way. The headquarters team was not happy. Mo, Juan's wife, was there and her sparkling personality helped immensely to lighten the mood.

Reports started to come in that voting was heavy, much more than expected. That lifted our spirits. Only a very few of the volunteers didn't show up. Since we had not had any requests for rides, one of the drivers said he would go cover a no-show precinct and that's where he voted. Mid-morning arrived, and we started to receive reports of precipitation—just a little snow. In an hour or two, the wind had picked up and the snow had turned to sleet. That essentially ended the opportunity of collecting names on clipboards as people were bundled up hurrying to their cars after voting.

Most of our people hung in there. None of the drivers got stuck. For the most part, the bag system seemed to be working well, with the new precinct workers going to their poll and finding the bag of materials to hand out even after there was a gap in coverage. There were only a couple of calls received from new poll workers who couldn't find their bag. In one case Rollie was able to track down the culprit. The departing poll worker didn't read all of the instructions and decided it would be better to take the bag to a friend of his living close to the poll because he was afraid it would be taken if he just left it there. But unfortunately he forgot to call headquarters and inform them. That information was eventually passed to the new poll worker who was then able to retrieve the bag and get on with her work. In one other case, the driver was able to deliver a new set of materials to a polling location and put the precinct worker back to work.

With the heavy turnout, the precincts started to have shortages of supplies, despite our entreaties to the workers at the beginning to push recycling. Turned out there were some voters who indicated they wanted to save the sample ballots as souvenirs. That was a first for Rollie! He had never heard that before! Tina graciously said she was willing to pay for a couple of thousand sample ballots to be reprinted at Staples, and the drivers were able to distribute them to those who had run out or were running short.

Rollie reported that after that rough start everything seemed to be working OK. They received very few calls at the office. They didn't have all the scheduled precincts covered as planned all of the time, but came close. Juan and Mo left the headquarters about 3 p.m. to catch a plane to California. Their only concern was the weather as the roads were getting slippery. They arrived in California by 7 p.m., Pacific Coast Tim, rented a car and were drinking margaritas in the resort pool by 10 p.m., hoping for the best. What a contrast to their day in Loudoun County!

So how did we do? Damn well, thank you Drew. What an incredible victory for Obama in Virginia, and what a decisive win in Loudoun County! There was a big turnout despite the frigid ice storm on Election Day, and Loudoun County gave Barack Obama a 62% to 38% win over Hillary Clinton. We outdid all the other counties in Northern Virginia except Arlington. And Barack received 23% more votes in Loudoun than all the Republican candidates combined! Not bad for a traditionally conservative county with an African American population much lower than that of the state as a whole—8% vs. 20%. The statewide vote was also definitive, with Obama beating Clinton 64% to 35%. These results again proved that as Loudoun County goes, so goes Virginia.

The Democratic voter turnout in Loudoun County was unbelievable—22% of all registered voters in Loudoun voted in the Democratic primary and only 11% voted in the Republican primary. In the last presidential primary in 2004, the Loudoun County turnout had been only 7%. An additional analysis was conducted to determine the percent of Loudoun's "Democratic base" who voted in the 2008 Democratic primary. This was a bit challenging since Virginia citizens do not designate a political party affiliation when registering to vote. It was decided that the best estimate of the size of a county's active Democratic base would be the number of people who had voted for the Democratic candidate for U.S. Senate in the most recent general election. The results showed that an amazing 85% of Loudoun's Democratic base voted in the 2008 primary—a higher turnout than any of the other Northern Virginia counties and the state as a whole.

I learned later from Ali McDermott that they had all the South Riding precincts covered all day as promised and that Darby had actually served as one of the precinct captains. The farmer and his wife that he had canvassed a several weeks earlier both showed up to vote and told him that they had actually followed his advice and voted for Obama—but still insisted he had no chance in November. We shall see, thought Darby. We shall see.

Obama's success was accomplished in Loudoun County by the early start, strong leadership, and hundreds of enthusiastic, committed volunteers spending thousands of hours reaching out to the greater community. Here's a review of what was done:

- Reached out to several specific groups such as young voters, seniors, local churches, veterans, African Americans, Latinos, Muslims, and more
    - Collected names for the petition
    - Promoted Barack Obama at local fairs and other events
    - Canvassed neighborhoods to spread the word Obama
    - Marched in the Leesburg Halloween parade
    - Made thousands of calls at our wild and crazy phone bank
    - Bought and distributed yard signs
    - Put together our own poster signs
    - Waved these poster signs near well-traveled intersections
    - Distributed flyers to bus commuters starting at 6:30 a.m.
    - Cheered Barack Obama at his local rallies
    - Updated our data base to prepare for GOTV
    - Stuffed packets for poll workers
    - Served as poll workers in nearly freezing weather
    - Drove folks and took material to the polls

Virginia really came through for Barack Obama and gave the campaign a momentum boost at exactly the right time. The Virginia primary was now a thing of the past, a boulder in the rear view mirror, and the grassroots campaign in Loudoun County shifted into an entirely new phase.

Those Who Know the Rules, RULE

> *"The application of parliamentary law is the best method yet devised to enable assemblies of any size, with due regard for every member's opinion, to arrive at the general will on the maximum number of questions of varying complexity in a minimum amount of time and under all kinds of internal climate ranging from total harmony to hardened or impassioned division of opinion."*—Robert's Rules of Order Newly Revised [RONR (11th ed.), Introduction, p. lii]

Rules are not my thing so before I get into them, I want to share a highlight of my own early campaign efforts.

It's March 9, 2008, and I am at my computer bringing up MyBO the Barack Obama website, to get a list of telephone numbers for a phone banking night. The list comes up, and it doesn't look promising—phone banking into the Mississippi primary scheduled for March 11. "This doesn't look like fun," I thought. "Mississippi has more racists than bluebonnets in central Texas on a cool spring day."

An hour into the calling and it happened. I made my standard pitch to a caller when the voice at the other end of the line said, "Son, I'm a Tuskegee Airman. Do you know what a Tuskegee Airman is?"

"Yes, sir, I do. My daddy was a fighter pilot flying P-38s in the Pacific during the War. He told me all about the Tuskegee Airmen. I'll bet you flew dive bombers out of Italy during the War."

"Son, I did," he said. "I was shot down three times, and three times I walked back to our lines. Each time they gave me a new plane to fly."

Then he digressed. "You know, living in Italy was wonderful for me. I could live anywhere I wanted to, I could eat in any restaurant I wanted to, and I could date any girl who would go out with me."

What he's saying, of course, is that for the first time in his life he was not living under the Jim Crow laws of the American South, the old Confederacy boiling with racial hatred and discrimination.

"When the war ended they put me on a ship to Brooklyn. I got off the ship and went to Grand Central Station and bought a train ticket to Birmingham, Alabama, where my parents lived. I got on that train and when the train crossed the Potomac River, the conductor came up to me and said, 'Nigger, we're in Virginia now. It's time for you to go to the back of the train.'"

It was a moment of high drama. He continued on. "Son, when that conductor told me that, I thought, 'I just fought in a world war for my country and in my own country I can't even sit in the train where I want to sit'."

At this point his voice began to break up. "Son, I never thought in my lifetime a Black man could be elected President of the United States, but I think this time it just might happen."

I thought for a moment and said, "Sir, I'm doing everything I can to make that happen."

With that, one of the most remarkable phone calls of the 2008 campaign ended.

I also remember the following week I came across an early 2008 March issue of England's *The Economist*. Loudoun County had hit the world press! *"A rapid influx of voters has thrown Loudoun County's politics into disarray. In 2006 the county narrowly plumped for Jim Webb, now Virginia's Democratic senator, after years of Republican domination in the area. Tim Buchholz, Loudoun's Democratic Committee Chair, says 'his party held just three of 29 elected county offices in 2003. Now they are running even with the Republicans."* This campaign was getting interesting!

The stakes had never been higher. It was time for a change at the national level. It was time to swing the states. And to swing Virginia, we had to swing Loudoun County. It's time to find out from Rollie about the local political process that took place after the primary in mid-February. Obama won big—in Virginia and in Loudoun County. But now what? I knew there were Delegates to choose for a couple of conventions plus all the minutia of party politics leading up to the National Convention in August. So I set up another interview with him.

I pulled in at our normal meeting place at the Rust Library in Leesburg just before 10 a.m., secured a meeting room for our use, and Rollie showed up ready to talk. To paraphrase Kasper Gutman from the movie "The Maltese Falcon," talking isn't something you do judiciously unless you do a lot of it. And he does a lot of it. I told him what I wanted to cover today, and he was ready—he even had a list of topics to discuss. Since I was not very anxious to learn about all the rules, I thought I would divert him.

"Rollie, before we get into the rules, tell me about what happened when the primary was over. You had a large group of volunteers enthusiastic about our huge victory here in Loudoun

County. Did you put them back to work?"

"We sure did! Well, actually, Marcia Carlyn did. She and some of the key Eager Beavers met to plan what LCO was to do next. One of the first things they did was to hold a big Brainstorming Bash at a local restaurant. She told me that more than 40 enthusiastic Obama volunteers showed up to offer suggestions. It was great fun, and they even picked up four new supporters who happened to be dining at the restaurant that night!

"The most important decision they made that night was to have the LCO begin spending time calling and walking primaries in nearby primary states. Even though we had done surprisingly well in our primary, Obama's nomination was far from certain, and the race between Barack and Hillary was still neck and neck. The next primary to be held in a state close to us was Pennsylvania, and they were right next door! Judy Ross also suggested a postcard project that she had seen described in an Obama blog. It was quickly taken on as a good project for those that didn't want to walk or talk."

"Tell me more about that."

"The project was to send personalized postcards to women from women. Here was the theory. Some people wanted to volunteer for the Obama Campaign but did not want to canvass, phone bank or do data entry. The strategy was to find something these volunteers could do to help the campaign that would appeal to them. Judy contacted the staffer in the Chicago Obama Headquarters for the details. She learned that if we would get the postcards ready to mail, including the postage, they would address and mail them. The volunteers would write a message to an undecided voter explaining why they were supporting Obama. Being hand written, the cards would carry much more appeal and a more forceful message than a pre-printed card. A typical message would read, 'my name is [First Name; Last Name]. I'm writing to you as a [mother/grandmother/woman] to let you know I am supporting Barack Obama for president because [2-3 specific reasons important to the author]. I hope you will give him your support, too. Sincerely, [First Name].'

"After locating a source, 5000 postcards were obtained, written, and stamped by LCO volunteers. We did a couple of Saturday/Sunday writing days in our headquarters. Also a number of volunteers picked up blank postcards and did them from their home (returning them to the office before shipment). When done, all 5,000 of them were bundled up and sent to the staffer in Chicago for labeling and delivery to the post office. We finished this very successful project in very early March. And, as a matter of fact we did a whole lot more of them which I'll tell you about later."

"What else did you decide to do?"

"Over the next several weeks, the volunteers called into Wisconsin, Ohio, Texas, Mississippi, Pennsylvania, North Carolina, and West Virginia using call sheets compiled by Obama's national campaign. In fact, many Eager Beavers even traveled to some of these states including Ohio, Pennsylvania, and North Carolina, to help them on the ground. In particular, Steve made several productive visits to Ohio to canvass in East Cleveland, Columbus and Youngstown. Remember, he was from there and could stay with family.

"Another of our more ambitious and successful projects the Eager Beavers organized was 'to adopt' a town in Pennsylvania to help get out the primary vote in this critical state. Marcia used MyBO to search for Obama groups located in south central Pennsylvania, not too far from Loudoun. Ben Flatgard, the Obama staffer assigned to Chambersburg, got back to her right away and welcomed LCO's offer to help them beat Hillary in their primary on April 22. The Eager Beavers were excited to help this town of about 20,000 which was quite different from Loudoun County (its median income was only $35,000) and an enthusiastic group set off on their first road trip from Leesburg to Chambersburg one Saturday in March.

"One of those joining the road trip was Joyce McLaurin. No story about the 2008 campaign parallels the heroism of Joyce. She joined the Chambersburg canvassing group and walked door-to-door. She was incredibly persuasive talking to whoever answered the door, and her fellow volunteers learned a lot by observing how she connected with people. And then one day, out of the blue, she hit them with it. Joyce told a few LCO friends that the reason she was having some trouble walking was because she had had a liver transplant operation within the last year. Here was a woman walking door-to-door who had recently had major organ transplant surgery! Later we also learned that when she was a lot younger, she was one of the first females to work on oil rigs in the Gulf of Mexico with her home base in Texas. Initially it was administrative duties, but not for long. She was assigned full rig duties and was paid accordingly. Yes, she was a persuasive lady. We'll be talking much more about her later in the story.

"They went to Chambersburg to canvass on six consecutive

weekends. Car pools were organized for the 1 ½ hour trip and one volunteer (Gillian Higgins) even once rented a van because of the large number of volunteers who wanted to participate. An unexpected side benefit turned out to be the bonding that took place among the Loudoun volunteers during these trips. The conversations were wide-ranging and people really got to know each other—our Eager Beavers were definitely turned on. When the groups arrived, they took their direction from Ben Flatgard, who always welcomed them with open arms. He let everyone know LCO was immensely helpful to his local group. During the final push, Ben summed it up by saying, 'You Loudoun County for Obama folks certainly are relentless!'

"On the last weekend of canvassing in Chambersburg just before the Pennsylvania primary, Judy Ross took Joyce to a big rally for Obama in Harrisburg, PA, about an hour's trip from Chambersburg. It was the first time Joyce saw Obama in person (there were to be others). They drove up to the event in front of the PA Capital building on a Saturday afternoon after canvassing. Steve Ames had arranged VIP seating next to the stage. They met up with him, and together had a great time. Although Hillary ended up winning the primary vote in surrounding Franklin County 59% to 41%, the vote in the nine Chambersburg precincts was very close—Obama only lost by a whisker (30 votes)."

"I didn't even know that was going on. Barbara and I called into a lot of states using their Obama's national website, but didn't have a clue there were organized teams going to other states from here in Loudoun County. That's impressive!"

"This was new for me as well. I have never known anyone from our county to go into another state to campaign for a presidential candidate. Of course it was done, but not by many. But remember that the Obama campaign had MyBO. That website made this possible. Now let me switch back to the LCO activities here in Loudoun."

"Ramble on, Mr. Winter, ramble on."

"Marcia and the gang continued to grow our community of local volunteers to help with all of our activities. Strategies included setting up a PR outreach group to write letters to the editor, organizing an Obama Works neighborhood cleanup team and food drive to help the Loudoun community, as well as arranging for folks to phone from home and knock on doors in numerous canvassing events. Steve Ames was into blood— lots of blood. He organized blood drives for the local hospital. And since we all wanted to mix a little pleasure with the business, there were several pot-luck Primary watching parties. They helped our Loudoun supporters get to know each other and provided an environment to spawn creative new ideas for getting Barack Obama elected in Loudoun County.

"We continued with numerous voter registration drives. We were very fortunate that Loudoun County's League of Women Voters had been registering high school seniors for years. Every May, the group sent out a cadre of LWV volunteers to speak to entire classrooms of 17-18 year olds in May—a captive audience—and discuss the importance of democratic elections and registering to vote. They encouraged the seniors to register on the spot and always told them to be sure to vote absentee if they would be away at school on Election Day. Knowing that the League would be contacting all the high school seniors, the Eager Beavers decided to focus on other groups in the county.

"A voter registration planning kickoff session was held in mid-May at Franco's office. Wynne Lundblad, the Obama staffer assigned to Loudoun and Arlington, attended the meeting and offered some great suggestions. We actually had little contact with Wynne as he saw we were continuing to find supporters and keeping the old-timers involved. The Eager Beavers decided to try a variety of approaches to register new voters, including setting up tables outside supermarkets, movie theaters, book stores, thrift stores, restaurants, and libraries and contacting potential voters at concerts, local fairs, churches, and shopping malls. Although LCO had substantial experience registering voters before the primary, the grassroots group was now much larger and could devote more resources to this activity, which everyone knew was critical to Obama taking Loudoun in November.

"Here's a snapshot of the system that was developed by LCO. Upcoming voter registration events were announced on MyBO and were included in Marcia's email updates to everyone on the Big List. Understanding how important it was to follow Virginia's voter registration rules, team leaders were well trained before each event so they could train the volunteers who participated. Each volunteer was given a clipboard and packet of materials in a 9 x 12 white envelope when they arrived. These materials included Voter Registration Tips developed by LCO, a Contact Sheet for recording email addresses, ten blank voter registration forms, and a couple of ballpoint pens.

"A Volunteer Checklist was taped to the outside of the white envelope to make sure each person knew how to contact their team leader, knew what to read before they started, reported their counts when they were done, and added their signature and date. All materials (including all completed voter registration forms) were returned in the same white envelope before the volunteer left for the day. Each team leader was also given a 10 x 13 yellow envelope in which they placed their team's white envelopes at the end of the day. A Game Plan for Team Leaders was taped to the outside of the yellow envelope which listed their responsibilities, the names and cell phones of the other team leaders, and a place for them to total their team's counts at the end of the day.

"Our grassroots volunteers learned a great deal about effective voter registration strategies in a variety of settings. For example, they learned the importance of always talking in person with a store manager beforehand to get permission to set up a voter registration table on the sidewalk, making sure not to block the entrance. Most store managers insisted on non-partisan drives (no Obama buttons or T-shirts) but it was usually easy to strike up a conversation about the election with potential voters. People who indicated that they liked Barack Obama were asked the question that had proven to be so effective throughout the campaign: 'Would you like us to keep you in the loop on our local Obama activities? All we need is your email address.' But regardless of his or her political preferences, everyone who wished to register to vote was encouraged to do so.

"Other strategies that worked especially well included registering folks standing in line at movie theaters (often a young crowd), setting up a table at the same place/day/time each week, working with local pastors to register voters after Sunday services, registering workers during their lunch hours, and asking store managers of fitness centers, car dealerships, restaurants, and others if their employees were all registered to vote and offering to register folks on the spot. Although many of the store managers might be Republican, their employees were usually young and more likely to vote for Obama. And, of course, our volunteers also went door-to-door to register voters (usually wearing Obama gear). We didn't consider voter registration to be soliciting, so apartment complexes were fair game."

My brain was spinning thinking of all these incredible campaign activities. I asked Rollie, "So what were you doing during the spring of 2008?" He responded, "I was busy putting together the

Loudoun Obama delegation to attend the local and state Democratic conventions. The major tasks of the delegation were to select the National Delegates to the National Convention, the elector to the Electoral College, and several party officials. At the same time I also helped to develop a strategy for those wanting to become National Delegates and will cover that story later. For now, I let me tell you about the Democratic organizations, conventions, and rules."

"The floor is yours!"

"To be effective, I had to know how the Democrats were organized from the National level down to the local level. I had to know how delegates were selected and how conventions worked. It's a dry subject, and I realize that many readers, especially those who don't live in Virginia, may just skip over the rest of this chapter; but for those who are interested in becoming politically active and being effective at it, knowing the rules of the Democratic organizations and their process is invaluable. And Virginia is not that much different from many other states. Later, when describing what happened here in Loudoun County, this basic information will help you more fully understand and appreciate what was accomplished here.

"As a young man, I learned that knowing the rules makes one much more useful and effective—so I became a lay parliamentarian. I have written operating rules for many new organizations in which I participated. I also developed the skills to preside or help others preside at meetings. This knowledge has served me well over the years and been very satisfying to me. I advise anyone who wants to become a political player in their state or community to do the same."

"How does this apply to the Democratic party? I believe it was Will Rogers who once said when asked about his party affiliation, 'I am not a member of any organized political party. I'm a Democrat.'"

"That's a funny line, and even though it often appears to the public that the Democrats are completely disorganized, it simply is not true. The party is extremely organized—at the National, State, Congressional District, and local levels. There are separate rules and/or different roles for each of these layers. All layers have a part in choosing our nominees for all levels of partisan elections and then working for their election."

"Partisan? Why did you use that word?"

"That means that the political parties first select their candidates, who then run in a general election under their party label.

In Virginia, however, most of the town elections only have a general election and candidates usually run as 'Independents'. However, in this partisan age, parties more and more often endorse one or more of those candidates, which is different from 'nominating' candidates for county, state or federal positions. This is defined in Virginia state law."

"I'm getting confused already; this is complicated! Aren't we getting too detailed here? Most of our readers aren't interested in this kind of stuff!"

"You're probably right. But it's this kind of 'stuff' that will set this book apart from other political history books. Putting this knowledge to work will let interested readers make significant future contributions to their local political organizations, so I'm just going to do it. They can keep it for reference if they decide they want to get involved. I warned you when we started this conversation that it wasn't going to be easy. In fact, we have barely started."

"OK, I'll try to stay awake. I'm ready for you."

"Generally, the two parties work the same way. At most levels choices can be made as to what process is used for each election. The most important of these is whether party candidates are chosen by convention or chosen by primary. In the former, the public is involved in the process by choosing delegates to a convention. In primaries, the public chooses their nominees directly by election. In modern times here in Virginia, Republicans use conventions more often than Democrats for state and local elections. However, both parties use only conventions to elect their party officials."

"For the sake of this discussion, let's just stick with Democrats and Obama's election."

"OK, here goes. I'll start by describing the party organizations. There are six layers or levels."

"You got to be kidding!"

"Nope. Six. At the very top of the political hierarchy is the National Democratic Party, run by the Democratic National Committee—almost always referred to as the DNC. Their rules are set forth in the Democratic Party Charter and Bylaws. Everyone is eligible to be a member of the National Democratic Party as long as you subscribe to their principles and support their candidates. You are not nominated or screened. There are little to no rules to follow, no officers to elect, no meetings to attend. You are a member if you consider yourself a Democrat and support them with your vote, money, or effort. The "Charter and Bylaws" of the DNC are readily accessible at www.demRulz.org under the 'references' tab. This website has a lot of useful information and is maintained by a very helpful and capable DNC committee member from Virginia, Frank Leone.

"The DNC is the big dog where all the power resides. It is comprised of the chairs and vice-chairs of each state, an additional 200 elected members apportioned among the states based on population, a number of elected officials serving in an ex-officio capacity (which means they are on the DNC because of the office they hold), and a variety of representatives of major Democratic Party constituencies. Note that 'chair' is political jargon. The chair is the person in charge (like a President) and a vice-chair is a secondary person in charge. Virginia now elects two men and two women to the DNC every four years at the State Democratic Convention held in presidential election years.

"Next in line are the State parties. Every resident of the Commonwealth of Virginia who believes in and supports the principles of the Democratic Party is a member of the Democratic Party of Virginia (DPVA). It is headquartered in Richmond, and has a few year-round, full-time employees, although they do beef up during election campaigns. The party is governed by the State Democratic Central Committee, which is comprised of 20 members from each of the 11 Congressional Districts (CD's) in Virginia, plus a host of other party officials and constituency representatives. They are required to meet at least four times a year according to the rules passed by the Virginia Democrats and their central committee, called the DPVA Party Plan.

"The central committee has a Steering Committee comprised of about 35 statewide party officials who do most of the planning. They set the agenda for the quarterly central committee meetings."

"And all of this is just at the State level?"

"That's right, Ed. Now let's move to the third layer, the Democratic Congressional District Committee, usually just called the CD. There are 435 CD's in the country, with 11 in Virginia, one for each Congressional District. Each CD is primarily responsible for electing a Democratic Congressman to the House of Representatives. The Party Plan for the state level contains the rules for the CD's along with the rules for the state party. A CD Committee is comprised of 20 elected members proportionally representing localities within the CD, one elected Senator or House of Delegate member, all county/city Democratic chairs, plus a number of add-on members representing various constituencies.

When I say 'proportionally' for the elected members, that refers to the Democratic vote in the three most recent state or federal elections. Thus, localities with high Democratic votes have more members on the CD than if it was based simply on population. CD boundaries are adjusted every ten years based on census data. Since Loudoun is a fast growing Republican-leaning county, it is usually under-represented in the 10th CD.

"The CD boundaries often slice through large localities. But all of Loudoun County resides within the 10th CD, picks up only a part of Fairfax County, and then all of eight other much smaller localities. As you will see, the CD plays a very important role in Democratic Party processes."

"And you're saying that the State Party Plan contains all of the rules for the second and third levels."

"That's right—for the State Party and CDs. In Virginia, the fourth layer is comprised of counties and cities and has their own rules, called bylaws. They are called that because you can actually consider them as being Bylaws of the State Party Plan, but they only apply to the locality. Although we also have towns in Virginia, they are always within the jurisdiction of a county. The Loudoun County Democratic Committee (LCDC) is our local organization. We write a lot about them throughout the book. The LCDC Bylaws govern their organization. They empower an executive committee to look after LCDC business in between monthly meetings. These bylaws also contain the rules for the final two layers."

"And what might those be? I'm beginning to feel quite layered!"

"We're almost done. In Loudoun County, there are eight magisterial (sometimes called 'supervisory') districts, each with their elected Supervisor on the Board of Supervisors, our local Government—not the party, the government. All LCDC members reside in a particular district and are automatically a member of that local Democratic district committee. Confusion can often arise with new party members when using the word 'district' since it is used in two ways: Congressional District and magisterial district. In this book, we will use lower-case 'district' when referring to the local district. In some of the very large counties in the state these district committees have their own bylaws, raise their own money, and meet more often than their county committee. This is the fifth level of party organization. We have eight districts in Loudoun County.

"The sixth and last layer is the precinct. Everyone in the country is assigned to vote at a particular place in a locality which is called a precinct. Across the country the precincts are named, numbered, or both. According to the Democratic Virginia State Party Plan, every precinct is to be represented on the local committee, such as the LCDC, by at least one person."

"What about block or street captains? I've heard those expressions used from time to time."

"Forget them—for a good reason. In the 20 years I've been here in Loudoun County, we haven't had nearly enough active party people on the local committee to make that feasible. In fact, we seldom have all of our precinct captain slots filled, much less have enough to get down to the block level. The larger, more sophisticated localities may have a fuller complement of precinct captains in their more densely populated Democratic areas."

"I just recently joined the Loudoun County Democratic Committee (LCDC). They told me I was an at-large member. How does that work?"

"When I moved to Loudoun County in the early 90's, everyone was elected at-large. At-large means you represent the whole jurisdiction, in this case, the County, not just the smaller area in which you live. A few years later the Democratic State Party Plan mandated that every precinct be represented on all local committees by at least one person who is designated the precinct captain. When adopting our new rules at that time, the Loudoun committee agreed with me to have a combination of all the precinct captains, and an equal number of at-large members. That same plan is still in effect today. And unless you have some more questions about the Democratic organizations, I'll move on."

"You mean there's more?"

"Sure is. What I've described so far are the permanent party organizations and structure. I haven't touched the campaigns. That's a whole different bunch of characters."

"I thought the Democratic political organizations you have just described run their campaign."

"Sometimes they do. First let me say that it has changed a lot in the last decade or two, with separate paid campaign organizations becoming more prevalent that are not controlled by the party organizations. There are no hard and fast rules. But generally, the factors that favor separate campaign organizations run by the candidates are big budgets, large electorates, candidate enthusiasm, high population densities, a non-dominant political party, and competitive races. If even one of these factors is missing, the party often runs the campaign. When the campaign is 'run by the candidate,' the candidate hires a campaign manager, who in turn, puts together the campaign organization."

"When Barbara and I decided to end our individual efforts for Obama through MyBO, somehow we found VV08, which turned out to be what they called a combined campaign, and we got our marching orders from them. How did they fit in with all of this?"

"Democratic candidates have been using combined campaigns for statewide campaigning for several years, and on the surface it makes a lot of sense. Candidates share office space, telephone lines, computer systems, utilities, campaign literature, the ground game, and even TV ads. But there are problems as well. One, for example, is how to split up the costs. Equally? What if one of the campaigns has difficulty raising its share? How do you handle the volunteers who want to work for one candidate but not the others? When it comes time to print your GOTV list (those you want to get out to vote), who do you include if the prospective voter doesn't support all three candidates? These are serious problems, and frankly, extremely hard to solve.

"This particular campaign highlighted for me what may be the biggest problem with having a combined campaign."

"And what would that be, pray tell?"

"It is the competition for volunteer resources. The CFC and VV08 paid staffers were praised or punished based on how many volunteers were recruited and how well they performed—as measured by door knocks and calls. Initially, there was virtually no coordination at all between them for volunteer outreach or neighborhood canvassing. They both used the VAN, an excellent tool for keeping track of the contacts made for each organization, but the contact information was not shared. This resulted in the same potential volunteer pool being contacted more than one organization to do the voter ID recruit volunteers. And also, on more than one occasion, street canvassing would overlap—even on the same day or weekend.

"I think I got it. Now let's get more specifically into the 2008 election. How was Obama actually chosen the Democratic nominee in the first place?"

"That's a big question! The simple answer is that he was

chosen by a majority of the 4200 National Delegates attending the Democratic National Convention on August 28, 2008 in Denver. About ¾ of the Delegates were pledged to vote for their candidate as a result of primaries or caucuses in their own states and territories. The balance were unpledged Super Delegates who were free to vote for any candidate. The unpledged included all DNC members, Democratic members of Congress, Democratic Governors, and other party officials. Since Super Delegates were not pledged to a specific candidate, there was serious speculation up to the end of the primary process that the Clintons would somehow be able to sway these 'unpledged' Delegates to vote for Hillary, thereby letting her 'steal' the nomination, in the view of Obama supporters. Because of Hillary's late surge, the press was all over this possibility despite the fact that Obama had a majority of the pledged delegate votes. She held out nearly to the end—announcing to a packed crowd at the National Building Museum Office in DC that she was ending her campaign in early June, no doubt influenced by the unpledged Super Delegates not breaking her way. I thought she handled the announcement of her decision masterfully.

"But the more difficult question to answer is: how were those pledged National Delegates chosen to do that job? I'll describe in some detail how it was done here in Virginia, but you should understand that many states have their own unique way of electing these National Delegates. And oftentimes within a state the Democrats and Republicans use different rules. For instance, one party may have a convention and the other a primary. Are you ready?"

"I'll not interrupt you unless you completely lose me."

"The DNC began the process a couple of years before the 2008 National Convention by appointing a committee to develop their national call to convention. This 'call' was simply the set of rules that specifies how the delegates and alternates are to be selected and also included dates, implementation schedule, location, number of Delegates and Alternates and how they were to be split among the states, and a lot of other party minutiae. I'm sure they started with the call used in 2004, had meetings, marked it up, solicited input from interested persons, debated and argued a lot, and then presented the proposed new call to the DNC. The DNC, in turn, fussed with it awhile and made whatever changes they deemed appropriate, adopted it, and sent it to the state parties. Since all the state parties are represented at the DNC level, the states were not surprised by what they received.

"The Virginia state party then went through about the same process to produce its call for the primary in February, the CD conventions in May and the state convention in June. It included the formulas used to determine the total number of Delegates and Alternates allotted to each CD (averaged five Delegates and one Alternate, divided between Obama and Clinton, based on the percentage vote in the primary), and set the number of At-Large Delegates and Alternates to be elected at the state convention, allocated according to the statewide primary vote. Then the CD's created the rules for their own District Conventions. These rules also directed each locality to produce their own call to caucus in their own communities. Rules, Rules, everywhere are Rules."

"Stop right there! I'm overwhelmed. I can't remember all of that. It's too much to swallow. I can understand the three conventions: National, State, and District. But what the hell is a local caucus? What's a caucus? What does it do? Never mind, my head hurts. Let's take this up tomorrow."

A few days later Rollie made a trip out to my home in Philomont. He took a diet Coke from the fridge (I buy them by the carton at a steep discount), popped the top, and looked ready to start.

"I've looked over the notes I made the last time we were together, Rollie. I can understand now why you went through the layers of the Democratic Party with me before talking about the election. That helped a lot. So, to make sure I have it right, I'll recap. To choose the National Delegates to the National Convention that elected the Democratic nominee for president, the DNC wrote a bunch of rules about the National Convention and sent them to all of the State Democratic Committees. The state committees, including Virginia, then wrote some rules about the state conventions and sent them to their CD's. And then the CD's wrote the rules for their CD conventions. I can understand there are three layers of the Party that hold conventions. We stopped our conversation just as you told me about a call to caucus. What's that all about?"

"That's great, Ed. You already know more than 99% of the people in Virginia about how we nominated Obama. In a few moments, as we talk further, you can call yourself an expert! We have described three party layers and three conventions, right? Now it's time to describe how the delegates are chosen to go to the CD and state conventions.

"As you said, we left off last time with the 10th CD having

sent the rules to the Loudoun County Democrats about holding a caucus. These rules instructed them how many Obama and Clinton delegates and alternates to elect and when it should be done. The call also instructed them how to publish in the local paper the details on how to run for these delegate and alternate positions, the caucus time, and the location. Information about the two conventions they are to attend if elected is also included in the published call to caucus. The elected delegates and alternates represent their localities at these conventions.

"And who can be a delegate? The answer may surprise a lot of people. Anyone! Anyone can file to run for these delegate and alternate positions as long as they live in the locality, are registered to vote, and are willing to sign a pledge that they will not support or work for an opponent of the Democratic Party in the coming general election!"

"I have to admit I didn't know anything about all the party mechanics and didn't even know you folks had a local convention."

"Join the crowd! Not many have any clue how this works. Voters had their first opportunity to make their voices heard in the 2008 Presidential election by voting in the February primary. The primary results determined the percentage of delegate representation for the presidential candidates at the conventions. And then the voters were heard from again by giving them the opportunity to choose the actual delegates to represent them from among the registered voters in their locality who wanted to compete for these positions. Cool, don't you think? The Republicans do the same, but sometimes in a little different way."

"So you're saying that all Democrats who are registered to vote can actually participate in these elections, called a caucus, and elect whomever they want as delegates?"

"Absolutely! As long as the persons they support filed their forms with the local party by the advertised deadline. It's a very open process."

"That is cool!"

"We are agreed on that. But unfortunately, I have to report that an extremely small percentage of people exercised their opportunity to participate in this caucus. In fact it was insignificant. Let me give you some statistics. Exactly 61 people participated and determined the 61 Obama delegates and alternates who went to convention. About 150 people chose the 38 Clinton delegates and alternates. So that's a little over 200 participants out of Loudoun's population of 300,000. You do the math. That's insignificant.

"As I said earlier, the call specified that the number of Delegates was divided between Obama and Clinton based on the February primary results. When the local people filed for Delegate or Alternate, they would specify the candidate they wanted to represent."

"So, in actuality, there were two caucuses held in each locality—one to elect the Clinton Delegates and one to elect the Obama Delegates."

"You could think of it that way. But in actuality, if there had been the need for two caucuses, they would be held at the same time and place, and the caucus voters would have simply specified they wanted either the Obama or Clinton ballot. We didn't need to have an Obama caucus."

"Wait a minute! Why didn't you need to have an Obama caucus?"

"We were able to file exactly the number of delegates and alternates required. All who filed were automatically elected without holding a caucus."

"How did you do that?"

"Ed, I'll tell you; and this is about a really important political tool to know and understand. The party insiders use it to maximize control over the process. It is called 'slate voting', and is authorized in the State Party Plan for all levels of the organization. The slate name is filed and then placed on the ballot with its own checkbox in addition to all the names of those who had properly filed for Delegate. In 2008, we were to elect 41 Obama Delegates, so I made sure to collect and file exactly 41 Delegate filing forms. Then I also filed a list of those same 41 persons by the deadline and requested that they be identified as the 'blue' slate.

The power of this process is twofold. First, the simplicity of voting the slate (one check by the slate name would vote all 41 names). Second, all 41 members of the slate promise to campaign (urge friends and family to come to the caucus) and vote for the slate. Think about it. It would be nearly impossible for any outsiders to file and expect to crack that 41-vote (plus friends) block. Of course I did the same for the 20 Alternates and also had to be cognizant of the 50-50 gender split for those on the slate."

"Did it work?"

"Sure did. As expected, we all won! Even better than that— the Obama caucus was cancelled! We didn't even have to go to the caucus and vote that day, because no one else filed! So all of us were declared elected, and the caucus was cancelled for Obama Delegates and Alternates. Not one person filed for delegate or alternate that I had not approved. All that preliminary work really paid off."

"How in the world did you make that happen? Seems like a logistical nightmare."

"I assure you it wasn't easy. You have to do a lot of dancing, bobbing and weaving, talking real smooth, being prepared to handle last minute glitches and follow-through failures. Again, this is where experience really paid off. I was prepared for last-minute unexpected filers and for those who just couldn't get me the necessary paperwork on time."

"Are you willing to share a little more of your technique? That could be very useful for those wanting to do something like this in the future."

"Well OK—since you asked so nicely. To begin with, Marcia did one or two of her magical memorandums to the Eager Beaver list, soliciting candidates for delegates and alternates. If interested, they called or emailed me. Frankly it is almost impossible for more than one person to handle the creation of a slate. You need to be an absolute dictator and make immediate decisions on whom to include and exclude. I've tried it the other way—especially for party reorganizations—and found that it becomes a nightmare if you have to make decisions quickly. I contacted old friends and all the party folks to be sure I would have a sufficient pool of candidates to pull from. Then I sent an email to those who showed an interest in participating with the details of the process and a questionnaire to help me make decisions regarding requesting a response. The full text is in the Appendix

"As they began responding to my emails and calls, I started to classify their responses and develop lists of likely Delegates and Alternates—keeping separate male and female lists. One of the keys to the process is to include a number of flexible people. By that I mean they let me use them where I needed them, and even drop them off at the last minute if need be. I would then assure them they would be added to the Delegation before the conventions convened because there is ALWAYS a 10-20% dropout rate from the elected delegates and alternates, and the delegation replaces them. Going into the week before the Loudoun caucus, I was pretty well set; but it was necessary to stay on top of it, as some of those who filed requested me to drop them and others decided at the last minute to participate."

"How did it turn out? Did you pull it off?"

"Here's what happened. I was at the LCDC headquarters all day, April 14, waiting to file my stack of Obama filing forms and my slate list at the 5:00 p.m. deadline. I went early just in case someone unexpectedly dropped by to file. The fact that filers could mail their forms or come into the headquarters up until 5:00 p.m. complicated the situation and made it necessary to stay close to the action. About 4:15 p.m., Phyllis Randall surprised me and came in to file her form. Phyllis and I were good friends, and she was very active for Obama. She said her life had been hectic and had not known of our efforts to form the Obama slate. She had mailed her form to LCDC, but then got concerned that it might not arrive by the deadline, so she decided to bring in another form to file in person if needed.

"It was a good thing she did bring it by, as the form had not arrived. So I had to make a last minute adjustment, adding her to the full delegation, dropping another Delegate to Alternate, and scratching an Alternate. Early contingency preparation had once again paid off."

"How did the Clinton folks do?"

"I had vigorously warned Dan Moldover and Robert Latham, the Clinton honchos, to be ready for a surprise filing from LaRouche supporters. They are abundant in Loudoun County since their World Headquarters is located in Leesburg. See the Appendix to learn all about them. They were smart political players, often concealing their hand until the filing deadline. I had several run-ins with them several years earlier and didn't want them to go through that again.

"Initially the Clinton crew was going to put together a slate as I suggested, but since they didn't see any evidence of a problem, they kissed off the preparations. Late morning on filing day, a fellow dropped by the headquarters and filed a couple of Hillary Delegate forms. I didn't know him or the other person he had filed. I immediately called Dan and apprised him of the situation. He said that in the previous couple of days he had received about 6-8 other forms from people whose names he also didn't recognize. I strongly urged him to do what was necessary to form a slate and file his list of names by the 5:00 p.m. deadline. They successfully accomplished that just in time to place their slate on the caucus ballot. But since the number of those filing as a Clinton Delegate exceeded the available Delegate positions, they had to hold a caucus. Of course if they had filed as Obama delegates, we would have been the ones to caucus."

"How did that work out?"

"I met with Dan and went over what would be necessary to be sure they were successful in winning their caucus election. We actually emailed our Obama lists to encourage them to contact their friends who supported Clinton to encourage their attendance at the caucus and vote for 'Slate A', thus voting for all of Dan's filers who agreed to run together. LCDC members were also contacted to do the same. We strongly suggested that Obama supporters not participate. That would not be right. I also volunteered to help out at the caucus as a LCDC representative. They accepted me, and I helped with crowd control. I had urged them to create a notice that urged a vote for "Slate A" and had them post some folks at the front door to lobby caucus participants to vote Slate A. It worked, and Slate A won handily with a big vote.

"However, there was one tense moment during the caucus voting when all of a sudden, a woman came up to me and said, 'Aren't you Rollie Winter?' 'Yes, I am.' 'Why in the hell are you here? You don't belong here! This is a Clinton caucus. You support Obama.'

"I explained I was representing LCDC and just helping to be sure the caucus was a success. Bob Moses, one of the VPs of LCDC, came over to explain I was asked to help because of my experience, which didn't mollify her at all. I ended the dispute by just walking away—she voted and left—and I then went back and continued helping. Never did find out her name or if she was a LaRouchee or not. I'd bet money on yes.

"While we were helping the Clinton people overcome the LaRouchee attack, we started to organize the Loudoun Obama delegation to the District Convention. We had a lot of planning to do to maximize our success."

"Sounds like you are about to get into the details of how we elected our National Delegates and elector. Let's get together another time to finish it up."

"OK by me. Let's go eat."

The Nitty Gritty Of Inside Politics

"One of the penalties for refusing to participate in politics is that you end up being governed by your inferiors." —Plato

Next time I went into the Rust Library to interview Rollie, I took my normal route and passed by Harrison Hall, now known as the Glenfiddich House, on the left side of King Street in Leesburg. General Robert E. Lee once was there to receive treatment for a broken hand. That evening in September 1862 he convened a war council with Generals James Longstreet, Lewis Armistead, Stonewall Jackson, and James Ewell Brown "Jeb" Stuart, probably the most famous cavalryman in the Civil War, to plan the Confederate invasion of Maryland.

From near Harrison Hall, Lee's army marched north on King Street, now Route 15, crossed the Potomac River at White's Ferry, owned by Elijah White's family and still in operation, headed to Frederick, Maryland, thence through the village of Sharpsburg, Maryland, where it collided with George B. McClellan's Army of the Potomac. The result was the Battle of Antietam on September 17, 1862, the bloodiest day in American history with 23,000 casualties. I told you this place reeks of history and I meant it.

Back to business. I wanted to nail down what happened at the local and state conventions and find out how well the Loudoun aspirants fared in the competition for National Delegates and other Party political plums. We're back at Rust, primed for action.

"OK, Rollie; all systems go. We finished up last time having our local convention delegates elected and ready to go to the District and State conventions. How did the National Delegates get selected?"

"Most of them were elected at the first of the conventions—the local 10th (CD) Convention; we in the 10th CD were to elect three Obama and two Clinton National Delegates and one Alternate for each candidate. As I was forming the local Obama delegation for Loudoun, I simultaneously started to track those who had an interest in going to the National Convention as a Delegate or Alternate for Obama."

"How many were interested?"

"There were a lot of them. Altogether, we had approximately

15 in Loudoun and at least another dozen in the rest of the 10th CD.

"With my past experience as a National Delegate and a good understanding of the process, I knew I could be a big help to them. Up to then, the only person I knew I would be supporting for National Delegate was Marcia Carlin. But the many calls I was receiving obviously indicated this was going to be a hotly contested election."

"I know Marcia went to the National convention. Was she a Delegate or Alternate?"

"I'll get to that. Be patient!

"I've already stressed the importance of 'What You Know' about party rules and procedures to be effective in politics. We are now entering the stage of the campaign when 'Who You Know' also gets major billing.

"The local Obama and Clinton campaigns and local party leaders also understood the importance of pulling together after the eventual presidential nominee was determined, so that we could maximize our campaign effort in the general election. As we approached the end of the primaries, I remember Marcia Carlin and Dan Moldover posing for pictures in front of a LCDC membership meeting as they exchanged their campaign buttons, promising to support the selected nominee if their candidate lost!"

"Was it your feeling that the general LCDC membership was leaning towards Obama at that time?"

"Most certainly. The private polling I had done of the LCDC throughout the campaign in 2007 was quite favorable for Obama—receiving nods from more than half of those willing to say whom they supported; that is, Obama had more support than the combined total of all of the other candidates still in the race at the time of each polling. And for most of the rest, Obama was their second choice. A sizable group continued to support Hillary after the Virginia primary, especially as she started to make a comeback, extending her race until June.

"From the beginning of LCO, we had been successful in recruiting a number of new LCDC members. Much later I learned there was a lot of speculation by the LCDC leadership about LCO's 'real' intentions regarding the party organization. They could see we were becoming a close-knit family throughout 2007 and speculated that by the end of that year, enough of us would be members of LCDC to essentially 'take over' the local party leadership. Since I was purposefully bringing a number of my new Obama friends into

LCDC, I could understand their concern. But we had no such intention.

"In December 2007, the LCDC went through its biannual reorganization at which time it was reconstituted and new officers elected. Chairman Thom Beres completed his term in office and was replaced by Tim Buchholz. The Vice Chairs, Bob Moses and Ellen Heald, were carried over to serve another two years. I strongly credit the four of them for staying positive about our efforts throughout 2007 and the Virginia primary in February. They were extremely helpful and encouraging."

"So, what you are saying, Rollie, is that you and Marcia had no interest in becoming local party officials, but wanted to continue to have free reign with the LCO operation."

"Exactly! And we did so until the general election. However, we were greatly affected when the paid staff from the Campaign for Change—the Obama Campaign—came to town in June 2008. I'll tell you about that later.

"After the primary was over in February, we began dealing with conventions and the selection of National Delegates. At this point, 'Who You Know' has increasing importance. Perhaps it's better to say 'Who Knows You!' It is rare that someone is selected a National Delegate who hasn't been a major leader in the campaign or a long-time Democratic Party official. The hopefuls usually have to have clout with the key people within the party or campaign—at the local and/or state level—to have much of a chance for selection. There is another minor consideration. Very few people know that Obama's official Virginia representative has final approval on the selection of Obama National Delegates! However, I don't know of a single case that a selected delegate was rejected by the national campaign. Although most who contacted me had little chance of winning a spot, I didn't disabuse them of their hopes."

"I seem to remember that the process isn't quite as closed as it used to be."

"You're right. The selection process has opened up a lot in recent years because the national Dems have mandated that each state delegation have certain percentages of specific demographic groups—50-50 split by gender, a certain percentage of young people, and defined minimums for minorities. This has opened up many more opportunities in the last three or four conventions for people who were very under-represented in past Democratic conventions. But it still usually comes down to raw inside politics that determines those winners and losers. I did coach our people on how to maximize their chance for success."

"What actually goes on at the National Convention? What's it all about? I remember over the years watching on TV a bunch of old men and women wearing funny hats and generally having a good time parading up and down the aisles. And they seemed always to be talking and not listening to what's going on. Does anything ever get done?"

"Well, yes. They are there to select our Democratic nominees for President and Vice President and to adopt our national party platform. The previous state Primaries or caucuses (based on state party laws) determine how many pledged National Delegates each candidate receives, based on results of votes received. In Virginia, 20% of National Delegates are called 'Super' Delegates. Unlike Delegates chosen through primaries and caucuses, they are not pledged to a specific candidate. Super Delegates are designated by state party rules and can include elected officials (members of Congress and governors), party committee members, and former office holders.

"In 2008, the Democratic Party decided that there would be 796 super Delegates out of 4,000 total Delegates at the National Convention. The winning candidate needed a majority of the 4,000 to win the party's nomination. Because of Hillary's late surge, the press was all over the possibility that most of these unpledged super Delegates would vote for her despite the fact that Obama had received a majority of the pledged votes from the states. And she held out nearly to the bitter end—finally announcing she was ending her campaign just after the last primary in early June. Although I thought she waited too long to concede, she handled the announcement of her final decision masterfully at the Museum of Building History in Washington, D.C.

"Ed, I told you earlier I was collecting names of those considering a run for National Delegate or National Alternate pledged to Obama. The 10th CD convention was to elect two male Delegates, one female Delegate, and one female Alternate. Just after the primary, I contacted Kevin Wolf to tell him the names I had accumulated."

"He was the guy who ran the Virginia petition effort, right?"

"Right. When I first reached him about this, he was very uncertain about the process of choosing the National Delegates, but believed it likely that Governor Tim Kaine and his key aides would be leading the effort. Since the Governor was the Chair of the Virginia Obama campaign, that made sense. My research of emails from that period revealed a number of interesting details that I had forgotten about my interaction with Kevin."

"What did you learn?"

"For starters, I discovered a copy of a letter dated late 2007 sent to the State Electoral Board and signed by Obama that clearly stated that Kevin was his representative in all matters relating to the selection of Virginia National Delegates. However, he realized he was really just a placeholder. About a week before the primary election, Kevin sent Marcia Carlyn and me this email:

There will be 5 Delegates (three men and two women) plus one female Alternate going to the National Convention from the 10th CD. HQ (in Chicago) needs to approve three times the number of Delegates it is allocated based on the results in the 10th CD on Feb 12.

'So, assuming we split roughly evenly with Clinton in the 10th CD, who would be the three men and three women, you would slate to be voted upon at the 10th CD Convention for Delegates from the 10th? Remember the need to designate diverse candidates.

'I have not heard from the Governor re who he would want from the 10th CD, so this is just getting from you suggestions for people from the 10th who endorsed early and who have been helpful and active in either the petition effort or the grassroots effort in the 10th. (Feel free to list yourselves as #1 on the men and women's side, respectively, by the way. That is my recommendation.')

"The HQ, in this case, referred to the Obama National Headquarters—and in particular, Jeffrey Berman, the person in charge of the National Delegate selection process. Unfortunately I could find no evidence, nor do I have a remembrance, of responding to this request. Marcia did respond, but only to say she was interested in becoming a Delegate. I do remember early on telling Kevin by phone that I had no interest in becoming a National Delegate as I had already 'been there—done that'. I did tell him of my interest in becoming an elector, and he promised to support me for that position. I know that neither Marcia nor I sent him a list of early Obama volunteers to be considered at this time for National Delegate. But Kevin's email was a clue that other CDs were starting to think about the Delegates to be elected at the CD conventions— and that we would soon start interacting with Charlie Kelly, who managed Tim Kaine's Political Action Committee (PAC), rather than Kevin.

"As you can see, Power Groups outside of Loudoun County

were starting to stir. Becoming a National Delegate has always been one of the biggest 'plums' of party politics. Major conflicts arise every four years as to who should be rewarded. On one hand, you have the presidential candidate enthusiasts who have not been active in local and state party politics before the particular election, but who have worked hundreds (and in many cases thousands) of volunteer hours for the winning candidate for several months. On the other hand, you have party regulars and leaders who have been working several years within the party hoping one day to get a shot at becoming a National Delegate, but only recently for the candidate. It leads to very bitter battles, and, as I said earlier, winning usually depends on 'What You Know' and 'Who You Know."

"We had a couple of big problems to overcome here in Loudoun County if we were to be successful in electing our four candidates. We only had 41 Loudoun Obama delegates out of the total number of 118 who would be selecting the Obama National Delegates at the District Convention. Fairfax had 46 delegates. So we would start five votes behind Fairfax walking into the convention hall. And we had an enthusiastic, but inexperienced, aspirants lined up to compete for the few National Delegate seats. Unlike Loudoun, Fairfax had been voting Democratic for several years and had a lot of old pros around who knew all about the process. Loudoun was stuck with me as their primary resource. And unfortunately, most of those thinking about running for National Delegate believed Loudoun County had earned the right to all four spots because of our early support for Obama and our surprisingly large win in the primary. I couldn't help but believe that this assumption was somewhat naive. It was time to start making deals."

"OK, I get that. So you had a tough fight ahead of you. And I know you had some success. How did you approach the campaign for National Delegates?"

"Well, I immediately got the lay of the land and verified that Kevin Wolf was no longer the decision maker. But clearly he still had clout, and his endorsement was important. Statewide, it was obvious that Charlie Kelly was going to be a key guy. Although he wouldn't be the decision maker either, he would be interacting with all of those who would be calling the shots. He wouldn't actually be making the final decisions but would be working closely with those who would. And locally we were going up against some very tough opponents in Fairfax. It was time to put together a strategy meeting for those in Loudoun interested in becoming National Delegates so we could coalesce around a couple of candidates."

"Did you know who was interested in running?"

"Sure—remember I told you earlier about compiling a list. Nearly all of those who had shown an interest came to the first Loudoun meeting. Unfortunately, someone turned up later, Ryan Myers, who had been overlooked—more about that later.

"We met at Franco Luz's place to thrash it out. I chaired the meeting and went through my spiel, drawing everyone out as to his or her opinions and concerns. After the meeting I sent an email to everyone summarizing what had happened. The full text is in the Appendix, but here's the gist of it.

"Marcia Carlyn, Gail Alexander Wise, David Kirsten, Larry Roeder, Robin Hyman, Steve Ames, and Juan Perez attended the meeting. Others who were interested in becoming National Delegates but couldn't make the meeting including Bahri 'Barry' Aliriza, Bernard Hill, Mike Turner, and Emma Ancrum. After those present were introduced I described the election process in some detail.

"I also told them that Fairfax had already formed a slate. Note that this slate was informal and not to be shown on the ballot. My suggested strategy included reaching out to the small delegations for support, attempting to make alliances with those who may want to run at the state level, promising to support them if they help us at the District Convention, and the most controversial of all: Unite behind one male Delegate and the female Delegate, leaving the other two spots open for negotiating support to and from others in the District.

"David Kirsten, one of the Delegate hopefuls, followed up that meeting with an email to all the participants which supported my position. I thought he expressed himself quite well and to the point:

Rollie had in mind for us to try to do some discussion on his proposal before our Friday meeting. I have not seen any response as yet. No one has ever accused me of being shy so I will chime in.

'I think Rollie's idea makes sense. If the Fairfax votes solely for their own slate without consideration of the minority blocks of the 10th, they could essentially shut themselves out of the running because of their greed for all the positions. Barack Obama's message all through his campaign has been for our nation to be inclusive rather than exclusive. We all realize that it has been the Loudoun County Obama movement that has done the majority of the work in this area to carry the day in Northern Va. but there were many hard workers from other areas of the District that worked too.

To shut them out as Fairfax is attempting would be wrong. By keeping a slot open for another minority block on our slate we could sway their votes and assure Loudoun representation at the convention, which is what we want. The one thing I have learned upon becoming a new-found Democrat in '98 and working as a minority Democratic leader since that time in what was a heavily Republican County, is that it is no fun at times to be in the minority, but with time and organization you can work miracles. The fundamental difference between Republicans and Democrats in my view boils down to one word—'empathy'. The Democrats have empathy for their fellow man where the Republican Party does not. We should show some empathy now for our fellow Democrats in the minority blocks of the 10th who would never have a chance to send a Delegate to the convention without our help.

"I attended and convened the next meeting. Since I was not running for National Delegate, I thought it best to let those who are running decide the process by themselves. After I answered a few questions, the group chose Marcia to moderate the rest of the meeting, and I left. Here are her notes of what transpired:

It was a really good meeting last Friday. We stayed together as a group and reached consensus in several areas.

First (on a personal note), thanks so much for backing me as our one female Delegate to the National Convention. I am truly honored and very appreciative of your support.

'Second, we agreed that Loudoun County would have a recommended slate of two candidates: one female Delegate and one male Delegate (who will be selected by secret ballot). We will also identify a backup male (for the other male Delegate slot) and a backup female (for the Alternate female Delegate slot) who will also be selected by secret ballot. The backup candidates will not be listed on our slate but they may prove to be useful later on when we are talking with other Obama supporters in the 10th CD."

'To select our male Delegate and two backup candidates, we agreed that we would each do the following:

1. Vote for two of the six candidates in the Male Delegate List (below).

2. Vote for one of the two candidates in the Female Alternate Delegate List (below).

3. Send me your votes by return email. The deadline for submitting your votes is 7:00 p.m. Monday, April 7. All votes will be kept confidential. The male who gets the highest number of votes will be chosen as the male Delegate on Loudoun's slate. The male who gets the second highest number of votes will be our backup male and the female who gets the highest number of votes will be our backup female for Alternate.

'Male Delegate List (vote for two): Bahri Aliriza, Steve Ames, Bernard Hill, David Kirsten, Juan Perez, Larry Roeder

Female Alternate Delegate List (vote for one): Robyn Hyman, Gail Alexander Wise

We also agreed that the two candidates on our recommended slate and the two backup candidates will each submit a Statement of Candidacy to be a Congressional District Level Delegate to the National Convention (or to be a Congressional District Level Alternate in the case of the backup female). There was also general consensus that individuals who were not selected would refrain from submitting a Statement of Candidacy to be a Congressional District Level Delegate (or Alternate). However, they could submit a Statement of Candidacy to be a State At-Large Delegate, or State At-Large Alternate.

I will send you the results of the vote on Monday evening. The next step will be to invite our 41 District/State delegates and 20 alternates to a meeting to explain our strategy and the process we used to select our proposed slate and backup candidates. We will explain our primary goal (to have at least two individuals from our grassroots Loudoun County for Obama group go to Denver as National Delegates) and we hope that the larger group will endorse both the process we used and the candidates we selected, but it is possible that they will have suggestions of their own. We will also discuss our plan to reach out to other Obama supporters in the 10th CD to identify folks who share our enthusiasm for Barack and our grassroots approach, find out what their needs are, discuss how we can help them in the coming months, and see if we can all reach consensus on a final slate of candidates.

The most important result of our meeting last night was that we were able to resolve these challenging issues in an amicable way that maintained the unanimity of our group. We really do represent the core values of Barack Obama! Please let me know if you have any questions or other interpretations of our discussion.'

"So, who won?"

"Gail Wise was chosen as the Female Alternate; no surprise there. She had Marcia's full support and had been an extremely valuable contributor all throughout the LCO efforts. It was a different story with the males, however. I really had thought Steve Ames would have been one of the two chosen. He was one of our early avid supporters and had shown real initiative in a number of areas. Instead, two really popular fellows were chosen, Bernard Hill had the top spot and Juan Perez was the 'backup.' They both had sparkling personalities and a good story to tell about themselves along with their hard work for Obama. Juan did tell me later in our interview for this book that his biggest regret in the campaign was beating Steve for the LCO endorsement. He opined that those making that decision just didn't realize all that Steve had done. But in retrospect, Juan and Bernard's personal stories carried the day."

"You must have been pretty satisfied with the outcome. Were you?"

"I did substantially agree with most of the decisions. A lot of egos took a backseat to the betterment of the group. However, I was not happy with the quasi-endorsement of the 'backup Delegate and Alternate' because that decision was coupled with the decision that 'the two backup candidates will each submit a Statement of Candidacy to be a Congressional District Level Delegate/Alternate to the National Convention'. This essentially nullified my strong recommendation to run only one male and one female. In reality, we now had a full Loudoun slate, which I really felt would limit our success, and perhaps leave us empty-handed. At the time, I strongly believed we could have gone to the Fairfax people or some of the other localities, worked a deal with them, and guaranteed two National Delegate spots for Loudoun, a fair outcome for us."

"What was the breakdown of the CD Obama delegate count again?"

"Fairfax had 46, we had 41, and all other localities totaled 31. To be successful, we had to keep our delegation voting as a block and needed to get votes from the smaller localities.

"Complicating the situation, EJ Scott, from the third largest locality, was adamant about running for the female Delegate slot, and if she lost, was planning to run for Alternate. I spent a lot of time encouraging her to accept our support for her for Alternate in return for her support for Marcia for Delegate, bringing her votes to our side. At her invitation, I even went to Manassas to their local committee meeting to explain the Delegate selection process, what would happen at the convention, and the rules that would be in place. There I met Jeanette Rishell, who eventually served as the Chair of the 10th CD Convention. (Later Jeanette asked me if I would be willing to serve as Parliamentarian at the Convention, which I subsequently did.)"

"Did you talk EJ into it?"

"She took it under consideration. But I knew that she and Marcia would have to get together to seal the deal. And, unfortunately, Marcia was already backing away from any deal that would result in Gail Wise not being on the Loudoun slate as the Alternate female. Marcia never did meet with EJ or seriously discuss it with her."

"What about Fairfax? I heard they filed a full slate."

"Sure did. I wasn't surprised, but it happened a lot earlier than I expected. I learned about it indirectly through Kevin Wolf. At that time he was still in nominal charge of the National Delegate selection process in the 10th CD, using me to help collect names of National Delegate hopefuls in our District. He forwarded an email to me in mid-March, originated by Eddie Eiches, an AFL union leader living in Fairfax, saying that he was interested in becoming a Delegate. Eddie had been one of the very few outside of Loudoun to help with petition effort, and I had already interacted with him several times.

"A few days after receiving that first email, I received another email from Eddie disclosing that he was part of a Fairfax slate which included him, Mary Lee Cerillo (the ringleader), Kristen Cabral, and Fred Mittleman. Mary Lee and Kristen were Fairfax district chairs and Fred, a long-time political operative in Fairfax Democratic circles. Kristen actually went to Harvard law school with Barack and was in a class with him. In our interview with her for this book, she told me about the time their class was to have a party, and her professor had written on the board 'bring deserts' [sic]! So she had the clever idea to bring a cake to class that had a 'desert' motif, and Barack had given her a thumbs up on her creativity. Fred served with me on the Temporary Rules Committee for the 10th CD Convention, a committee which had only communicated by email, so I really didn't know him either. I also didn't know during the rule-making meetings of his own plans to run for National Delegate and also for elector.

"These four people lived in two Fairfax magisterial districts that together were able to send 37 of the 46 Fairfax delegates to the 10th CD Convention. As it turned out, some of the Fairfax Delegates who were not in these two districts probably voted for some non-Fairfax candidates at the convention, but we didn't know at the time that the Fairfax delegation was not unified. This was obviously a very strong slate. Kevin Wolf and I discussed the fact that it was interesting that neither of us had any interaction with them in the early Obama campaign. Their lack of visibility in the petitioning effort to put Obama on the primary ballot was the case in point.

"It was clear that we had our work cut out for us. So Marcia and I and our core group of Eager Beavers started a major outreach program to the 10th CD delegates and alternates who supported Obama and lived in the other localities comprising our District. She contacted a number of these folks and sent them tip sheets and other materials LCO had developed, offering to help them expand their own grassroots campaign. Our core team also drove out to meet in person with some of them."

"Did you help in this effort?"

"Somewhat. There was EJ Scott, whom I mentioned already. I was still perturbed about our strategy on the full-slate issue as I felt certain this made it much more difficult to be successful. I was also on good terms with Paul Hampton, Winchester's party chair and a big supporter of Obama. He dropped by the LCDC headquarters a number of times in late 2007 and we gave him significant amounts of Obama material that were then in very short supply. I remember lobbying him to support our slate.

"Earlier, when I was working with Kevin regarding the tracking of the National Delegates in early March, I made a major effort to reach all of the local party chairs in the 10th CD to learn who the main Obama go-to person was in their locality. This included the three chairs of the Fairfax districts that had the balance of the Fairfax delegates to our 10th CD Convention. I was reaching out to the non-party Obama supporters in the Fairfax delegation to get them a shot at becoming State delegates, as most of them were new to politics and didn't have much of a clue how to participate in the local and state conventions. Unfortunately, I had limited success, with only two or three of them getting back to me."

"Rollie, I can understand that—these local party chairs you were contacting were either already in close contact with their Obama volunteers, or wanted to get their own allies and party people to the conventions. You were probably seen as someone trying to take some control from them."

"I'm sure you're right. And they had me pegged accurately."

"It seems to me that you and Marcia really had full plates—she with the volunteers and projects, and you with the rules, caucuses, Delegates, and conventions. How could you cope with all of this?"

"Ed, that's a real good question! While doing all this political work, we both had part-time business ventures going as well. We needed some additional leadership help. Gail Wise and Judy Ross were helping Marcia a whole lot, but one fellow in particular kept coming to our attention—Steve Ames. He was our regular go-to guy as soon as he linked up with LCO in late 2007. He had a job with some flexibility and really got very involved with a lot of the activities of the group—walking, talking, going on out-of-town campaign trips, designing outreach strategies, and spearheading many other activities. And best of all, he had a very understanding spouse, Anne Marie, who also pitched in and helped. They hosted a couple of the debate parties—his Ashburn home was centrally located and well suited for these events. They also allowed staffers and volunteers to stay with them until they could secure other housing. Steve has a terrific sense of humor and a sarcastic wit which I especially enjoyed. He was a definite leader and had already played a major role in the campaign.

"You may remember that Steve came to our attention during the primary. He worked closely with Marcia and Daniel Dennison for the Get Out The Vote (GOTV) effort at headquarters. He also headed up the visibility effort as we neared the primary and on primary day.

"After our Loudoun Obama delegation for the local convention was put together and officially elected, Marcia and I agreed to ask Steve to serve as the Chair of our Obama delegation to the convention. He turned out to be a terrific choice. We must have had half-dozen events between then and the local convention. Our first meeting was in late April on the night of the Pennsylvania primary—at Steve and Anne Marie's home. It was a terrific social event despite the disappointing results from PA. About 30 delegates and alternates of our delegation attended the meeting, along with several other supporters. I put together the agenda and chaired the meeting. Steve was nominated and elected 'Temporary' Chair of the Obama delegation. It was only 'temporary' because the rules called for a 'permanent' chair to actually be elected at the 10th CD convention. Steve was then in charge of subsequent meetings. He added great organizational skills to our Loudoun Obama team."

"How did that first meeting go? Were the newbies excited about going to their very first political convention?"

"Yes, interest was high. It went extremely well. Everyone was particularly committed to elect our Loudoun slate for the National Convention. And I announced my intention to run for elector.

"I went over the details of selecting the National Delegates. But then I dropped the bombshell: The Fairfax slate now included one of our own Loudoun delegates to the local convention! Wow! Eddie Eiches, originally thought to be on the Fairfax slate, told me that the other three participants on their slate had a little caucus of their own and dropped him. I later learned that they did not believe that they officially included him in the first place. They decided, in their wisdom, that he wouldn't bring much to the table. Since he also lived in McLean, including him would result in three of the four candidates living in just one locality, and the others in their Fairfax delegation wouldn't look very kindly upon this lack of geographical diversity.

"They had done the math and even though they had the largest delegation to the convention, they realized they did not have the necessary votes to take them over the top. So they ditched Eddie and reached into OUR delegation to find someone to include. They figured that this would drive a wedge into our delegation and peel off enough votes to guarantee them total success. They were successful in recruiting a Loudoun Delegate, and Ryan Myers agreed to join them. Thus they now had their own unified slate to promote.

"You must have been a very surprised camper when you learned what had happened."

"I was absolutely shocked! It was political genius! If Ryan could whittle away just four or five of us, we would be in a real pickle—and it would be very unlikely we would secure any of the four spots. They had adopted precisely the strategy I had been suggesting to our aspirants all along.

"By the time I learned of this, we had already chosen our four folks to promote. I called Ryan Myers to discuss his decision. He strongly believed that he had made it absolutely clear to Marcia and me several times over the prior year that he was running for National Delegate, period. I barely remembered some very early talk about him going to the convention, not necessarily as a Delegate, but I thought as an observer. And unfortunately, Marcia did not remember any conversations with Ryan at all about his desire to run. I apologized profusely about not remembering our earlier conversations and thus not including him in our slate selection process. By this time he had already committed to the Fairfax slate.

"Later I reached out to him again to see if he would back off from the Fairfax folks, remain neutral, and vie for the one male slot we wouldn't be contesting. He declined, believing it was in his best interest to keep his commitment. In response, I unilaterally indicated he would therefore not be included at our caucus gatherings preceding the convention that I was putting together for training and socializing. Thus he was not invited to this first meeting.

"When I opened the floor for discussion on this development, there was a strong feeling that we would not be true to the Obama spirit of unity and conciliation to continue to exclude him. It was a teaching moment for me. We agreed to invite Ryan to all our future gatherings except strategy sessions aimed at getting our Loudoun folks elected. I was proud of the civility displayed and that this decision was reached. I thanked Thom Beres for beginning the discussion of this very sensitive issue. It was even suggested we invite all of the other Obama National Delegate candidates to let them have a shot at us—and that met with general approval as well, although no one followed up on it as I remember."

"Why do you think Ryan missed out on the opportunity to be included in the Loudoun process for marshaling support behind an endorsed Loudoun slate? Didn't you spread the word?"

"We absolutely did! I would estimate that Marcia and I contacted at least a hundred or more possible candidates. Although I later verified that Ryan told me in late December that he was interested in volunteering, and he was getting Marcia's emails, he was not active in our local Obama effort and it simply slipped my mind. I rarely ran into him and there had been no recent opportunity for him to remind me of his interest. But it is important to understand that it was extremely unlikely that our grassroots people would have endorsed him if he had participated. Essentially no one knew him except members of LCDC who, with few exceptions, were not prominent in LCO.

"In the two interviews I had with Ryan for this Swing County project, we discussed at length what actually happened. Here's the scoop. Very early on, about the time I was putting LCO together in spring, 2007, Thom Beres, the Chair of LCDC at the time, had put me in touch with Ryan. He was pretty new to Loudoun County, and I had yet to meet him. Thom told me of his very strong interest in Obama, since, it turned out, he had had previous contact with him. But when Obama first announced, Ryan didn't give him much of a chance—a common view held by most of the professional African American community at that time.

"Soon after we began our discussions on how best to work together in Loudoun for Obama, an opportunity presented itself for Ryan to run for the Loudoun School Board. The Democrats had no candidate for the school district in which he lived. I put him in touch with John Stevens, the Chair of the Loudoun County School Board, to help him get up to speed with the issues. We both clearly remember that I strongly advised him at that time not to identify himself with any presidential candidate—especially one who was then supported by fewer than 10% of the Democratic voters. And this was a non-partisan election. Such a move just wouldn't be prudent if he was seriously committed to his school board election.

"Ryan didn't win, but before he could get involved with the Obama people, he was asked if he would accept the position of Secretary for LCDC. He believed that was a good idea, as it would put him on the local LCDC Executive Committee, and give him good visibility in the local party. But it also created a self-imposed problem regarding active involvement with the Obama campaign. Most of the Executive Committee felt pretty strongly that they shouldn't publicly endorse or show partiality towards any of the candidates—sort of an unwritten rule. So he stayed uninvolved with LCO."

"So why did he think he had a good shot at winning a National Delegate spot?"

"He just didn't understand the process. He thought that being on the LCDC Executive Committee would propel him to victory, not knowing that the local leadership had essentially no influence in the selection of National Delegates."

"You mean that even Tim Buchholz, the LCDC Chair, couldn't be elected?"

"Not likely. Not if he just suddenly appeared on the scene as Ryan did. The Obama people in the grassroots crowd were just too tight. However, since Tim was an excellent Chair of LCDC and a very popular leader, if he had subjected himself to our selection process, he would have been strongly considered. But I doubt anyone else could have pulled it off."

Ryan believed all he had to do was to file, put together his resume describing his work and loyalty to the Party, and, on his own, become a National Delegate. He had no knowledge of slates likely being a part of the process. And he didn't attempt to confirm his assumptions until it was too late. He learned that we had selected our 'slate' after the fact. He was hugely disappointed and one pissed-off Obama supporter. His calls to me and to Marcia were very heated.

"In our conversation, I told him that of course he was not precluded from filing. He could still run for National Delegate, but would likely have little support from the Loudoun delegation. And he went ahead and filed with Rich Galecki, the Chair of the 10th CD. Upon request, Rich would send anyone the current list of those filing with him, and Mary Lee Cerillo of Fairfax likely stayed on top of the filings. When Ryan's name popped up, she did some checking and found that Ryan was not endorsed by the LCO, was an 'up and comer' in Loudoun politics, and thus might be just what the Fairfax

Committee needed to solidify their slate. Three of them met, decided Eddie Eiches wouldn't bring enough to their ticket, and agreed to approach Ryan about joining them to form a new cross-county ticket. If Ryan had anywhere near the clout they thought he had in Loudoun, they would all be going to Denver! When we learned of this new alignment, we were shocked, disappointed, and quite concerned as to how this would affect our chances for success.

"It is common in Virginia for many local committees to hold their own annual Jefferson-Jackson (JJ) Dinner to raise a significant part of their annual income. Loudoun and Fairfax are no exceptions. These are usually black-tie affairs at big hotels, and thousands of dollars are raised through ticket sales and brochure advertising. One of the statewide elected office holders can usually be counted on to be the main attraction. This year, 2008, was no exception. Although our LCO team wasn't smart enough to attend the Fairfax dinner, the Fairfax slate attended our Jefferson-Jackson dinner in full force. Ryan introduced them around at cocktail hour, and I chatted with most of them myself, especially Fred, since we served on the Rules committee together.

"Not too long after this event, Tony Barney, the Sterling district chair in Loudoun, announced that he was going to sponsor a Forum for anyone in the 10th District who may be interested in learning how to become a National Delegate. As a member of the 10th District Committee, he thought that would be a good use of his time. He has always been one of the people in Loudoun politics interested in rules and procedures, and we have worked together a number of times. I didn't expect that he would have many people attend because our Obama aspirants had been trained by me, and had already filed to run.

"I was right; only a few showed up. But the Fairfax unity ticket was there except for Fred—Mary Lee Cerillo, Kristin Cabral, and Ryan Myers. It was a bit awkward, of course. They didn't expect me, and I certainly didn't expect them. This was Loudoun territory. They didn't belong here! (Yeah, I know that wasn't PC thinking—but I have faults too.) We were stiffly and awkwardly polite to one another throughout the session. When it was over, as I was leaving, I noticed them in deep and serious discussion. I would have loved to be a fly on their shoulder. There were only four or five others at that meeting, none of whom filed.

"A couple of weeks later, Ryan announced that he was going to have a barbecue at his home to introduce their unity ticket to the

Loudoun Delegates and Alternates. He used Evite, an Internet application that many of you savvy readers have used in the past. What was of particular interest to me was that the invitee list and their responses are tracked in the application and available to anyone who received an invitation. Since Ryan was a member of LCDC, he emailed an invite to all its members. I was then able to track who had accepted or declined the invitation. I considered this event a direct assault on our LCO efforts to elect OUR candidates at the 10th CD Convention, so this information was very valuable. I remember calling a couple of those who replied in the affirmative and made sure they understood the purpose of the party—which resulted in them changing their minds and not attending. (I can see the frown on some of your faces, but folks, this is just practical politics.)

"Dave Poisson, our very popular member of the Virginia House of Delegates whom I had previously lined up to be Loudoun's Delegation Chair, signed up to attend the party. After intense pressure from many of us in LCO, and from some others, he realized it may not be such a good idea and changed his mind. He later told Ryan that he had never been so intensely lobbied on any issue in his four years in office as he had been on his attendance to a simple backyard barbecue!

"Remember, all of this happened after our local Obama delegation to the conventions had been settled, and it would be these delegates voting to elect the National Delegates at the District Convention. I described earlier how I put together this slate of Obama delegates, which did include Ryan. Not all of them were active in LCO, but most were. Some were just some of my political buddies, and others were old friends of mine on the local Democratic Committee. Only a handful of them were 'friends of friends' whom I didn't know at all. We were certain that we had their full support for our Loudoun slate. As it turned out, we didn't have as much control as we thought.

"Mary Lee Cerillo ran the show for the Fairfax slate. They put together a four-color handout, ordered pins with the unity theme, and lobbied the Delegates throughout the District prior to the convention. They did a much better job than we did. Ryan made a valiant effort to gather in some votes for him and his new slate, but he had a formidable task. EJ Scott from Manassas was conducting a lonely battle for support for National Delegate, mostly by email.

"As for my campaign for elector, I was so wrapped up in what I was doing for LCO and the campaign that I didn't go after it as hard as I should have. I did ask for support from my delegation, and didn't take them for granted. And since the entire delegation would be voting for the elector position (Obama and Clinton Delegates), I reached out to the Clinton leadership here in Loudoun as well—with success. I had gotten full support from Dan Moldover and Robert Latham. They were the ones running the local effort for Clinton for several months, and remembered that I had helped them with handing out their supplies at headquarters and the Lyndon LaRouche invasion of their Caucus at the time they elected the local delegates.

"Initially I had an open field when deciding if I was going to run for elector. No one had yet filed. Later, I heard that Barbara Lee from Clarke County was running. She had been a good friend to me way back in 1995, when I ran for House of Delegates. I really like her—a good long-time, important Democrat in this county, who also had served on the 10th CD Committee for many years. However, Barbara supported Clinton, as did many of the Loudoun 10th CD members. They knew Barbara well and would likely vote for her. But because of the lopsided advantage that the Obama delegates had over the Clinton delegates, the odds were that an Obama candidate for elector would win, and so I decided that I would be that Obama person.

"A few days later I learned that Fred Mittelman, who was on the Fairfax National Delegate unity slate, had also filed for elector. With that large Fairfax delegation behind him, I thought he would be my strongest opponent. And if we were to split the Obama vote, perhaps Barbara would slip in and win. Four others also decided to run for elector, but they were to have no significant bearing on this competition.

"All of the pre-convention jockeying was over. All interested parties had filed. It was District Convention time. Game on. I'll tell you what happened at the convention the next time we get together."

Convention Combat

> *"The life of the individual is a continuous combat with errors and obstacles, and no victory is more satisfying than the one achieved against opposition."*—Gustav Stresemann

It is time for me to go see Rollie Winter again at the Rust Library in Leesburg for another interview to learn more about the Great Campaign of 2008. This time let's go by way of the village of Hamilton up Business Route 7 so we can take a look at that nursery in Ivandale. Ivandale is a tiny little village over a mile north of the town of Hamilton, seven miles west of Leesburg.

Ivandale is the home of the Ivandale Farms Nursery, which has 20,000 trees in stock. The place started in 1900 as the Ivandale Floral Company, growing huge numbers of flowers which were shipped into Washington, DC, some 48 miles to the east. The flowers were delivered on the Washington and Old Dominion Railroad. In its day, the nursery dominated the Washington floral market. It's still an incredible sight, even more remarkable because it is located in the middle of almost nowhere.

Rollie was there at our usual 10:00 a.m. starting time and I ask him, "Tell me about the 10th CD Democratic Convention in 2008. I'll not interrupt you unless you confuse me."

Rollie's response was right to the point. "Saturday, May 17, the Convention convened at the auditorium of Heritage High School, just outside the town of Leesburg and across the street from where I regularly vote. It was a bright, beautiful late spring day—reaching 78 degrees by early afternoon. Our delegates and alternates had been trained; our Obama Delegation Leader, Steve Ames, chosen; and our candidates for National Delegates and elector had speeches ready. It was time for the BIG show."

"There was a whole lot of politicking going on outside the entrance and in the lobby. Many of the candidates were introducing themselves and trying to get support. The folks on the Fairfax Hope Happens slate were wearing their buttons and handing out their fancy four-color brochure touting their experience, diversity, and how hard they had worked for Obama. Unfortunately, they certainly outdid our efforts.

"Dan Moldover was lobbying for National Delegate votes

from the Clinton delegations. I had expected him to win as there didn't seem to be a strong candidate from Fairfax. However, there was a last-minute hat thrown into the ring by a flamboyant, talented, former LCDC Chair, John Flannery.

"John Flannery and I had crossed political swords a few times in the past, and I had been somewhat reluctant to ask him for support for my bid for elector. His wife, Holly, was also a Clinton Delegate to this District Convention. I ran into them in the lobby before the convention started and did ask them for their support—which they gave me. Later in the day, they approached me to reaffirm that I would indeed vote for Hillary at the Electoral College if she were to be nominated. They had 'heard' that I had indicated that I wouldn't vote for her if she was nominated. I pointed out I had made that commitment in the handout I gave to all the delegates that day. 'Of course I will vote for the Democratic candidate for President, whoever it turns out to be! I'm a Democrat!'"

"While checking in at the convention, I noticed we were missing a number of delegates, but it was still pretty early, and all had confirmed their participation. I had also given them my cell phone number to contact me if there was a glitch and they were to be late or had to cancel altogether. Noting there were a few absences just before convening the convention, I conferred with Steve Ames and put a couple of Alternates on the floor. It wasn't really important that early because the voting wasn't to begin anytime soon. The delegates took their seats down by the stage, with the Alternates of all localities gathered in the back, ready to be called if needed. As usual, there was some confusion as to how to handle the replacement of a Delegate with an Alternate, but eventually everything was straightened out. This is ALWAYS, ALWAYS, ALWAYS a big problem at our Democratic conventions. Someday, someone smart is going to get this figured out.

"One important convention rule is that if delegations are short because of no-shows and insufficient Alternates, they can fill in with Alternates from other jurisdictions. These fill-in delegates could very well affect election outcomes. But of course the Fairfax bunch also knew the rules. All too often, the Alternates seated by vote time were those who were more aggressive in making themselves available when vacancies occurred. I kept running back and forth making sure our Alternates were speaking up when Alternates from other localities were needed, but had mixed success. The main problem was that the Alternates strongly preferred to wait so they could sit with the Loudoun Delegation—with their friends. If I had known just how close the elections were to be, I would have placed much more emphasis on this role and done much more training.

"Temporary Chair Rich Galecki called the meeting to order. All the Convention's movers and shakers, including all the committees, were 'temporary' until the Convention, by motion and vote, made them 'permanent'. By motion, the Committees were made permanent.

"Loudoun County's own very able State Senator, Mark Herring, gave a spirited welcoming address, after which State Senator Creigh Deeds was introduced. He unsuccessfully ran for governor the following year. The roll call of jurisdictions showed that there were 175 delegates present on the floor out of the 199 delegates authorized; these totals included both Clinton and Obama delegates. This first count also showed that there were more than enough Alternates present to have a full count. Fairfax was there in force, 72 of their 76 present, along with 7 Alternates; Loudoun had 63 out of their 66 seated, and 14 Alternates. Significant shortages were noted for Fauquier and Prince William Counties (total shortage of 11 delegates with no alternates present). My mistake was not to approach these delegation chairs and ask that they fill in with some of our Loudoun County Alternates.

"Thus a quorum was declared present (enough delegates present to conduct the business of the Convention). Rich Galecki and Barbara Lee were then voted as Permanent Chair and Secretary, respectively. Keynote addresses were given by State Senator Margi Vanderhye of McLean and State Delegate Dave Poisson, the Chair of our Loudoun Delegation.

"The tension was building. Loudoun and Fairfax were now fully represented. A few of our Alternates had been seated in other localities—but just a very few. The Convention Rules were unanimously adopted with no discussion. I was very pleased with that because of my involvement in their production. Sam Crockett and the Rules Committee had done an extremely good job handling all the complexities. There is nothing like a rules hassle on the floor to sour a convention.

"Next up were the two candidates for the 10th District Congressional seat: Mike Turner and Judy Feder. We had to choose one of them in a Democratic primary in July to take on Frank Wolf, who had been our representative since 1980. Judy, from Fairfax, and thought by many to be a Clinton supporter (she wasn't), had run a very credible race against Wolf two years earlier. Mike, from Loudoun, was the first candidate running for Congress in the nation to endorse Barack Obama for President. Both gave spirited speeches and the response to their addresses was warm. Mike, particularly, gave a great speech—but the Clinton people in the audience were not very pleased with him. As it turned out, Turner carried Loudoun (by one vote!), but Feder won the nomination easily because of the Fairfax vote.

"Finally, it was time for the real fireworks to begin. The first step was to divide the delegates according to whom they represented, so the Clinton delegates and Alternates (since their group was smaller than the Obama group) left the floor and went to the cafeteria to have their caucus. Tony Barney chaired the Clinton Caucus. The Obama delegates remained in the auditorium. Jeanette Rishell from Manassas Park, who had been appointed temporary Chair of the Obama Caucus, was then confirmed as permanent chair.

"In the Obama Caucus, Jeanette made some opening remarks, including the rules for candidate presentations. We started with the selection of one female National Delegate. In addition to Marcia, Mary Lee, and EJ, there were two others: Sheila McConnell from Manassas and Margaret Richardson of Delaplane. Both were virtual unknowns to the vast majority of the delegates and had little chance to win.

"Presentations were made—one minute each. All did well, although some nervousness showed through. I thought Marcia hit her speech out of the park. The ballots were then distributed, marked, and collected for counting. Ro Pelletier, a Loudoun friend, was the head teller; she was a member of the 10th CD Committee but was not a Delegate to this convention. As we waited, the tension built, and it felt like an eternity before the results were finally available. The announcement was made: Out of the 118 votes cast (46 from Fairfax, 41 from Loudoun and 35 from all other localities), Mary Lee led the field with 50 votes and Marcia closely followed with 48. EJ had 11 votes, and Sheila McConnell was just behind her with 9 votes. It was a damn close race!

"Since no one had reached 50%, the delegates were asked to cast a second ballot to decide between Mary Lee and Marcia. Out of the 118 eligible voters, two dropped out and didn't vote. Marcia only picked up five votes, and Mary Lee the balance. A huge sigh of disappointment was expressed by our delegation. The final tally was 63—53 and Marcia had lost. What a disaster. I couldn't help but remember that if we had been successful in cutting a deal with EJ, Marcia would have won. It was a crushing defeat for Marcia and for Loudoun County. Since all of us believed that Marcia was clearly our strongest candidate in our slate of four, there were a lot of glum faces in our pack of delegates. Our 'hopes', driving us for more than a year, were severely dashed. It appeared very unlikely that we would go home with any winners.

"Next up was the female Alternate. Gail Wise was our Loudoun nominee. Gail was Marcia's main go-to person, and after the Obama campaign arrived in June, she turned out to be the major gate-keeper at the Obama headquarters in Leesburg. She was up against the Fairfax powerhouse, Kristin Cabral, and EJ Scott of Manassas, who had filed for Delegate and Alternate. The rules allowed filing for both positions and if losing the Delegate election, the candidate could run for Alternate. After failing to win the Delegate seat, EJ gave a second, very passionate and emotional speech, imploring the delegates to give her a shot, and not just go along with their delegation choice. The vote was taken, and again we sat and waited for what seemed like forever to get the result. It had become apparent to all of us that the number of folks assigned to the counting task was insufficient. The head teller, Ro Pelletier, came forward with the results in hand and conferred with Jeanette, who then called me over for a conference.

"What's the problem, I wondered? It turned out that a few MORE ballots were cast than the number of delegates present to cast those ballots. Some folks had accidentally (or purposefully) cast more than one ballot! This was a first for me. I've been attending these conventions for over 40 years and this had never happened. Jeanette and I conferred and decided that the only thing to do was to redo the vote. But this time, after new ballots were distributed, every person from every locality filed up the stairs to the stage, crossed over to the middle, put their ballot in a ballot box, and continued across the stage and exited stage left. Again, we waited for the result.

"At last, they were in. 115 votes were cast. Kristin had the most votes with 46, shy of what was necessary for a majority. Surprisingly, EJ came in second with 35 votes, and Gail received only 34 votes. Unfortunately, three delegates didn't even vote! EJ's personal story had been very effective with some in our Delegation, since at least seven of our bunch had not voted for Gail. And other than Ryan, I doubt that any voted for Kristin. Since Gail had the fewest votes by one, she was dropped from the list and a runoff was held between Kristin and EJ. She lost by one lousy vote. Rats; double rats. ONE LOUSY VOTE! We were totally screwed!

"As you can imagine, Gail was very upset, as was most of the Loudoun delegation. I wished I had done more to help her. When putting together the delegation no one was included whom I had not approved. I had assumed all of them would naturally support the Loudoun folks we had selected for the slate, but did not make it absolutely clear that this was expected of them. I should have known better. Secondly, I should have contacted all the localities ahead of time, found out who was their delegation chair, and made it clear to them I had the Alternates to use if they were short. Since the results were so close, doing either of these things could have made the difference in these first two elections. Gail especially had the right to be upset with me. In the runoff election, only 107 voted and Kristin beat EJ 57—50. And I'll say it again—if a deal had been made between Marcia and EJ, they both would have won. Instead, they both lost."

"Now we had to sit through another likely debacle—electing two male delegates. Ryan had gotten at least a couple of Loudoun delegates to support him—maybe more. If Gail was right, he had been more than a little successful.

"Our candidates were Bernard Hill and Juan Perez. Both have a great sense of humor, but Bernard, particularly, had a tough time asking people for support. Neither knew delegates from the other localities. They were somewhat reticent to ask for votes in the hall as the delegates were arriving. We helped them earlier in the month to improve their words, style, and delivery. Naturally, they would be quite nervous—which might affect their impact upon the listeners. I was not optimistic.

"The two heavyweights up against them were Ryan Myers and Fred Mittelman—Hope Happens ticket. There were eleven others running as well. Eddie Eiches from Fairfax, however, ended up not running because he was at a labor union meeting—running for its President! Since he had no chance here, he obviously had a more important function to attend. It turned out he won.

The only other candidate with some chance of winning was Bruce Roemmelt of Prince William County. He is a popular, long-time Democrat and well liked. Back in 2007, Bruce took on the extreme conservative Republican incumbent Bob Marshall in a House of Delegates race. In his campaign letter to the convention delegates and alternates, Bruce stated: 'I felt then as now that we must fight in every district to turn Virginia blue. There are some who say in the heavily Republican 13th it was a lost cause, but look at what we did. We fought a fight where no Democrats had run essentially since redistricting in 2001. We knocked on over 20,000 doors in four years. Not only did we ID voters in 2005 and 2007, but we worked tirelessly for Judy Feder and Jim Webb in 2006, and Senators Herring and Colgan, Loudoun County Board of Supervisors Member Stevens Miller, and candidates Karen Schultz, Mike George, Corey Reiley, and Kevin Turner in 2007.' It was a good message, and although his support list mentioned some Loudoun 'heavyweights', none of them were delegates to this convention. Net, net—I didn't really expect him to be a problem against our nominees.

"There was one other man running for National Delegate from Loudoun County: Thomas S. 'Tommy' Dodson, who wasn't a part of our delegation. Although I knew him politically very well, he had not told me of his interest or intentions. Tommy came from a political family in Middleburg; his dad was Mayor for many years. When his dad died, Tommy, at 27, was elected to take his place. At the time, he was the youngest mayor in the Commonwealth of Virginia. Tommy and his father had each served in that position during an era when public office was viewed as community service. Tommy used to say, 'No one even knew if there was an 'R' or a 'D' by your name. The towns were completely nonpartisan, and holding office didn't confer anything important except the opportunity to serve. Councils and boards cooperated together to find solutions to local needs.' A few years later, Tommy offered to serve instead on the County Board of Supervisors and worked in that capacity for 14 years. When a great job opportunity came along that required him to resign from the Board, he took it. That was about the time I moved to Loudoun and met him.

"Soon after Obama announced, Tommy became very active with the campaign and independently started to work for him door-to-door, even traveling to other states. He loved getting back into politics for this candidate and especially liked working with all of the inspired young people. With Tommy's independent, moderate stance, it's easy to understand why Barack Obama's positive message that *'there are no red states or blue states, there is only the United States of America,'* resonated with him. Tommy dared to hope that a focus on all of us cooperating and coming together to solve the nation's problems could return. His own history led him to believe that we are capable of doing just that. But, as I said, I was really surprised to find him among the list of those running for National Delegate.

"But now it was decision time. Juan and Bernard gave great speeches—much better than their earlier practice attempts. Their preparation and practice really paid off, and I could sense from the applause that they were well received. Could we be in for a pleasant surprise? The ballots were distributed. And because of that earlier snafu, we continued to have each Delegate walk across the stage to put their ballot in the ballot box. Since there were two positions to fill, everyone had two votes to cast."

"OK, OK, Rollie. Get on with it—who won the damn election?"

"This time all 118 eligible delegates voted. Only nine of the fifteen candidates received votes, and those with five or more votes included: Bernard Hill—54; Juan Perez—51; Ryan Myers—44; Fred Mittleman—31; Bruce Roemmelt—26; and Frank Costanza—14! WOW! Loudoun candidates ran first and second. At least 15 of the 46 Fairfax delegates didn't even vote for Fred. Big surprise! Ryan ran third, and I was astounded that he did better than Fred. No one had received a majority, so we had more voting to do. Frank was dropped from the list, and we voted again. Two convention delegates had gone home (maybe mad), and this time Juan jumped 9 votes to 60 which made him a winner! Bernard came up to 57, just two shy of what he needed for a majority. Ryan picked up 5 votes, but Fred actually dropped 4 votes. Bruce was way behind. Now we're looking good.

"We then went to the third ballot. Juan because of the win, and Bruce because he placed last, were both dropped from the ballot. Five more people left for home, so only 111 people voted, and Bernard was elected with 62 votes, followed by Ryan with 28 and Fred, 21. Astounding!

"So the LCO candidates, although suffering a couple of agonizing losses, ended up with two wonderful wins. In fact, with Ryan's showing at the end, the three Loudoun men ran 1-2-3. An amazing outcome and one we truly savored.

"Our delegation had stayed together up until this result was announced, but it was running late so we did have to pull in a few of the Alternates. Our Alternate pool was thinning out as we or other localities made them delegates. It had been a long day. We had been voting for more than two hours, and we still had business on the agenda.

"While all of this was going on, the Clinton delegates had

concluded their business and were waiting for the full convention to reconvene. Turned out they had surprises of their own in their Caucus."

"Tell me about it."

"Their business was to elect one male National Delegate and one female National Alternate."

"I have a feeling there's more to this story. Keep going."

"Tony Barney was elected Chair of the Caucus, John Flannery of Loudoun was elected the Clinton National Delegate and Eula Tate from Fairfax was elected the Clinton National Alternate. John's election was a surprise to me since I had no idea he was running. Apparently he had done a lot for the candidate that convinced the caucus attendees that he was worthy of the position. I really had expected Dan Moldover would win the trip to Denver. I knew how hard he had worked for Clinton. But John once ran for Congress and Commonwealth's Attorney. He is a very charming, passionate and persuasive speaker, and I'm sure he blew away all the competition at the Clinton caucus, despite other candidates' long and somewhat lonely hard work for Hillary.

"Now that the two caucuses were done, the convention reconvened as one body a few minutes later. We still had important work to do, including choosing the elector. If the Democrats were to win the state in November, the elector chosen here would represent the Virginia 10th CD at the Electoral College in December.

"Other than reaching out to some of the Clinton delegates in Loudoun, I made little person-to-person contact with those who were not Loudoun Obama delegates prior to the convention. We had a two-minute speech limit. That plus a bio-handout at the convention was all the campaigning I took the time to do.

"As with the National Delegates, all the elector candidates had to prefile their applications. However, neither the Party nor the Campaign endorsed any of the applicants. We were on our own, and it was a wide-open race. Seven candidates had filed for the job including Fred Mittleman, the fellow who had run for National Delegate from Fairfax. I expected him to be my toughest opponent as Fairfax had 76 total convention delegates compared to our 66. There were 57 in all of the other localities, combined.

"The sentimental favorite for the job was Barbara Lee. She is a wonderful person and a long-time Democrat from Clarke County. I had met her when I ran for the Virginia House of Delegates back in 1995. She did a lot of campaigning for me at that time. She also had served a long time on the 10th CD Committee, so she knew several of the key people in the localities outside of Fairfax and Loudoun. However, she was a Clinton Delegate, and since the Obama delegates at the Convention readily outnumbered the Clinton folks 118—81 that gave the Obama nominees a decided advantage.

"The rules stated that it took a majority vote to win the National Delegate and Alternate seats, but specified that all other elections would be determined by plurality vote. That meant the winner would be determined by whoever received the most votes on the first ballot. We had done that to speed up the process. And by the time the election for elector came around, many of the delegates had left the hall. Although I was not able to confirm it, I was pretty sure we still had most of the Obama component of our delegation intact, along with a majority of the Loudoun Clinton folks.

"Only four of the seven candidates spoke, and I was last. Two of the missing was a married couple, John and Margaret Richardson from Fauquier County. They must have filed on a lark because to have any chance at all, only one would have filed. The other man who filed who failed to show was Tapan Banerjee from Fairfax. The first of the four to speak was Anthony Hines, a man who was dressed in a good-looking dark suit and looked very impressive. He had a four or five page single-spaced typewritten speech in a three-ring notebook that he placed in front of him on the podium. And then he started to read it, word for word. He of course was nervous as all get-out as we all were, and I immediately started to feel very sorry for him. I knew he couldn't even come close to finishing his speech within the two-minute time limit. When the moderator announced that his time was up, he was still on his first page, and he tried to keep reading. But he was then, more firmly, cut off.

"Barbara Lee was next, followed by Fred. I thought Barbara had the best personal story and she presented it well. And by seeing how this convention had previously responded to strong personal stories, I felt she would do well in the voting. Fred followed without problems. Now it was my turn to make my case. Here was what I said:

'What is an elector? Most of us are a bit fuzzy about that. So I have provided you that information on the back of my handout.

'As a young man, I decided I wanted to make a difference. My political road was often bumpy, but it has always been interesting.

'Some advice for newcomers: Pick your party, work your butt off, and

always, always support your party's nominees.

'Over time you will find you are becoming more and more influential—and you will start making a real difference.

'Then, when you've put in your time and paid your dues, you too may have the chance to run, and the honor to become, an elector.

'I am proud of my accomplishments; I have earned your vote.

'I'll end by using my 7th grade campaign slogan when running for Vice President of my junior high school:

'BE JOLLY, AND BY GOLLY, VOTE FOR ROLLIE!'

"That got a good laugh, and I received a good round of applause. I then went back to my delegation, received my ballot and as I was walking up to the stage, several people gave me a lot of support. One in particular I remember came from a young lady whom I didn't know from Fairfax. She introduced herself and said, 'I'm going to vote for you; you snagged me with the slogan!' That helped to reduce my tension. I was anticipating success.

"The results of the vote were announced. With 141 voting, I received 65 votes, Barbara Lee 46, Fred Mittleman 21, and Anthony Hines 9. So, I had done it! What a thrilling experience! I potentially could be one of 13 **Democratic** electors representing Virginia at the Electoral College. All we needed to do now was to carry Virginia in the fall—no small task! The last time Virginia had a Democratic elector was in 1964. We had our work cut out for us.

Marking Time

"Well they often call me Speedo because I don't believe in wasting time. Umm hm hm.... Well now some may call me, Joe, some may call me, Moe, Just remember Speedo, He don't never take it slow."—The Cadillacs from the song, Speedo.

I'm going to Hillsboro. Now this is a town 52 miles west of Washington, DC near the foothills of the Short Hill Mountains. By 1802 it sported 40 villagers, making it the fourth largest village in Loudoun County. It is an interesting place with an old stone school and old stone houses, some dating from the 18th century. It now has nice vineyards and a wonderful organic market where almost everything is grown or raised locally.

Things got really exciting there in October of 1859. On the 17th of October of that year, this joint was jumping. That's when John Brown conducted his famous raid on Harper's Ferry, 10 miles to the north of Hillsboro, to seize the federal arsenal of 100,000 rifles and foment a slave uprising in the South. Brown deeply believed that slavery was wrong, that the slaves should be freed, and that they would have to rise up and free themselves.

This caused extreme fear and a deep pile of excitement throughout the white oligarchy that ran the Southern economy. You see, by 1859 the net capital investment in African slaves in the South exceeded the total capital investment in railroads and manufacturing plants throughout the entire rest of the United States. That's why this was such a big deal; we're talking big money here, and big money talks. If you wanted to know why the Civil War happened, you just got your answer. The way the oligarchy saw it, the entire ballgame was on the line, and they didn't take kindly to it. The uprising had to be stopped, and stopped now. Never mind that John Brown came with only 21 men to raid the arsenal; this had to be nipped in the bud.

Here's what this has to do with Hillsboro. The village called out the militia, mustered into companies and marched off to Harper's Ferry, less than a day away on foot. There they placed themselves under the command of an obscure West Point graduate named Robert E. Lee. Lee thought Brown was insane but should get a fair trial and then hanged. Sure enough, Lee's boys captured Brown on

October 18, 1859. Brown got his fair trial and they hanged his ass in Charles Town, West Virginia on the lawn of the courthouse 15 days later. *Sic transit gloria mundi*, peeps.

Well, now I'm headed out of Hillsboro and back to the Rust Library to talk to Rollie Winter about what happened next in the Great Campaign of 2008. The primary was over; the District Convention ended. And although Obama had a lead in the committed Delegate count, Clinton had started to rack up some victories and narrow his lead. And there was great uncertainty about how the Super Delegates would break nationally. Many felt the Clinton machinery would somehow snatch victory from the 'Hope for Change' enthusiasts.

Rollie and the gang thought they would get a nice rest between then and the State Convention in mid-June in Hampton. I wondered what he did during this 'slow' period, as there hadn't been many of them. I also wanted to know how the State Convention turned out.

"OK, Rollie—tell me how you relaxed and took it easy between conventions. Did you take a break from the political world?"

"I sure thought about it. But there were some loose ends to tie up after the District Convention was over. Number one was to make every possible effort to get Marcia to the National Convention one way or another. And, as I saw it, the best way to get that done was to use what influence we had to have her included on Tim Kaine's 'Slate' of 16 National Delegates who were to be elected statewide at the Virginia Democratic Convention. Charlie Kelly, the fellow I mentioned earlier who ran Kaine's 'Moving Virginia Forward' PAC, was the one to contact. He worked with Kaine and the party leaders to put together an 'approved' Slate of candidates to be Obama At-Large National Delegates—six females and six males. Those included on the Slate were most certain to be elected and go to Denver. Charlie, of course, got a lot of direction from Kaine and other prominent Democratic leaders in the state. You can imagine the difficulty of that task. Hundreds of activists thought they had a right to be on the Slates.

"Of course, we started lobbying Kevin Wolf and Jane Van Ostern. We believed that if they in turn lobbied Charlie and other decision makers on Marcia's behalf, she would be a lock. A day or two later, Kevin came back with the bad news/good news result: The bad news was that Marcia would not be included on their Delegate Slate. However, the good news was that she would be recommended for the National Convention Rules Committee. That came as a complete and welcome surprise! She was subsequently elected to serve on this Rules Committee by the State Convention, which gave her a pass to the National Convention. It opened a lot of doors, gave her access to the Convention gallery, and relieved her of Delegate obligations throughout the business sessions. Our connections with Kevin Wolf, Jane Van Ostern, Tim Kaine, and Charlie Kelly really paid off. The travesty of Marcia's possible exclusion at the National Convention had been avoided. It was very heartening to discover that the Obama Campaign really did appreciate our grassroots efforts.

"And remember EJ Scott? She was the lady from Manassas who also lost in her quest for National Delegate at the 10th CD Convention. She was appointed to the National Convention Credentials Committee, so she also went to Denver. Fate took an unexpectedly good turn for both of them."

"What else went on while you were waiting for the State Convention?"

"I ended up getting pretty busy. I advised Robert Latham when he started a Young Democrat Club in Loudoun and helped to organize one of their early meetings, attended a Democratic National Committee (DNC) Rules Committee meeting in DC that handled the Michigan and Florida National Delegate disputes, and processed many requests made to the Loudoun County for Obama website for local activities and events. We used this website on MyBO to announce upcoming events and screen email requests by folks wanting to communicate with our group—this was the same LCO social networking website I had set up way back in February 2007, and it continued to be very active throughout the campaign. Also I advised and helped several other Loudoun folks who were running for the At-Large National Delegate openings at the State Convention, despite the fact that there was little chance for their success."

"On a personal note, just after the District Convention, I emailed my family and several of my non-political friends to tell them of my successful bid to become an elector. I attached my bio and my elector information sheet that I passed out at the Convention. Some of these relatives and friends were Republicans and many were Independents. Among the replies were many enthusiastic congratulations and quips. Here are a few I received that I found encouraging and amusing:

From Cousin Nancy, I am a Hillary supporter, so I'm in mourning. Hopefully I'll get over it and get behind Obama. Another male with charisma. What else can I say?

'From long-time Loudoun friend, Al, who now lives in Florida: Be jolly and, by golly, vote for Rollie! That has to be one of the best campaign slogans I have ever seen or heard.

'From my sis-in-law, Chris, living in Northern California—former CA State President of AAUW: Hi Rollie...I loved it! Congratulations on your election. It's nice to actually know one of the infamous electors. This is really terrific. I do hope you have a job come December.

'From an old boss, Jeff, in MD (I once ran marketing for the company): Congratulations...this is terrific news, and I certainly hope you become fully employed!! Even in 7th grade, you showed signs of marketing brilliance.

'From very long-time friend Nancy in Virginia Beach: You are a great American, and I'm very proud that you count me among your friends. Way to go Jolly Rollie!!! I'll spread the word, by golly.

'From my youngest bro, Jeff, in Yorba Linda who has never cast a Dem vote in his life: By golly I'm jolly I have a brother as wonderful as Rollie! Seriously! Congratulations!

'And lastly, from a fraternity brother, Al, living in Washington State: Bravo!! And let's hope that later in the year you will be casting a vote for Barack Obama. If Virginia goes Democrat, the nation will too...I say this as a recovering Republican.'

"Some of your activities sound pretty interesting. Tell me about the DNC Rules Committee meeting; what was that all about?"

"This was an interesting sidelight to our efforts in Loudoun. It was a pretty big deal nationally at the time and very controversial, especially because the delegate counts for Obama and Clinton were tightening, and there were only three primaries left. The dispute over the Michigan and Florida delegates could determine the nomination outcome. Clinton was scratching for every delegate she could get and hoped to get the rules changed to affect the outcome in her favor."

"But surely all of the Rules for primaries and Conventions were put in place many months before, weren't they?"

"Yes, they were. Let me give you a little background. In 2007 the DNC adopted timing rules for the state primaries. They set February 5th as 'Super Tuesday', and specified that only Iowa, New Hampshire, South Carolina, and Nevada could have their primary before that date. Any state violating this rule would lose all their delegates and not be seated at the Convention. All candidates agreed with these rules, which also included a pledge not to campaign or advertise in any state violating them."

"But weren't there a couple of states that did violate that

rule?"

"Yes. And that's why we found ourselves at this Rules Committee meeting in late May, just before our Virginia State Convention. When Michigan and Florida announced they were moving their primaries up to January 15 and 29, 2008, the DNC immediately warned them that if they followed through with these new dates, their delegations would not be seated at the National Convention, nor their votes counted. The warnings were ignored, and Michigan and Florida went ahead and had their primaries.

"Clinton ended up winning Florida with a small plurality and did even better in Michigan, where Obama didn't even have his name on the ballot."

"So it was to Obama's advantage not to have those states counted at the National Convention?"

"Absolutely. But Clinton had a lot of clout at the DNC, and she and her people started agitating for a retroactive rules change so that these delegations would be fully seated and counted. In her appeal to the Democratic National Committee, she pointed out that 'More than two million voters in Florida and Michigan cast votes during the Democratic Primaries . . . The current posture . . . denies these voters who took every possible step to have a say in the election from doing so. It also jeopardizes our ability to reclaim the White House and expand our majority in Congress this November. Democrats in Florida and Michigan must be fully represented in the nomination process, and our leaders in those states must be encouraged to work hard to promote our Party's interests. One guiding principle alone should govern the resolution of these challenges: the preferences expressed by these voters must be honored.' Her persistence paid off, and she won the opportunity to present her case once again at the Rules Committee meeting, which was set for May 31 in Washington, DC at the Sheraton Hotel."

"I imagine it was pretty hard to get a seat to that show!"

"It was essentially impossible for the general public. But since it was relatively local—in DC—Steve Ames contacted the usual suspects and suggested a road trip to join the crowd expected to demonstrate for Obama outside the venue. Theresa, Bernard, Juan, Maureen, and Marcia decided to make the trip with him.

"Then the Associated Press (AP) reported that hundreds of Clinton protesters planned to rally outside the hotel to encourage the Rules Committee to find a way to punish Michigan and Florida without completely disenfranchising Democratic primary voters from those states. Several busloads of Clinton supporters were expected to arrive from Florida and perhaps scores of people from Michigan. Obama's campaign sent out news releases discouraging any kind of counter-protest, although his supporters competed with Clinton backers for the limited number of public seats available inside the meeting. There could have been trouble.

"The day before the Rules Committee event, Kevin Wolf sent an email to me, Marcia, and Kevin Vincent of Arlington, saying that Jeff Berman had 50 floor tickets and wanted us to use them as bait to recruit supporters who would provide muscle to discourage any strident Obama partisans who might gather outside the hotel. Once that was handled satisfactorily, our supporters could then attend the Rules Committee meeting. Our gang jumped at the chance and grabbed five of the tickets. But there was another wrinkle to this story."

"What's that?"

"A few days earlier, Steve Ames had found and sent us the online procedure that would be followed to give the public an opportunity to gain admittance. Some of us, myself included, decided to try to get them online because if we were successful, we wouldn't have crowd duty.

"Anyone wanting a ticket was directed to a website that was going to go live precisely at 10:00 a.m. on the 29th, a couple of days before the meeting. There were approximately 400 tickets available. Since thousands of requests were expected, the likelihood of success was slim. But when the time came, I was prepared. I had my cell phone available that had the EXACT time. I went to the site about ten minutes early, and once I got connected, I filled out the request form, and waited. At exactly the right moment I hit the *send* key. Amazingly, it was accepted! I was feeling pretty smug, I tell you. I was the only one from Loudoun who procured a ticket through this system, although several told me they had tried.

"I ended up driving separately to the event because I wasn't to be involved with crowd control. When the gang showed up for duty, they found Kevin Wolf and received their tickets. Things were relatively calm, so Kevin asked if two of them would volunteer to keep an eye on the situation outside the hotel and try to calm things down if needed. Steve and Theresa agreed to do so. The rest proceeded to their seats.

"Turned out the prior efforts by the Obama campaign to discourage any sort of protest had worked well. There were only a handful of Obama demonstrators on site. And the Clinton protesters were in the scores, not hundreds. Since there was no trouble, Steve and Theresa soon came inside and joined their friends. They all sat together close to the action. I, however, was with strangers in the balcony, and missed sitting with my friends, but had a good view of the assembled tables around which the 30 Rules Committee members sat.

"There were several passionate speeches delivered in debate—the Clinton advocates, led by Harold Ickes, said the full delegations should be seated with a full vote because to disenfranchise the voters of Florida and Michigan would be disastrous in the November elections, and the Obama people responded they would be open to some compromise.

"So how did it turn out?"

"The Florida debate went reasonably well. There was no dispute about the number of delegates to which they were originally entitled. But because of the violation, the original rules specified that none were to be seated. The committee and the candidates agreed to a compromise—seat all of them, but halve their vote. The result was in Clinton's favor as she had won the state. Michigan was a different matter. Obama had not received ANY votes, as he decided not to be named on the ballot because Michigan had broken the DNC rules by scheduling their primaries earlier than permitted. Voters were encouraged to vote 'uncommitted' if they did not support those listed on the ballot. Clinton received significantly more votes than those cast uncommitted. A 'Michigan Compromise', adopted by Michigan's Democratic political leaders, was submitted to this Rules committee meeting for their consideration. The Rules Committee modified that plan by switching four Delegates from Clinton to Obama, which greatly distressed the Clinton forces. Even with this change, Clinton narrowed her delegate gap with the final decisions made that day. But it could have been a lot worse.

"Frank Leone, one of the four Virginia members of the DNC, sent out an excellent full account of the meeting which is posted in the Appendix with permission. Note that he wasn't a member of the Rules Committee—just an observer at the meeting.

"I have one other personal story I'd like to relate. When it came time for the Rules Committee to vote on the motion to set the final rules for Florida, they went around the table and voted one by one, and when the teller reached the Chair, she demurred and said something along the lines, 'As Chair, I cannot vote on the resolution as I have to remain neutral!' She again abstained when the vote was taken on the Michigan resolution. As a lay parliamentarian, I was really surprised!

"Just for grins I made my way to the floor when the meeting was over and cornered the parliamentarian. She had been seated next to the Chair during the discussions, which was normal for these kinds of meetings. I introduced myself said 'I have a question for you. When the Chair said she couldn't vote'... she immediately interrupted me and said, 'she was wrong'. We both knew that it was not appropriate for the parliamentarian to correct a Chair during the meeting—the committee members alone were able to bring a point of order. She went on to tell me that she would be sure to let her know of her misunderstanding of that rule. Other than this minor error, the Chair was very competent and did an excellent job running this contentious meeting.

"I then encountered Mame Riley, a member of the Rules Committee and a Clinton supporter. I've known Mame for years, and after some chit-chat she asked me for my support for her re-election as one of the two Virginia Female DNC Delegates who would be elected at the Virginia State Convention in a couple of weeks. I told her as long as I could count on her support for the eventual nominee of the party, I would do so. After an enthusiastic yes, I added I could round up some Loudoun votes for her. She was pleased."

"Shortly after the Rules Committee met, Robyn Hyman, one of our Obama delegates to the State Convention who was running for National Delegate, forwarded me an interesting email. She had heard from a woman living in the 3rd Congressional Convention in response to an email Robyn had sent to all of the Obama delegates attending the State Convention asking for support. The sender warned Robyn that during the 3rd CD Convention, a motion had been introduced to accept the Slate endorsed by Tim Kaine/Charlie Kelly's state campaign committee to avoid the need for balloting. It was defeated. But the purpose of her email was to warn Robyn that they might try the same at the State Convention. Passing that resolution would have eliminated the voting. I sent emails and made calls and eventually was assured that the balloting would proceed as scheduled.

"Just when was the State Convention?"

"On Saturday, June 14, in Hampton, Virginia—a couple of weeks after the National Rules Committee met. We were busy preparing for it. Steve was getting our delegation squared away by processing the local delegates who had dropped out and replacing them with alternates. He took over the Loudoun Obama delegate training and organization during this period between Conventions. He kept the delegation informed about what was going on and what they needed to do. He and Marcia also worked with our supporters who hoped to be elected as National Delegates at the Convention, and they helped Joyce McLaurin and Arlene Donnelly plan a 'Unity Party' for Friday night in Hampton, the Convention locale. All of the Loudoun Clinton Delegates were especially encouraged to attend. Car pools were arranged and Jack Beavers flew Steve Ames and another delegate to Hampton. I missed the party because I was staying with friends in Virginia Beach. I remember Joyce hitting me up for $50 to help pay for the food and drinks. She wasn't bashful. The cupcakes made by our delegates and brought to the party were a big hit. There were a lot of drop-ins from other parts of the state who were staying at the same hotel. It was considered a huge success.

"Our Button Lady, Patti Maslinoff, came through with a complete, professional set of individualized name tags for our Loudoun Obama delegates and alternates. A lot of the attendees from other jurisdictions commented about how much they really liked them. Unfortunately, Patti couldn't make it to Hampton to join us. We missed her."

Most of the Loudoun delegates went up Friday and stayed at a local motel near the Hampton Coliseum where the Convention was to be held the next day. There were a number of optional events Friday and Saturday nights sponsored by the Convention Committee, State Party, and a few candidates for State offices in 2009. Very few were free. Our delegation's welcoming 'Unity' party was an exception.

"I drove over to Hampton from Virginia Beach early Saturday morning and had to wait for the doors to open. As did all of the delegates and alternates, I signed in at the specified registration desk for the 10th CD and picked up my badge and program, found my assigned seating area, and watched the hall fill with excited, enthusiastic Democrats ready to rock and roll. I passed out some flyers for those running for National Delegate, and saw several old political friends, some of whom I hadn't seen in years. Then all of a sudden I saw Gay LaRue, my first wife, come up the aisle. She lived in Hampton, and their delegation was sitting up front. She was hunting for me.

"After a quick 'hello' she went on to say, 'you won't believe this—but I'm here as an Obama Delegate!'

"That WAS a surprise. For all of 2007, she was an adamant Hillary supporter. She is very progressive, and from time to time, very involved in the party or specific campaigns. In the early 70's, one of her biggest gripes about the political process was the glass ceiling, and she was not a happy camper about that. In fact, when she ran for Virginia Beach City Council, no woman had ever been elected as a Councilman. She didn't win but did quite well against a popular incumbent.

"I went on to say, 'but didn't you vote for Hillary in the primary?'"

"Yes, I supported Hillary. But I became disenchanted the day she started campaigning for John McCain—that is, when she said that 'only John and she were ready to be Commander-in-Chief'. This happened shortly after our Virginia primary. The weekend prior to the primary, I attended a rally in Chesapeake with Bill Clinton (got to shake his hand) and another in Virginia Beach for Obama (also got to shake his hand). Unfortunately, I was not able to get what I wanted from Obama's rally, i.e., a clear understanding of what it is about him that gets people so fired up! That was mainly because the sound system was so bad that I couldn't understand anything he was saying. So I decided to get his books—'Dreams From My Father' and 'The Audacity of Hope.' I was completely hooked after reading his biography. His success at raising himself above the politics of anger and frustration and molding himself into an incredible leader was absolutely spellbinding for me.

"In addition to all this, I have a sister-in-law who is an avid Democrat. After Mother died, I didn't have anyone to talk politics with, so Maxine and I started having lunch and discussing the campaigns. Now we are we are both Hillary-supporters-turned-Obama-diehards. Having someone to help me flesh out all the stuff on TV and on the Internet has been both fun and very helpful." She congratulated me for my successes and rejoined her Hampton Delegation.

"Steve held a brief Loudoun caucus just before the Convention started in which some last-minute adjustments were needed to finalize the delegation composition. Changing the schedules of the elected delegates and alternates had to be handled formally by vote of the delegation. During their earlier meetings, Steve had kept track of which delegates couldn't make it to Hampton, temporarily penciled in the open positions from the alternate pool, and then added alternates from our waiting list. At this caucus just before the Convention started, a number of individuals who had not been voted into the delegation at the previous two meetings were officially added; a little later we added five more.

"Steve worked closely with the 10th CD Chair, Rich Galecki, throughout the early morning, and all of our alternates were the first in the 10th CD to be promoted to delegates. In the end we were able to promote all but two of our alternates to be delegates in other localities. Furthermore, there were another seven individuals from Loudoun who came with their spouse or a delegate friend who was also pressed into service as delegates for a total of 68 voting Obama delegates on the floor from Loudoun by the time the voting started—a 60% increase in our voting delegation size! Good job, Steve!!

"The Convention started near the scheduled opening time of 10:30 a.m. Initially it was still loud and boisterous—lots of people milling around. But they settled down pretty quickly. Saying the Pledge of Allegiance and hearing the *Star Spangled Banner* usually works well for that purpose. Then Richard Cranwell, the Virginia State Democratic Party Chair, who also served as Convention chair, continued with the agenda. At one point Steve counted those present in the Loudoun delegation and reported the result—a full Delegation. Mark Warner gave the keynote address and the Convention was well underway. We heard a parade of speeches, including one from each Congressional candidate. After lunch there was some business to attend to and further speeches, after which the Convention divided into Obama/Clinton caucuses to elect the additional National Delegates.

"Tell me more about these other Obama National Delegates. What was that all about?"

"The Call to Convention specified that pledged Obama National Delegates elected at the District Conventions would be augmented by 12 elected At-Large Delegates at the State Convention—six males and six females. Historically, party leaders and the presidential campaign operatives create and present a Slate to the Convention delegates. Anyone who is not on this endorsed list is rarely able to obtain a ticket to the National Convention.

The Convention's Clinton Delegation left the hall and met separately to choose their At-Large Delegates and Alternates. A very delighted Dan Moldover, one of the two local men who ran the Loudoun County Clinton campaign, was on their Slate, and he was elected a Clinton National Delegate.

"The Obama Delegation stayed in the main hall and did their voting. The Kaine/Kelly team did offer a full Obama Slate of their preferred delegate candidates. They also sent an email to all of the Convention delegates in advance of the meeting to push their candidates."

"How many filed to become National Delegates?"

"There were many more than usual. Obama had really stimulated Virginians with his call for 'Hope' which led to our large active grassroots campaign throughout the state. Even though their chance for success was slim, many wanted to be candidates in order to say to their grandchildren that they had been a part of history. Altogether, there were 71 male candidates and 79 female candidates for the six open slots for each gender. Candidates running for National Delegate who were not on the Slate faced a daunting task.

"Most of our candidates put together flyers and polished up their speeches. The original rules stated that they would have two minutes to make their case. We had five males and one female running from Loudoun: David Kirsten, Bahri Aliriza, Larry Roeder, Mike Turner, Ryan Myers, and Robyn Hyman. Most of them took this very seriously. They did a lot of campaigning as the Convention doors opened and the delegates arrived. Some recruited others to help distribute their material."

"How did they fare?"

"Unfortunately, they all lost by a pretty wide margin, but they did a little better than I expected. The winning candidates had about 500 votes each. But compared to those who were not on the Slate, we did pretty well. Robyn, our only female candidate, placed 9th among the women with 103 votes. David Kirsten, Bahri Aliriza, and Larry Roeder placed 9th, 10th, and 11th, with about 85 votes each.

"What surprised me most was that the 1,200 Obama delegates only cast about 2/3 of the votes they were eligible to cast. My guess is that many of them just voted for the few they knew or had just met during the campaigning done that day. Less than half voted for the Slate, a much lower percentage than I had expected.

"It took me several weeks to obtain the official results. Calls to the state party organization in Richmond were largely ignored. Finally I contacted Frank Leone, a Virginia DNC member who was the Virginia Democrats' Rules guy, and he promised to push the party staff to send me the results. The folks who wanted to be able to say, 'I ran for Obama National Delegate back in 2008' can now boast for the rest of their lives that not only did they run, but they did quite well compared to the non-Slate vote of previous years.

"Tim Russert had died earlier that week and someone in our delegation thought it would be a great idea if we could get a resolution passed at the State Convention to honor him. A couple of our better writers took on the task, and Gail Wise put it into its final form. Dickie Cranwell was running the Convention; he was the Virginia Party Chairman as well as the Convention chair. Since I knew him personally, I volunteered to take the resolution to him at the chair's table at the front of the hall when there was a lull in the activities, before the voting.

"I went up to the platform and presented the idea to him, and when he said that he would let us offer the resolution near the end of the Convention, I returned to my seat and let everyone know he had agreed to recognize us to move the resolution. We were very pleased."

"Did you get it passed?"

"We did, but not in the normal fashion. After the votes were cast for those running for state party officers and National Delegate, the ballots were turned over to a Tellers Committee appointed by the Chair. We then went into recess, expecting the count to take about 30-40 minutes. After the recess, the results would be read to the assembly, there would some last-minute business (including passing our resolution), and then we would adjourn. According to Robert's Rules of Order, the results HAD to be announced to the assembly or the balloting would be void.

"During the recess, a hubbub ensued in the hall. A lot of folks went outside to find food and drink and then returned. We waited and waited. A large number of people left and didn't return. Remember, we had started with about 2,500 people in attendance. After a couple of hours had passed, I made my way to where the counting was taking place, was stopped at the entrance by a Marshall, but finally was able to talk to the fellow in charge, who said they only had one more District ballots to count (ours). So I went back to my seat and passed the word. In about ten minutes, workmen showed up and started to dismantle the stage. Another 30 minutes passed. Our Loudoun folks were about the only ones left in the hall. Cranwell and crew had fled the scene much earlier, and it appeared likely that the Convention was over. We weren't going to get the count. They did, however, tell us that everyone on the Obama Slate had won.

"At that point, someone in our Loudoun Delegation (I don't

remember who) suggested we just pass the resolution ourselves—as if we were in session. I expected to do it right there where we were sitting—but one of our Delegates, Natasha Kotecki immediately said, 'I'll do it!' I accompanied her up to the foot of the stage; she strode up to the podium and called the Convention to order! Her voice boomed from the mike throughout the nearly empty room. She then read our resolution honoring Tim Russert, asked if there was any debate and seeing none, asked for the ayes and nays (all ayes). She then declared the resolution passed and adjourned the meeting! We were ecstatic! What a moment. It was just extraordinary to see and hear our own Natasha, who was participating in her first election. She handled the resolution with incredible poise and intelligence, as if she had been a Chair all her life.

"Was it legal?"

"Of course not. But it sure was fun, and it was the right thing to do. And I have to add something that really made it special. While doing research for this story, I did a quick web search, entering a few generic words regarding this Convention. Interestingly, out of the thousands of search results, the following was listed among the top dozen hits (posted at www.mydd.com):

The Sense of Convention Statement—Tim Russert
Virginia Democratic Convention
June 14, 2008
Tim Russert Remembrance: Virginia Democratic State Convention

'At the Virginia Democratic State Convention on June 14, 2008, Loudoun County for Obama introduced this Sense of the Convention statement in memory of Tim Russert and his outstanding service and commitment to unbiased journalism. It was unanimously adopted at the Convention on the evening of June 14th.

In recognition of Tim Russert's outstanding commitment to the American people; to fostering clear and insightful political debate and discussion; his tremendous contribution to promoting and strengthening our democracy; and most of all, in recognition and appreciation for the example he set as a son, father, husband and American;

The delegates of this Convention add our voices to those of millions of Americans and those around the globe to express our gratitude and appreciation for a life that touched and enriched the lives of all of us.

'The Sense of Convention statement was moved by Natasha Kotecki, a member of the Loudoun County for Obama team in Virginia's 10th Congressional District. Gail Wise wrote it, and she

was also a member of LCO.'

"I was bowled away coming across this reference. Apparently someone in our delegation decided to post it on a blog for posterity. I still don't know who did it.

"To wrap up the Convention, Steve sent everyone an amusing email in which he creatively imagined public reaction to Loudoun's presence:

'Here are some notable quotes and headlines (fresh off the presses):

'Loudoun County for Obama Wows at State Convention!

Front-page headline from the Richmond Gazette/Inquirer

'That Obama group from Loudoun showed enthusiasm never before seen by mankind! J. Harbaugh, Stanford University, Head Football coach

'Never have so many suffered, so that so few could be so very happy. Maj. F. Burns, SITCOMPAC

'How did those people get in here? All kidding aside, that 'Natasha gal showed real leadership potential. Chairman, Virginia Democratic Party

'Will those Loudoun Obama guys and gals ever go home? Henrietta Sweeper, Head Housekeeper, Hampton Roads Convention Center

'Can't those people from Loudoun County take 'NO' for an answer? Unidentified, exhausted Dem Convention official

'No we can't, because YES WE CAN!! Constant refrain from the LC Obama delegation

'The Obama Delegation from Loudoun County was the best damn delegation I've ever seen! Thomas Jefferson Everyman, Great-Great-Great-Great Grandson of Thomas Jefferson who has attended Conventions since 1932 as a ten-year old.

'Steve Ames'

"I couldn't have said it better myself. Despite the National Delegate selection process, it was a great Convention, and Steve was a terrific Delegation Chair.

"All the party work was done. Now it was time to rev up the general election campaign. We were ready. But soon after the convention, Joyce McLaurin told us she wasn't feeling very well. Her new liver wasn't behaving, and she started making frequent visits to the local hospital for treatments. Once while in the waiting room, she had a sudden inspiration. She approached and negotiated a deal with the administrators at the hospital to let her set up a voter registration table outside their cafeteria. Marcia remembers getting a surprise call from Joyce one day that started out: 'Hi boss, I've worked out the details on something you're gonna love!' She was right; Marcia loved this creative idea and Joyce's ingenuity in pulling it off. This voter registration initiative turned out to be a great success. Other Eager Beavers soon volunteered to help out at her table, and they registered a lot of hospital workers and folks who were visiting patients. That was Joyce for you—turning lemon into lemonade.

Dramatis Personae

"For an actress to be a success, she must have the face of Venus, the brains of a Minerva, the grace of Terpsichore, the memory of a Macaulay, the figure of Juno, and the hide of a rhinoceros." —Ethyl Barrymore

A successful presidential campaign in Loudoun County in 2008 required an inspirational candidate, several cooperating Power Groups, and thousands of volunteers to all converge at the same time. That convergence would be a truly spectacular political event—and for many individuals, a once-in-a-lifetime experience. This chapter describes the gathering up of these people and their organizations. It also tackles some of the difficulties learning how to work together throughout the summer of 2008.

First and foremost was Barack Obama himself, who is arguably the best orator in the history of American politics—certainly since William Jennings Bryan. He was a remarkable candidate who hoped to bring out the young, poor, and minorities who historically voted in low numbers. His campaign was able to motivate millions of them to register. This effort significantly expanded his voter base. He inspired new volunteers to come forward in large numbers to help win the campaign and raise money. He was a money making machine. He was able to raise significantly more money than McCain, providing enough funds to impact states like Virginia which normally were not considered favorable to Democrats. And we cannot overlook the huge emotional impact and significance of attempting to elect our first non-white President. We could feel down to our bones that we were making history in unison with this gifted man.

Now to the Power Groups. Every campaign has them. But we had them in abundance this election—organizations scrambling for power and resources to elect our candidate. I'll start with the Loudoun County for Obama (LCO) grassroots organization. It had been up and running for well over a year by the summer of 2008. LCO continued its work finding Obama supporters and recording them in the computerized Big List. By the time the Virginia primary was held in February 2008, the Big List contained contact information for over 2,500 supporters which grew to nearly 3,000 by July. We called the most ardent of these supporters the "Eager Beavers."

The second Power Group was the combined Democratic campaign called Virginia Victory 2008 (VV08), funded by the Mark Warner for Senate Campaign, the various Congressional Campaigns, and the Democratic Party of Virginia. VV08 flooded the Loudoun zone, to speak in football terms, with a large number of field organizers of extraordinarily high quality, who were assigned the difficult task of campaigning for the three Federal campaigns for President, Senate, and House of Representatives. High quality means focused, motivated, hardworking, and highly effective at recruiting volunteers to help in the effort. Dan Chavez managed this team, who were veritable animals on the campaign trail, working long hours for low pay but with big results. Their contributions were never well appreciated among the Great Unwashed because most people thought the staff was all a part of the "Obama CFC Staff." This was not true. They worked for Obama alright, but also for the U.S. Senate candidate, Mark Warner, and the Congressional candidate, Judy Feder. VV08 should get significant credit for what happened in Loudoun County in 2008. They were a very unrecognized component of the campaign.

Third, Obama's "Campaign for Change" (CFC) arrived in Loudoun in early June in the person of Sophia Chitlik, who was quickly followed in mid-June by Shira Sternberg, who was put in charge. She was a Regional Field Director for the Virginia CFC, responsible for Loudoun and a couple of other nearby counties. Shira managed the Leesburg office the entire campaign. Six Obama 'Fellows' soon followed (carefully selected volunteers who had been trained elsewhere, assigned to Loudoun, and who knew they would have to work their tails off to earn the right to become paid Obama field organizers). Furthermore, there were a few unpaid interns, expecting to work only during the summer before going back to school in the fall. She compiled the results from her assigned localities daily and passed them on to the state headquarters. And by daily, I mean seven days a week. Like VV08, the members of the Loudoun CFC team were of exceptional quality. They were up and running in mid-June, a couple of weeks after VV08 was on the scene. The Obama staff worked no less hard than VV08, and with the jump start provided by the grassroots organization, they recruited, trained, and managed thousands of volunteers in Loudoun County. They were tightly directed from Richmond by Mitch Stewart, the State Director for Virginia's CFC, who in turn reported to the national CFC.

Fourth, the local Loudoun County Democratic Committee (LCDC) had its own ongoing political structure in place, including eight magisterial district chairs (or coordinators) and their 62 precinct captains (or coordinators), although not all of the latter positions were filled. Tim Buchholz, LCDC Chair as of January 2008, appointed Kevin Turner Chair of the Precinct Operations Committee, with responsibility for developing, managing, and coordinating campaigns occurring during his two-year term, including this 2008 election. LCDC primarily concentrated their efforts on finding drivers and poll workers to work inside and outside every precinct on Election Day. Many LCDC members also were members of LCO and volunteered to help VV08 and CFC in their phone banking and canvassing efforts.

Fifth and sixth, the Mark Warner and Judy Feder campaigns had their own State/Congressional campaign structures which they funded. However, VV08 managed the Warner ground troops in Loudoun County and throughout the state. The Loudoun Feder campaign staff was separate but co-located in the VV08 office in Loudoun, and was directed and funded through the Judy Feder Congressional campaign organization headquartered in Fairfax.

Certainly many other organizations could also be considered Power Groups. How about the DNC? State Democratic Party? Congressional District Committees? Labor Unions? NAACP? Other ethnic organizations? League of Women Voters? Occupiers? Teabaggers? MoveON? There are scores of them, constantly recruiting activists. Some of them were very important to the Great Campaign of 2008, but the list of the six Power Groups above are those that directly affected the on-ground campaigns in Loudoun County and their volunteers.

Furthermore, many independent and unorganized volunteers also worked for Obama in Loudoun County who were not a part of any Power Group. Several different types of volunteers fell into this category, and altogether, they made a substantial contribution to Obama's eventual success. Unorganized volunteers were not directed by any of the formal campaign organizations. For instance, one set of volunteers were motivated to contact the national MyBO website or other national organizations like MoveOn.org. No staffers were telling them how, what, or when to volunteer. Instead, these motivated volunteers learned of opportunities through new automated email and website systems. They canvassed and telephoned in Loudoun, but their telephoning efforts were not limited to Loudoun County, especially during primary season. They complemented the work of the Power Groups themselves. My wife Barbara and I, along with Robin Hyman, typified these efforts. And there were those who were even more independent, like Ali McDermott, Diana Denley, Daniel Dennison, Larry Roeder, Carolyn Ronis, and Timothy Wyant. I will tell you all about these independent characters in this and following chapters. Their stories are extraordinary.

You now know the major actors in this play. Now I'll start setting the stage. I'll begin with the paid campaign groups. In a zoo, the objective is for the zookeepers to keep the animals on the inside, while the zookeepers stay on the outside. For CFC and VV08, a political campaign is like a zoo in reverse. You have to get the animals on the outside while the zookeepers stay on the inside. Translated into English, this means you have to get the volunteers out on the street and on the phones while the staff deals with the inside administration, number reporting, and keeping the higher-ups off the backs of the volunteers, lest the volunteers quit and go native on you. When volunteers "go native" then nobody controls them—they get off the boat; they self-direct, sometimes with very good results. But native mode was very disconcerting to the paid staffers because after they lost control, they didn't get any credit for what work the volunteer accomplished, which could result in failing to meet their daily goals. Reaching their daily goals was their obsession—imposed upon them from on high.

Throughout the campaign, more and more of the reliable volunteers became rookie zookeepers to handle the onslaught of new volunteers. So now the paid staffers became trainers and managers of their new zookeepers. A side effect of all this was that when the volunteers became zookeepers, things didn't always work as well as the paid staffers wanted. These rookie zookeepers were unpaid volunteers and couldn't always be relied on. It was a question of perspective in many cases; what worked well for the locals didn't necessarily work well for the paid staffers. They saw things differently. The locals were incredibly effective, but stuff happens. The paid staffers wanted credit with their bosses; the locals didn't care. They wanted results, and the credit didn't matter. This was a critical difference. A lot of the locals wanted to make a difference, and they didn't give one red damn cent about the credit. They weren't looking for credit; they just wanted to do whatever they felt would help Barack Obama. Now let's turn our attention to the paid zookeepers.

First in town was VV08. The first two paid staffers on the ground in Loudoun County were Rachel Fulk and another staffer who was gone in two weeks. They arrived in very early June 2008 and initially occupied in the LCDC headquarters in downtown Leesburg. They quickly needed a much larger space and found suitable headquarters in the Ashburn area, five miles east of Leesburg, towards the more developed part of Loudoun County, and just off Route 7 (the Old Colonial Highway), and the most traveled road in Loudoun County.

Ashburn is best known as the headquarters for the Washington Redskins football team. This suburban area with over 70,000 residents also happens to be the headquarters for Verizon Business Unit and the Old Dominion Brewing Company. Ashburn was once known as Farmwell, but old locals will tell you that the name "Ashburn" came from a lightning strike on an ash tree in 1896 on Senator William Morris Stewart's farm. The tree burned and smoked for several weeks, and if legend is to be believed, gave its name to the area—Ash Burn.

Rachel Fulk had heard that the Democratic Committee of Virginia was hiring field organizers for the "Combined Democratic Campaign," called the Virginia Victory '08 Campaign." We called it VV08. Rachel received her training in Wakefield in the Tidewater region of Virginia over the weekend in late May, which included how to canvass, phone bank, collect and input data, and recruit volunteers.

At the end of the training she was assigned to Loudoun County. Rachel had really hoped the campaign would send her to Harrisonburg in the Shenandoah Valley, because that was where her home was located. However, the VV08 staff explained that Loudoun County was absolutely pivotal in the coming election, and that the Democrats had to win Loudoun to win the state of Virginia. They really needed her in Loudoun, and they needed her there soon. After a few days off to get her personal life squared away, including attending her own graduation ceremony, Rachel Fulk headed off for Loudoun County.

Rachel reported to a regional VV08 campaign official who was replaced before the end of her first month. Campaigns are often like that—fluid dynamics! Some people work out, some don't. So she was left on her own. The VV08 Campaign did arrange to get good housing for her in the Eastern part of the county.

LCO did not give Rachel access to their Big List. That was

reserved for themselves and the Obama staffers. She actually didn't even know of its existence. (After the campaign was over, Rachel said she would have eaten nails to get her hands on it.) She recruited for weeks by phoning strong Democrats available from a list mentioned earlier known as the 'Voter Activation Network,' nicknamed 'the VAN.' As she recruited volunteers, she put them to work canvassing, mostly on weekends. For most of the first month, she grew her volunteer list and built the foundation of the VV08 campaign on her own with no help except from the volunteers she recruited.

Canvassing is sometimes called "door knocking." It is direct face-to-face conversation with potential voters by staffers and volunteers. Contrary to the conventional impression, canvassers did not go house-to-house speaking with anyone who came to the door. Canvass lists (turfs) produced by the VAN identified specific houses and specific people to speak with in those houses. On the Democratic side early in the campaign the canvass lists focused on strong or leaning Democrats to confirm probable Obama voters. As time progressed, the canvass lists expanded to include known independent voters and later those not yet identified. Late in the summer, in certain neighborhoods, they even included Republicans.

Canvassing Monday through Friday during daytime hours is usually unproductive because most of the people are away at work. Those who knocked doors during this period seldom found anyone home to speak with. The canvasser would then leave promotional literature on the doorknob or the front steps. Initially, only paid field organizers conducted canvassing on weekdays.

On weekends the canvassing scheme changed dramatically. Many volunteers who worked during the week also volunteered to knock doors on either Saturday or Sunday, and many worked both days. Although canvassing is an effective method of voter interaction, it is notoriously inefficient. About 75% of the door knocks would go unanswered or the specific person of interest wasn't at home to interview. The typical canvasser would knock about 50 doors a day and would be able to speak with 10-15 people targeted on the canvass list.

Nighttime was the best phone banking time because people were at home. Phoning in the middle of the day was usually unproductive because most people were at work. Door knocking in the daytime in the middle of the week found few people at home, but at least the canvasser could leave campaign literature at the door.

Another key field operation for VV08 and CFC was data

entry. Those volunteers who were uncomfortable contacting potential voters directly could help the campaign by entering data. The VAN database was updated daily with data gathered from canvassing and phone banking in order to categorize the contacted voter using the five-point system described in an earlier chapter, essentially recording the prospect as being for or against Obama, or undecided. Those voters who clearly indicated they were voting for Obama would not be contacted again until it was time to get out the vote; those opposed would be ignored; and the undecideds would later get a "persuasion call."

Strange things often happen at doors. Here are a couple of canvassing stories that will not soon be forgotten, especially by the participants.

Rachel was responsible for a rough and tumble neighborhood in Sterling to canvass. One day she knocked on a door, and this guy came out. She got into her bit and the guy at the door said, "Get the 'F***' off my porch, or I'm going to get my shotgun and blow your 'effin' head off." She left. Who wouldn't?

Marianne Bowen and Tim Buchholz (the LCDC Chair) were canvassing the streets of Ashburn, and while it was hot, it was fixing to get a lot hotter. However, these two were tougher than nails and could handle anything. So Marianne walks up to this door, but she doesn't get a chance to knock because there standing in front of the door was a woman waiting for her. It's always been my experience that if the door meets you on the porch before you knock, chances are, the thing will go circus on you. And this thing went Roman candle right off the bat. The lady had seen the Obama stickers and proceeded to tell Marianne that she was a "baby killer" and began to lecture her on the evils of abortion. Marianne, meanwhile, tried to argue that Obama would actually reduce abortions with good policies on female health, but the woman would have none of it. She continued to lecture her on the evils of abortion and the evils of Obama. The two began to argue the issue when Tim Buchholz came up and told Marianne to let it go because it had degenerated into a hopeless dispute.

The two walked off to the next house on the list, but the woman started following them. It was a circus. All the while she kept telling Marianne what a baby killer she was and what a baby killer Barack Obama was. Then the woman threw in the pièce de résistance—if Obama was elected, he was going to force Republican women to have abortions so in a generation there would only be

Democrats remaining. Sounded like Fox News. The lady trailed them to the next four houses, all the while railing against the evils of abortion.

It just goes to show you. When a canvass goes circus, the last person to know is often the canvasser. What goes circus usually stays in circus, complete with dancing bears, scary ladies, alligator men and the whole bit. As Job would say, "I have escaped by the skin of my teeth."

Back at the office, sometimes things got so unpredictable nobody knew how to handle it. One day a phone banking volunteer approached Rachel Fulk with a dilemma. The volunteer didn't know how to record the results of a particular phone call. When she asked to speak to a certain person, the response from the other end was, "Well, he can't come to the phone because he just died, and we're waiting for the ambulance to come and pick up the body." That check box wasn't on the response sheet. Others, hearing the story, were of the opinion that this was a novel way to deal with unsolicited campaign calls.

Just a few weeks after Rachel started at VV08, Dan Chavez entered the scene. The son of a migrant farm worker from the Los Angeles area, Dan comes from a family heavily involved in politics for years. His father (Daniel Chavez, Sr.) was such an interesting man; I just have to tell you about him. His biography could have easily come straight from a Horatio Alger novel. At the age of seven, his father picked grapes as a migratory farm worker in central and south central California to support the family. He graduated from Carson High School in Carson, California. Later he enrolled in law school at San Francisco University, graduated near the top of his class, and got involved in politics with Caesar Chavez (no relation). Dan Chavez, Sr. was a Regional Field Director for the Al Gore Campaign in 2000, directing operations in 13 western states. He worked for the Clinton campaign in 1992 in California, and when Bill Clinton was elected President, he gave him a presidential appointment in the Labor Department. Often he took son Dan with him on his political travels. Dan learned politics from the bottom up.

Dan Chavez, Jr. grew up mostly in Fairfax County, Virginia, took a degree in political science from Northern Arizona University, and applied to the national Obama CFC organization. He was not happy with their offer and turned it down. Later that year he received a much better offer from the Hillary Clinton campaign and for several months worked in Nevada, California, Texas, Wyoming,

Pennsylvania and North Carolina. He ended with the Clinton campaign as a Get Out The Vote (GOTV) Director for eastern North Carolina. When Clinton dropped out of the race, Dan and hundreds of other political professionals no longer had a job.

He used his contacts in the Obama campaign to get a line on a new job with VV08, as there was not a comparable job still available for him in the Obama campaign. The VV08 officials recognized his abilities and selected him to head up operations in what was regarded as a critical swing county in a swing state. That was us, folks.

A veteran campaigner, Dan needed no training in the basics of field organizing and was assigned to run field operations in Loudoun County. And that meant Rachel reported to him. He checked in for action on July 4, 2008. Shortly thereafter, two more staffers reported in, Amanda Millard and Kurt Gonska.

On arrival, Dan immediately reached out to Rich Culbert, Mark Warner's political director for Loudoun County and several other Northern Virginia localities, to get his take on Loudoun politics. As you may remember, Rich was working on a State Delegate campaign in Loudoun and was present at that very first LCO meeting in the LCDC headquarters held over a year earlier when Rollie and Marcia met the first time to form LCO. Rich urged Dan to reach out to Rollie, Tim Buchholz, LCDC Chair, and the LCDC Vice Chairs, Bob Moses and Ellen Heald. These guys and gal could best give him the lay of the land. Rich told Dan that the Democratic organizations in Loudoun had vastly improved. What Rich didn't say was that he, Rich, was probably one of the major reasons for the improvement in that he personally had served as a very effective field director of campaigns in Loudoun for the previous two years!

On Dan's first day, he marched in three Fourth of July parades—Leesburg, Purcellville, and Manassas. Quite a beginning. Also that day Tim Buchholz called and invited him to a meeting he had set up for all the key Loudoun players in the coming campaign. It was held in the LCDC headquarters and was to start immediately after the LCDC monthly Executive Committee meeting the evening of July 7. That turned out to not be such a good idea. Too many of the LCDC Executive Committee members decided to stay and meet the new kids on the block. It was July. It was hot. And the AC wasn't working well. There must have been more than 25 people stuffed into a hot little room built to hold less than a dozen. But all the lead actors were there. That was a good thing. Rollie came in a little late and was barely able to squeeze in and find a place to sit on the floor.

Tim did a great job facilitating the meeting. Introductions were made, along with a brief description as to who they were and why they were there. There were good feelings all around; they were on a holy mission that demanded cooperation from all to be successful in November. At the end of the meeting, Rollie asked to be recognized and said that he had observed over the years that attempts to coordinate ALL parties in a campaign had rarely been successful. The room grew very still. He went on to say that despite what he had experienced, he was optimistic at what he had heard that night, and that if communications were kept open, there was a good chance we could achieve victory on Election Day. It was a grand success; Tim was a great facilitator. But this was the first and last "coordinated" meeting held with all parties in attendance.

Tim believed the reason for not attempting to put this gathering together again was the intense focus and energy each group put into their own campaign organizations. He felt that after that one meeting, everyone knew their roles and knew each other well enough to coordinate activities as necessary. Much later in the campaign Kevin Turner, the person handling LCDC Precinct Operations in 2008, hosted several weekly telephone conferences regarding Election Day. Those telephone conferences played an important coordinating role.

Steve Ames, the LCO "go-to guy," graciously provided housing for Dan. Steve also went on the web to Craig's List, found a source for some free office furniture, rented a truck, picked it up, and delivered it to the newly rented headquarters in Ashburn. That was typical of Steve. He often saw the needs and then filled them.

In mid-August, more VV08 cavalry arrived. They were field organizers Conrad Chaffee and Amanda Millard. The VV08 Campaign now had five paid field organizers, including Dan as the Regional Field Director in charge of the whole operation. They spent seven days a week recruiting, phone banking, canvassing, and entering data. They were now a full-blown 'rock and roll' band with the arrival of Conrad and Amanda.

I want to define 'entering data' for the reader as we use this term frequently throughout the book. We have already discussed the VAN database of registered voters. What made this database so useful is that every attempted contact made, and the result obtained, was entered by computer, along with codes that described the voter's affinity for Obama and the date of the transaction. 'Not homes' and 'no answers' included. This new data was then inspected and considered when creating new call or walk lists. It took many thousands of hours to input this data. But this information was the lifeblood of the campaign.

In mid-June, right on VV08's heels, the next major Power Group to arrive in Loudoun was Obama's Campaign for Change, with Sophia Chitlik leading the pack. What was especially remarkable about Sophia was her age; she was only19 years old. After graduating from a Southern California high school in 2007, she got the "political bug" and ended up a year later here in Loudoun. She was very mature for her age and handled immense responsibility like a seasoned political pro. She was a take-charge young lady, and was not shy in telling people what to do and how she wanted it done.

Within a week, Sophia had her own on-site boss: Shira Sternberg. The newly appointed regional field director was in town and charged with 'Running the Show' for Obama in Loudoun and a few surrounding counties. Shira was a whole lot older than Sophia—in her early 20's! She had studied politics and international relations at Bennington College in Vermont and, after signing on and completing her Obama training, was assigned to Loudoun County. She was a good listener, very capable, and a steady performer throughout the campaign.

The entire tenor of the 2008 campaign changed for LCO with the arrival of CFC. LCO was no longer the sole voice for Barack Obama in Loudoun County, and that was a difficult adjustment. Initially, Marcia and her Eager Beavers volunteered extensively with CFC, but did keep the grassroots movement active. Marcia suffered the brunt of the change because Rollie went off to help LCDC. In terms of the sheer volume of volunteer hours, the CFC and VV08 organizations were soon dominant.

Soon after Shira's arrival, Marcia Carlyn and Gail Wise met with her at LCO's "headquarters" (Franco Luz's place) and gave her a key to the place (with Franco's approval, of course) to use until the CFC could set up its own office in Loudoun. It turned out to be quite a challenge to find a good place for that new office—something centrally located with lots of parking and enough space to serve as Obama's main field office in Loudoun. Shira was under strong pressure from the state and national campaign to find an office quickly, but much to her credit, she didn't rush this important decision. Two good possibilities were in Ashburn and Sterling on the eastern end of Loudoun County (towards DC). Marcia and Gail went with Shira to check these places out, but they much preferred to have the office in Leesburg since it was more centrally located geographically, and LCO had shown that volunteers from all over the county would come to Leesburg. Shira heeded their advice even though that significantly delayed finding a suitable place. As it turned out, the large office that Sophia ended up finding on Market Street proved to be a fantastic spot for Obama headquarters. It was in downtown Leesburg not far from the Loudoun County Courthouse, the seat of county government, and the LCDC office.

A week or two after the office was set up, Juan Perez came by after work to see how they were wired up for telephones and Internet service. That was his specialty. He found the systems almost inoperable, offered his services gratis, and then he did his magic! In short order he created a highly functional, sophisticated communication and data center that met their immediate and long-term needs. He came by regularly throughout the next several months, keeping everything in good working order. Here was one of the best examples of a LCO volunteer providing a key component to the success of the Obama campaign in Loudoun County.

Soon after CFC landed in Loudoun, one of the first things Marcia did, with Rollie's OK, was to share with them the Big List, (excluding email addresses). She also gave them the list of the "Eager Beavers," about 60 volunteers who were especially zealous in their support of Obama. She partitioned the Big List into Loudoun geographical areas, which was not an easy task, but it was definitely worth doing since it gave them an enormous jump-start. In addition to using MyBO to recruit volunteers, the CFC was able to hit the ground running, working from that list of 2,500 supporters and several hundred volunteers. Rachel Fulk and Dan Cahill of VV08 had to start recruiting from zero; CFC started with a whole bunch of potential volunteers.

In return for giving them this contact information, Marcia secured an OK from Shira to ask walk-in volunteers if they would like to be "kept in the Loudoun loop" on grassroots activities in Loudoun County. This was easily accomplished by adding a check box to the volunteer registration form provided by the campaign for new volunteers when they came to the office. Other check boxes were also added to identify the particular interests of each Obama volunteer including reaching out to women, African Americans, teachers, faith-based groups, seniors, veterans, Republicans, African

Americans, Hispanics, other ethnic groups, canvassing, phone banking, phoning from home, entering data, doing other office work, registering new voters, hosting a house party, writing personal notes to potential supporters, providing housing for out-of-state volunteers, promoting Obama through the arts, and helping on Election Day. One of the Eager Beavers copied the forms each day for Marcia so could add this key information to the Big List.

This was the strategy that had made LCO's grassroots movement so successful—identifying each person's unique interests so they would be inspired to do more and come up with some creative ways to help Barack Obama win in Loudoun County. This procedure worked like a charm for a couple of months for LCO until higher-ups in the CFC found out about it and realized LCO activities were diverting a few new Obama volunteers from the three activities the national campaign emphasized—canvassing, phone banking, and entering data. But you know the relentless Marcia Carlin pretty well by now. She tried several times to explain to the Obama staffers how important it was to understand each person's unique interests to "catch their spark," but it was not to be. Shira and the staffers were reluctant to defy those in charge of the Virginia campaign who were applying incredible pressure to deliver on their numbers. They went back to the original form, and LCO was cut off obtaining that information.

Needless to say, Marcia was not happy that the Obama campaign reneged on their agreement. They had abruptly ended a very successful system for giving volunteers different opportunities to contribute. Rollie was not surprised at their intransigence on this issue. They simply had reverted to standard state and national campaign mode. They had our names and now wanted full control over their participation. For Rollie, it was politics as usual between Power Groups.

I had a lengthy conversion with Rollie about all this. I had never considered that those working for Obama's election weren't all part of one big monolithic, coordinated group of people. As an example, Barbara and I had been working for VV08. I thought they were the whole show. Here's what he had to say about it:

"Well, Ed, up to this campaign, I had often witnessed and resented how paid campaign outsiders came into our county representing the candidate, worked like hell with their own agenda, found and consumed all the energy from new volunteers, then left immediately after the campaign was over without sharing the knowledge, results, and relationships they had forged. Strong personal bonds were made between volunteers and staffers which weren't readily transferred to the leaders of the local political organizations. It had been a recurring theme. This philosophy over time resulted in a much weaker local party than would otherwise be possible.

"That was the main reason I was so surprised that the Obama campaign had the foresight and intelligence initially to set up the MyBO website, empowering local groups to begin their own grassroots organizations. Marcia and I had hoped that when the Obama staffers came into town, there would be a close cooperative effort between LCO and CFC. But the honeymoon was of short duration.

"But it is also important to understand that this conflict was a direct result of the pressure exerted on the local staffers received from the Obama state campaign staff. Our quarrel was really with the leadership of the state professional organizers, not with local paid staffers. They were just following orders. The locals had to deliver their numbers; anything that diverted potential volunteer resources from this directive was not welcomed. Marcia and I were definitely out of step with CFC people by late summer, and had an uneasy relationship with them throughout the rest of the campaign."

The light dawned. I can now understand much better what went on between the Power Groups. They all wanted power and influence, including Rollie and Marcia. This reach for control caused problems. So I asked him, "How do you think this problem can be solved?"

"I can see only one way to do it, and it must come from the top of the campaign structure, and built into the campaign plan. The value of local grassroots initiatives and local party organizations should be recognized and encouraged by the field directors. Those running the campaign should implement a rating system for regional and local field directors that include, as a significant component of their evaluation, a subjective rating done by the key local leaders. When the staffer's overall competence is measured, this rating would be factored into the evaluation along with the numbers achieved. That would make a significant difference, especially over the long-term."

Interesting, I thought. Perhaps another example of a Power Group conflict would be useful for this discussion. Here's one that happened between Marcia and the local staffers of CFC soon after

CFC's arrival. The new staffers started promoting their canvass meetups and other activities on the LCO MyBO site. Marcia and Rollie were still the co-administrators of that website, but MyBO web managers had given staffers the authority to post their events without approval. That actually did make sense; Rollie and Marcia would have had a hard time keeping up with all their postings. However, Marcia had learned early on how important it was to post accurate and complete information on MyBO for each upcoming event. In fact, she had developed a checklist for LCO event coordinators to use to make sure the participants knew exactly where and when to meet.

Unfortunately, the field organizers started out making the same early mistakes that LCO had made a year previously. How to post events obviously had not been included in their training. Marcia started getting calls from volunteers who told her they had gone to a canvassing event they read about on MyBO and finally left because no one showed up. When she talked with the field organizer who had posted these events, she realized what had happened—the meeting place had been misunderstood by the volunteer because it had not been clearly described on MyBO. Wanting to prevent any more volunteers from being "turned off" by these errors, Marcia urged the field organizers to use the LCO checklist to minimize future misunderstandings. This good advice was ignored by some of the paid staffers, mistakes continued to be made, and Marcia continued to bring them to their attention. They felt badgered and apparently resented this type of interference so much that they complained directly to state headquarters. Marcia was then strongly invited to butt-out of the process. A much better solution would have been for the local Obama team to work it out with Marcia directly. That kind of cooperation was no longer happening.

About this same time another kind of Power Group conflict arose; this time it was between VV08 and CFC. They both used the VAN for all of Loudoun County's core data such as name, address, precinct, and other demographics. However each organization had their own place in the database to record their results obtained by their calling and canvassing. They could not see or use each other's data. Although Loudoun is a big county, they soon started stepping all over each other. Callers from one organization would often be told that they had already been called. Canvassers learned that the home had already been visited by the other group the previous week, or even in a couple of cases, earlier the same day.

After several days of contention, Tim Buchholz, the LCDC

Chair, finally called the parties together and worked it out. They kept their separate files but divided the responsibility for precincts between them. From that point on, it was like Loudoun was really two separate counties as far as the two official campaign organizations were concerned.

One very important point that Rollie and Marcia stressed over and over with me when writing this book was that new volunteers had little to no knowledge about the occasional dissension that flared among the leaders of the Power Groups. The staffers knew, but not the volunteers. That was a good thing.

Throughout the summer months, the national Obama Fellowship program recruited and trained more unpaid Fellows—more actors for our play. They were then sent to swing states throughout the country. Some of them would become paid staffers, but this was rare. One of the new Loudoun Fellows was Diana Denley, who was a real actor! Unfortunately, she got off to a rocky start with the local CFC, but it makes for a great story! Diana ended up as one of our independent characters in Loudoun County. She actually had been a director and actor in Australia, Europe and the US, and eventually served on the Arts Policy Committee for the national Obama '08 Presidential Campaign as its Virginia Chair. Although she spends considerable time in Sydney, Australia, Diana has considered Loudoun her home ever since she was a small child living in rural Northern Virginia. Like so many others, she wanted to express her strong feelings for the vision Barack Obama laid out in his 2004 Democratic Convention speech. So she applied to be an Obama Fellow for the 2008 campaign. She made the cut and after her training was sent to the Loudoun environment she understood so well.

However, the local CFC structure, with its strict marching orders, did not allow for the use of her diverse talents. And she was often piqued with the young staffers who simply didn't want to deal with older volunteers not fitting in with their generation's use and love of technology. So, on the side, she started volunteering for Obama's National Arts Policy Committee and quickly met with great success promoting Barack Obama in the local, state, and national artistic community.

After some lengthy and spirited discussions with the local CFC staff in Loudoun, and with support from LCO grassroots leaders, Diana was able to abandon the Fellows program and commandeered a small desk to work from in the Leesburg CFC office, which she used throughout the entire campaign. She found ample opportunities to coordinate events and fundraisers, including art shows, parade floats, picnics, concerts, and policy development. For instance, she coordinated a fundraiser in Reston which raised $30,000 for the Obama campaign. She even convinced a Loudoun County arts group to project Obama imagery onto barns, houses, and stores so they would be visible to folks driving by—a very creative promotional activity! Her considerable database of artists attests to the fact that Obama's connection to the arts community held sway. And her perceptive evaluation of the issues surrounding the merging of a national campaign staff with an in-place grassroots organization provides a pearl of wisdom future campaign managers will want to pry free and take with them. There are some examples of her work in the Appendix at www.swingcounty.com.

Monica Vickers-Root was the famous Bus Lady. We're telling her story here because it is another prime example of the problems that local volunteers with initiative had in working with CFC. Monica was an early supporter and member of LCO. She volunteered to help Rollie staff the LCDC headquarters way back in early 2007. She was born in the United States Naval Hospital, Jacksonville, Florida, moved to McLean with her parents when she was six weeks old and later lived in Washington, DC, Mexico City, Boston, Spain, and Paris, then back to Northern Virginia. The lady did get around. Monica grew up in Mexico and is completely fluent in Spanish. She worked with Americans living in Mexico for the Gore and Kerry campaigns in 2000 and 2004. By 2008 she had moved to Loudoun County.

At an early age Monica was involved in a serious car accident, and has refused to drive a car ever again. Instead, she takes the bus everywhere she goes. Most people who use bus transportation in the United States are poor or disadvantaged. Monica didn't fit either case, but she had a special history. When the campaign of 2008 kicked off, Monica realized that people who ride buses were a natural Democratic constituency. So why not register them to vote and then persuade them to vote for Obama?

Working for the grassroots campaign and the LCDC, Monica obtained voter registration forms and campaign literature and began campaigning while taking bus trips. She registered new voters and handed out Obama literature to other riders. She found a very receptive audience and did quite well campaigning on her trips. Her experience was a perfect example of a local volunteer adapting very effectively and creatively to local and personal circumstances.

When the Obama Campaign opened up shop in Leesburg, Monica pitched her idea of bus campaigning to the local field organizers. "It's a natural Democratic constituency," she advocated. The Obama Campaign didn't want to hear it. They were going to do things their way, and what the locals suggested received very little consideration. The Campaign was utterly blind to the opportunities of campaigning among a natural Democratic base. But in fairness to the local Obama field organizers, the Obama State Campaign paid their salaries and directed them to follow their playbook.

Like many other grassroots volunteers in Loudoun, Monica said to hell with them. She got her own voter registration forms and campaign literature and continued to go out on her own. She didn't need supervision, especially negative supervision. She understood the demography of the bus riders even if the Obama Campaign did not. She continued to campaign because she was so inspired by the candidate, Barack Obama. Under a different candidate, someone such as a Monica Vicars-Root might just decide that this type of campaigning isn't worth the effort. But she believed in Obama, so she just ignored the paid staff and continued to do what she knew best. She kept on very good terms with the LCO people and had a lot of 'unofficial' support. She registered scores of new voters and continued to campaign on the buses.

When looking back on the last few months of the campaign, Marcia believed it likely that a lot of problems could have been avoided if there had been better communication between the Obama field organizers and the LCO grassroots leaders. There was only one meeting directly between the two groups, an initial social get-together hosted by Steve Ames when the CFC first arrived in Loudoun. After that, the Obama Fellows and field organizers were too busy to take time to sit down with the grassroots group to let them describe their own accomplishments and "lessons learned" during the previous 16 months. But of course, that was not in their manual. They had their marching orders. Hup! Hup! Hup!

During this summer, while all of these adjustments were playing out, we learned of some terrible news from Joyce McLaurin. Her physicians diagnosed her with spine cancer. Her physical condition quickly deteriorated, and she was admitted to the same hospital where she had set up her voter registration table. However, being hospitalized did not stop Joyce McLaurin. Her room became campaign central! She decorated the walls of her hospital room with Obama campaign posters and began canvassing other patients and staff right in the hospital. The Eager Beavers became her support group, as she had no nearby family. Bernard Hill, Steve Ames, Judy Ross, Gail Wise, Marcia Carlyn, Eva-Marie Suntum, Peggy Suntum, Juan Perez, and Maureen Jules would bring food and visit with her at the hospital and later at her home when she was occasionally discharged. They shared a lot of laughs hanging out in her bedroom, watching Obama on TV, and telling stories about the campaign. LCO essentially became her extended family. Despite the bad news that her disease was likely terminal, her spirits remained high. She had an election to win!

Another one of our major independent supporting actors was Timothy Wyant, the Farmer's Market Campaigner Extraordinaire! His stage was the Farmer's Market in Purcellville. He had his bit-players ready to go and had gotten the OK to hang out the eight weekends before the election, starting Labor Day weekend, at the same Purcellville location he had covered the four previous years. In fact, the market operator was expecting him. Tim was all set except for handout material. When he asked CFC and VV08 for signs and stickers, he found an abundant supply for Mark Warner and Judy Feder, but to his dismay, nothing for Obama. The Obama campaign just wasn't into signs and literature. I'll tell you what he did about that problem in The Big Rumble chapter later in this story.

I remember once in July 2008 during the Obama campaign I was knocking doors in a gated community in north Purcellville near the Giant supermarket. It was a Sunday, and I was working for Katherine Grant, an Obama field organizer,. She was the daughter of Linda and John Grant, early members of the LCO crowd, and the only paid staffer in the campaign who was actually from Loudoun. It was hot enough out there to bake biscuits. I mean, I could literally bake biscuits, fry eggs and bacon on the sidewalk, and have breakfast alfresco. All I needed was silverware to eat it. Damn, it was hot and humid, but that's Virginia in the summer. The sign out front said "No Soliciting" but that never deterred me. A sign like that really said to me, "Catch me if you can." Well, as it turned out, they could.

So I was knocking, knocking, knocking doors and encountering some very strange characters in this place, including one utterly and completely stoned dude sitting on his second story porch wearing a cowboy hat and sunglasses while smoking a marijuana pipe, holding forth that he was voting for Hillary Clinton as a write-in candidate. The guy was wasted. The smoke was so thick I didn't need my own joint. I just needed to breathe. Whatever;

Hillary had taught us it takes all types to make a village.

So a half hour later I'm knocking on another door and out comes the property manager. When she heard what I was doing she booted my ass out of there so fast I couldn't even whistle the first stanza of Dixie. It was my first merit badge. Unless you've been kicked out of a few places, you haven't done enough work for the campaign.

I hustled back to the parking lot of the Giant and started telling VV08's Kathryn Grant about this guy with the marijuana pipe. "No problem," she said, "we have a special team just to deal with Hillary supporters." I thought if the campaign was that well organized, it could win. It was a memorable moment. That was the exact time I came to the conclusion that Obama could win the election.

Let me tell you more about VV08 during the summer of 2008. Barbara and I threw over our independent ways and decided to work for them. Dan Chavez would typically get up early in the morning and drive to the VV08 Regional Headquarters in Ashburn. At 9:00 a.m. every morning there would be a 15-30 minute conference call with all the other regional field directors and the statewide field director. They would all report their numbers—how many volunteers recruited, how many volunteers actually showed up, how many phone banking calls made the night before, how many house parties thrown, how many people came to the house parties, and how many doors were knocked. Dan reported the numbers to Matt Robinson, who in turn reported them to Pete Cavanaugh. They collected more data than the CFC campaign.

Dan would then meet with his paid field organizers and get everything in place to receive incoming volunteers. It was extremely important to have something for the volunteers to do the minute they walked in the door. Detailed priorities on the day's activities were given to the field organizers, followed by another call to Deputy Field Director Matt Robinson to discuss activities from the previous day. An hour later there was another conference call with Matt and three other Regional Field Directors in Northern Virginia to discuss activities—including Fairfax, Spotsylvania, and Prince William counties. This done, Dan would put his Loudoun field organizers on the phones to make calls recruiting volunteers from 10:00 a.m. to noon Then he was off to lunch followed by more field organizer training and door knocking.

Recruiting volunteers worked on the "three no" system. A

field organizer wouldn't give up on the prospect until he or she was told "no" three times. Then it was on to the next prospect. The highest priority was recruiting canvassers for the weekends. If a prospect said "no" to a canvass pitch, then the organizer would try to get the prospect to come in to do phone banking. The organizer would not quit trying to recruit until the third "no."

The state campaign assigned specific daily objectives to each of the Regional Field Directors. Each region was given a goal to knock a certain number of doors and make a certain number of phone calls. The goals never remained constant—they increased all the time. Conrad Chaffee, one of the VV08 field organizers, said that if you "made" your numbers, it was guaranteed that those goals would increase for the next week. Dan Chavez said the goals seemed impossible, but by the end of the campaign VV08 was exceeding its goals on a regular basis.

In addition, the 'universe' of registered voters to contact constantly changed. At the beginning the field organizers recruited "SDs," strong Democrats identified from the VAN. Then the universe expanded to include "LDs," leaning Democrats. Next were the "INDs," independent voters who voted either way. They next went after the large number of voters who had not been previously identified. As Election Day approached, the universe even encompassed "LRs," voters leaning Republican, and "SRs," strong Republican voters. Each expansion made recruiting more difficult and ratcheted up the pressure on the field organizers. It was a high-pressure environment with the pressure rising steadily as Election Day approached. Remarkably, from June through the election in November, only one field organizer burned out. All the others stayed the course.

Let me tell you about two of the new kids on the stage that arrived mid-August for VV08. The first, Amanda Millard, was born in Virginia involved in Democratic politics with her dad. She took a degree in English and Africana Studies from Lehigh University up in Pennsylvania in May 2008 and was knocking doors in Alexandria with her father in June when she heard that the VV08 Campaign was hiring field organizers. She applied, interviewed, and was hired. She received one day of training emphasizing cold calling to recruit volunteers, canvassing, and phone banking. Then Matt Robinson told her she was headed to Loudoun County.

Matt also explained more about the job. He hoped she was prepared to give up all free time for the next four months. At that

Amanda asked, "Does that mean we don't get weekends off?" "That's right," said Matt, "no days off." Nothing in her comfortable urban existence prepared her for what was to come next.

From the minute Amanda walked into the Ashburn field office, the pressure to get the job done was overwhelming. No college course could ever have prepared her for the stress of how important this mission was. The pressure not to flub it up was intense. She had just walked into the world of Dan Chavez, Rachel Fulk, and Kurt Gonska—all battle-hardened veterans—and was as green as Loudoun County corn in early July.

Amanda's first order of business was to borrow some furniture from Franco Luz's office to use at the Ashburn office. Then they gave her on-the-job training that continued the instruction started back in Alexandria. At the beginning it was mock phone calling to recruit volunteers. Then she hit the streets canvassing. Then it was recruiting volunteers on the phone, this time for real. One of the first she recruited was none other than yours truly, Ed Robisheaux.

The pace of work for the staffers was unbelievable—12-15 hour days, seven days a week. Amanda later said the pace was so hectic that "I have no timeline. It all flashed back, flashed into a ball, when I looked back on it." Extremely long hours and almost never a day off turns the mind into mush, and Amanda had a one-and-a-half hour commute back to Alexandria every night.

Conrad Chaffee's story is another of the more remarkable of the Great Campaign of 2008. He was born in Iowa City, Iowa, raised in Binghamton, NY, took a degree in history and East Asian studies from Oberlin College and came to Virginia because of a job opportunity. When Conrad was nine years old he had the good fortune to live for a year in Japan. In college Conrad learned Japanese and later lived and worked two years in the Tochigi Prefecture in rural Japan. At the time our story opens he was working as an Assistant Correspondent at the Washington, DC Bureau for a Tokyo newspaper translating political news for Japanese readers back in the home island.

The Tokyo newspaper gave Conrad press credentials, so he traveled to all the primary states to cover the primaries. He was in Iowa, New Hampshire, South Carolina and others. He covered the campaigns up close and helped the Japanese correspondents make sense of it all for their readers. He had a unique vantage point from which to follow the campaign.

He was also a committed Democrat appalled at the damage done the country by the Bush Administration. He vowed to become more active in politics and do what he could to elect a Democrat to the presidency. He volunteered for the VV08 Campaign, but soon wanted to do more. There was, however, a small problem. Conrad's wife was pregnant with twins. In spite of this, Conrad quit his job at the Japanese newspaper, and applied for and was accepted as a field organizer for the VV08 Campaign. Matt Robinson, the same guy who hired Amanda Millard, also hired Conrad. At the ripe old age of 31, Conrad was the oldest field organizer in the state of Virginia. Field organizers aren't paid a lot of money, around $2,000 a month, so this was a big financial sacrifice for them and their growing family.

Like Amanda Millard, Conrad Chaffee was given one day of formal training. The emphasis was the same as Amanda's—how to make a hard sell recruiting volunteers. The basic theme was you don't take "no" for an answer. You push hard and see if the volunteer will go out and knock doors on Saturday. If the answer is "no," then you stress the need to win the campaign and "can you come out Sunday?" If that answer is "no," then you ask them when they can come out. If the prospect didn't want to knock doors, then you asked him or her if they would phone bank. If they didn't want to phone bank, then you asked them if they would do data entry. If that option was also a "no," then you asked them what they could do. When you get three "no" responses you let them go but call them back on another day.

Conrad later said that the most important training lesson he received was not one he fully appreciated at the time. He was trained to turn his found animals into zookeepers. A field organizer trained volunteers to do what the field organizer did. Ideally a field organizer recruited enough volunteers so that they in turn begin to recruit new volunteers and the field organizer's job transforms itself into managing volunteer team leaders rather than making voter contacts. The team leaders liked the new responsibility. For some, telling people what to do can be a lot more fun than doing it. This leveraged the power of the field organizer into that of a manager. This was the same basic game plan used by CFC.

Conrad recruited Deborah Morbeto as a volunteer to work for the VV08 campaign. Born in Boston, with her degree in Art History at the Massachusetts College of Art, Deborah was a graphic design artist and marketing expert who made her way to Loudoun County by way of marriage. As a volunteer, she ran phone-banking operations for VV08 out of the LCDC office on King Street in

Leesburg. Later she knocked doors, assigned homes to walk by canvassers, did data entry and just about every other type of activity for the campaign. More recently, Deb helped Rollie, Ann, and me by doing the graphic design and marketing of this book, Swing County. She's a pistol. Thanks, Deb!

Let me get back to Loudoun County for Obama (LCO). The grassroots movement had grown to well over 3,000 supporters by July 2008 and their enthusiasm didn't let up when the other campaigns arrived on the scene. In addition to the Eager Beavers, LCO had hundreds of volunteers who now had a lot of campaign experience under their belt. Strong friendships had been formed during the previous 16 months due to their shared passion for Barack Obama, the large number of campaign events they had initiated or experienced, and their frequent socials (debate watching parties, house parties, phone parties, post card writing parties, and brainstorming parties) where the fare was potluck and everyone was welcome. Diversity prevailed, with all stripes and colors. Excitement was in the air. There was a feeling of purpose, optimism, and goodwill.

A host of new grassroots activities were initiated by LCO Eager Beavers in the summer of 2008, despite the lack of interest and occasional outright antagonism by CFC and VV08. Steve Ames and Theresa especially were inspired by Obama's call to create positive change in local communities, and they launched a variety of Obama Works projects, including military care package drives for our soldiers in Iraq and Afghanistan, food drives (which resulted in hundreds of pounds of food being donated to Loudoun Interfaith Relief), community cleanups, blood drives, and a volunteer call center to help hurricane victims. LCO also spread the word to join the Obama caravan in Leesburg's Fourth of July parade and a lot of supporters came early to decorate the Democrat/Obama floats. LCO also started a blog to encourage supporters to share their views about Obama, offer suggestions, and review the calendar of upcoming Obama campaign activities in Loudoun.

On July 10, Barack Obama held a town hall meeting in Fairfax and a group of Eager Beavers were fortunate to be selected to sit in the bleachers behind him (what fun)! Back in Loudoun, two major meetings were also organized to give all our supporters an opportunity to recommend policies for the Democratic Party Platform—one meeting was about Education, Economy, and Faith and the other focused on Energy, the Environment, and Global

Climate Change. More than 50 people attended each meeting and participated in lively discussions, including Alice Germond, an incredible woman who served on the DNC Rules Committee and was serving her third term as Secretary of the DNC. Much to our delight, Alice loved us and continued to be active in Loudoun County for Obama from time to time.

There were a couple of other major events in July that were very successful, thanks to the help we received from the national campaign. In response to an urgent request from LCO volunteer Hari Sharma, Trista Allen (Southern National Field Director) arranged for Barack Obama to send a personal letter greeting the attendees of the American Nepali Association Convention on July 4, 2008. We heard that this letter, in which Senator Obama mentioned his childhood years in Indonesia, was truly appreciated by the 10,000 Asian Americans who attended the convention.

A few days later, another LCO volunteer, Charles Avery, requested a letter from Senator Obama to be read to the graduates of Douglass School who were attending the 40th reunion of the closing of this school, the first high school for African American students in Loudoun County. Marcia immediately contacted Mitch Stewart (State Director for the Virginia Campaign for Change, CFC). We were worried when we heard that a representative from the McCain campaign was driving up from Richmond to read a letter from Senator McCain, but Mitch responded to the request very quickly and sent Charles a personal letter from Barack Obama which he read at the reunion.

Whenever Marcia received requests, concerns, or suggestions for the national campaign from supporters who were getting her emails, she forwarded them to Trista, Mitch, or Nikki Sutton (Southeast National Field Director). Most went to Nikki, who was very responsive and forwarded them to the appropriate person in the national campaign. For example, one supporter urged Obama to hold a town hall meeting with Warren Buffett to discuss the current financial crisis (he was way ahead of the curve with this suggestion!); another supporter offered suggestions on how Obama could reach out to gun owners in Virginia; and several others urged Obama to respond more forcefully to the lies and distortions of the McCain ads. These are examples of what can happen when there is good communication between grassroots activists and a national campaign.

On August 2, LCO supported the very successful kickoff meeting of Loudoun Women for Obama. CFC did support this effort. A throng of women (and a few men) showed up at the Leesburg office to discuss how to reach out to Hillary supporters, Latinas, and women who hadn't been involved in the campaign thus far. Soon after, our grassroots activities caught the attention of the media and some of the Eager Beavers (Gail Wise, Lina Burton, and Marcia Carlyn) were interviewed by NBC-TV, which was soon followed by a half-hour interview of Gail, Marcia, and Juan Perez by Mary Jo (MJ) Stemp at her Ashburn TV production studio. A second interview focused on LCO's strategies and goals, and was shown many times on local TV stations in the weeks that followed. Arts for Obama, led by Diana Denley, also held a big picnic in August, and sponsored a poster competition to Turn Virginia Blue. And, of course, many of the women also volunteered for CFC and VV08 with canvassing, phone banking, and data entry.

The Obama folks had correctly anticipated the large need for free, temporary housing for staffers and scores of other folks who were expected to pour into this swing county, especially as we got closer to the election. These potential volunteers primarily came from noncompetitive states (the Reds and Blues) as well as from foreign countries. This was a first for Loudoun County, and the locals agreed that the least we could do was to rustle up some housing for those willing to come to our county and help with our campaign. Gail spent many hours helping the Obama staffers find, track and book sleeping spaces for out-of-towners needing a place to flop at night. Free housing was always in short supply, however, and those who did provide housing often let multiple political vagrants stay a night or two and get refreshed.

OK, I've covered the LCO, CFC and the VV08. How about our local Democratic Committee, the LCDC? This is where Rollie spent most of his time, supporting the LCDC Precinct Operations Chair, Kevin Turner. It was July and time for Kevin to start planning for Election Day. Although this was a new responsibility for Kevin, he brought a lot to the table. Born and raised in Campbell County in Central Virginia, youngest of seven siblings, he was the President of all four of his classes in high school, graduated from William and Mary in Political Science and received a Master's in Business from George Washington University in DC. One summer, he worked as an intern for Virginia Congressman L. F. Payne, Chairman of the Ways and Means Committee.

After graduation Kevin joined the high-powered Price Waterhouse company as a consultant, married, and came to Loudoun

County in 2003, after a two-year stint in Fairfax County. He maintained his interest in politics and government, joined the LCDC in 2003, and ran for the School Board in 2007. He lost, but he put on a good show, especially considering the short period of time he had lived in Loudoun County.

When Tim Buchholz put him in charge of Precinct Operations in January 2008, Kevin had already decided to support Obama, but he kept that pretty quiet as did the others on the LCDC Executive Committee. In the February primary, he decided that he could best serve as a non-partisan election official, and he worked all day as the head judge. By the time Rollie started working with him in July 2008, Kevin was working for IBM in their Education Products Division.

Kevin appreciated the fact that an old pro, who had handled precinct ops for several other county-wide campaigns over the years, was willing to help him out for the November election. They met in late July for lunch in South Riding and Rollie agreed to draft an Election Day plan. A few days later he sent a rough copy to Kevin, who then added major input, wrote it up, and created an extremely professional power point presentation of the plan. Kevin presented it at the LCDC August meeting. The members were extraordinarily impressed, and Kevin was lauded mightily for his presentation skills. The plan was enthusiastically accepted as presented. It specified that Kevin and Rollie would each keep tabs on four of the eight district chairs to help them reach their goals for precinct coverage. Since Kevin had a significant full-time position with IBM, they also agreed that Rollie would handle all coordination with the other Power Groups, transportation needs, Election Day materials, and the headquarters operation on Election Day. Of course Rollie was not to do all the work himself; he would recruit managers and be sure they did their jobs.

One of the first items on Rollie's list was to line up a couple of people to develop and manage the transportation plan. Someone was needed to develop and implement a plan for the Route Drivers. They were the drivers who circulated through the polling locations several times on Election Day to be sure all was going OK. There were 62 precincts to cover in over 500 square miles. They were the eyes and ears of the Election Day activity.

We needed someone really special and talented for solving the kind of problems we experienced in the primary with our Route Drivers. It needed to be laid out well in advance. Rollie knew just the right person, and that was Jack Beavers. Jack had been hunting for a way to become involved in the campaign. He didn't like talking (phone banking) or walking (canvassing) so he didn't find his niche until Rollie talked to him in September about the need for a manager for the route driver activity.

This job was perfect for him. He had the temperament, skills, and creativity to do something quite extraordinary with this responsibility. Jack put together the best, most sophisticated, and successful routing system Rollie had ever witnessed. Let me tell you more about Jack—an incredible person. He was the pilot we discussed in earlier chapters. He and his wife had started a software company and sold out at a good time. This election was his first time to be involved in a campaign, and when asked, "Why Obama? Why now?" he told us of his first impressions: "Every time Obama opened his mouth, out came an extremely reasoned answer given with deep understanding; he was the smartest guy in the room, by far." Jack came to Loudoun originally from Pittsburgh by way of New York. He was the son of left-wing Democrats, but he preferred a more centrist approach as expressed by Obama.

Jack went looking for people to put him to work on the campaign, searched the web, and found LCO and Marcia Carlyn. He was energized by the "disaster" of the George W. Bush administration. Joining the Loudoun grassroots group just before the February primary gave him an outlet for his determination. He was one of the brave ones who worked all day out in the sleet on primary day, passing out sample ballots at his polling place.

In May, Jack flew his small (and very cool) high performance single-engine Diamond Star plane to North Carolina with the spirited Joyce McLaurin and Steve Ames on board to participate in GOTV canvassing for their primary. The trip was exciting for him as he learned just how sophisticated an operation Obama had put together. On the North Carolina primary night, the three Loudoun volunteers attended a huge raucous rally in Raleigh, where Obama continued to impress.

Now Rollie needed someone to handle the other transportation needs. Bob Moses agreed to handle the recruitment of the Rovers and Runners. The Rovers were those who would be available throughout the day to handle any emergency driving needs, particularly taking people to the polls. That can be a time-consuming job, as the driver sits and waits at the polls until the voter completes their voting and then takes them home. Typically, there was a very small need for this service, but this time it could be a lot different. The National Obama campaign was planning to heavily advertise a national 800 number to call for rides. And as the several hundred volunteers visited homes on Election Day, they were to arrange transportation for anyone they came across who needed a ride. Bob Moses also was to recruit and manage the Runners who would be at the beck and call of the CFC or VV08 campaigns to move people and material around between the campaign offices and neighborhood hubs on Election Day. He was to provide a couple of drivers, working in shifts, assigned the whole day to each of the five hubs.

Bob Moses is one of the great heroes of the Great 2008 Campaign. Bob knocked thousands of doors during the campaign, and also served as the LCDC Vice President. If there was a Democratic event in Loudoun, he was there. He worked diligently for the Loudoun County Democratic Committee on numerous administrative tasks needed to help the campaign organizations handle the throngs of volunteers who showed up to help. Bob's interview on the website, www.swingcounty.com is an operations training guide for efficient, effective canvassing.

One of the memorable Bob Moses stories involved the Halloween Night Parade in Leesburg just before the election. While riding in the parade he was accosted by a vicious sounding Republican who said he hated him. Bob looked at him and said, "But I love you," and the confrontational moment was instantly defused. The hater probably had never heard anything like this and immediately changed his whole attitude. If there is one thing in this world Bob Moses can do, it is defuse a tense situation.

In addition to transportation, another strategy of interest to Rollie was implementing a voter check off system he had used quite successfully in a number of previous elections. For decades or more, local campaigns have used a variety of ways to identify their supporters and then get them to vote on Election Day. Before 1970, small white index cards were the storage medium of choice. Rollie believes he was the first person in Virginia to actually develop and use a computerized version of this technique. He did this back in 1971 in Virginia Beach. A compact alphabetic computer-generated supporter list was prepared a day or two before the election. Inside each polling location, volunteer Democratic poll watchers checked or crossed off the names of those who actually voted. Depending on the size of the precinct, there could be as many as five or six inside people working from 6 a.m. to about 4 p.m. The lists would then quickly be taken to a phone bank where callers would contact those not struck from the list and remind them to go out and vote, by saying, "we have not seen you at the polls yet," or words to that effect. Depending on the availability of drivers, callers would ask if transportation was required and arrange it with the Rovers.

The LCDC Election Day plan was to include inside poll checkers for the check off system. But CFC had a lot of uncertainty as to whether they wanted this done, and if so, would they want to assign the responsibility to LCDC (Kevin and Rollie). Rollie explained to me that he could understand their hesitancy. Their major strategy was to use all available volunteers on Election Day to finish the six 'touches' that were to be done the last four days of the campaign, including Election Day. Since all of the identified supporters were to be reached this many times regardless of whether they had voted or not, they were not very interested in a checking system. Logistically, there would be a problem deleting those who voted from the walk sheets and call lists. It was just easier to contact everyone regardless if they had voted. They put off making a decision about checkers until the GOTV team was to be in town in early October. So LCDC put this activity on hold. Names of people interested in the checking activity were accumulated, but it was given low priority.

While Kevin and Rollie were putting together the LCDC Precinct Operations Plan, the LCO ladies were expanding their grassroots activity. A few days after Sarah Palin's speech at the Republican Convention, Loudoun Women for Obama held a second meeting at the Leesburg office. There was an overflow crowd and the energy in the room was palpable. It was clear that Palin as a possible VP had provided the motivation. The group felt strongly that they needed to reach out to undecided women to help them understand the striking differences between Obama/Biden and McCain/Palin on issues of special interest to women. The decision was to organize a Women's Issues Forum with nationally known speakers who would take questions from the audience. A planning committee was soon formed led by Toni Boyd. They did an amazing job over the next three weeks to secure a large auditorium, recruit top-notch speakers (with help from the Obama campaign), and publicize the forum.

On September 6, Amy Klobuchar (U.S. Senator from Minnesota) stopped by the Leesburg headquarters, along with her husband and their two engaging daughters. They came all the way out to meet us despite the pouring rain! The Senator and her family were welcomed by an enthusiastic group of Obama supporters, and she enjoyed answering our questions, including queries about Sarah Palin's position on different issues. On September 19, there was a rally for Joe Biden in Sterling. Loudoun's grassroots leaders were invited to meet Senator Biden in a tent set up next to the stage (very exciting) and many LCO volunteers got to shake his hand and talk with him after the rally, including Joyce McLaurin who was now in a wheelchair. She was hanging in.

Later in September, Barack Obama and Joe Biden held a huge rally in Fredericksburg, about 60 miles from Loudoun County. It was their first joint appearance in Virginia, and Joyce just had to be there. She really was hoping she would have a chance to meet Obama before she was too weak to do so. Using all of her persuasion skills, she started in on Judy Ross and Steve Ames, the eagerest of Eager Beavers, who were looking after her closely. They received the brunt of her entreaties, and Judy finally relented, even though the weather was looking bad, and it was an outdoor event! Judy sent several of us an email with a vivid portrayal of the Fredericksburg rally:

"*Hi Marcia and all...*

"*I just got home from the Obama/Biden rally with Joyce from Fredericksburg! Midnight nearly. It was a long, tiring...and great day. Thanks to VIP-ADA placement, we were up close, right next to the fence line...though to the side of the backstage area...so during the speech we were seeing the backs of heads. But yes, Joyce got to shake Barack's hand...not really "meet" him...and shake Biden's hand again too (he was very personal with her again). And yes, we got wet, wet. Luckily we had an umbrella and rain coat...so mostly only Joyce's legs got wet (and in my case, most of me!). Mind you everyone was wet...including Obama and Biden...who took their suit coats off when the rains came again...and swam with us in the rain! What a guy!*

"*We weren't up close to start...but after the rain chased some 'light weights' away, and it was raining, and many of the wheelchairs were in the back (where they would never see or have a chance to shake hands), I and a mother took over...took down chairs and set up 4-5 wheelchairs next to the barrier. Where there's a will!*

"*Joyce was sitting next to a really sweet young man (cerebral palsy), and she and he hit it off. Joyce shared her umbrella with him, gave him a flag which he happily tied to his rain poncho...and together they listened to the speeches and shook hands. His mother was really nice...she and I hit it off. After the event was over, she told Joyce that she made her month, for the way she took care of her boy. And he, haltingly shared, it was 'a once in a lifetime experience.' It was a really sweet meeting. Everyone was soaked (for the second time)...but oh so happy!*

"As now the grass where parked on was soaked, I found a really nice young, strong man to help me push Joyce to the road. I had found a parking place not too far from the VIP entrance...but required going down a pretty steep hill. So we did wheelchair slalom, switch-backing back and forth down the hill so that we didn't go into a run-away Joyce! First time I ever did wheelchair skiing! Was quite exciting!

"When we got to the car, we were soggy dogs! Joyce had a quilt in the trunk, so I bundled her up. And we had a nice warm, dry ride home. We sure laughed a lot. I've had a few crazy road trips with

Joyce...but we both agreed this took the cake!! For those who have road-tripped with Joyce, you know what fun you have...and the conversation was rich...even on the way home, when we were both beat.

"Don't think she got too chilled...but was very worn out by the time I got her home...into bed...and a cup of tea. Pretty sure she will be spending tomorrow quiet in bed! And truly hope the experience was worth it all for her.

"So that is a brief recap of our amazing journey! I too am beat. But boy, I do love Joyce road trips! Happy Saturday night!

Judy"

I promised you earlier that we would tell you more about Larry Roeder, the Indiana Jones of the 2008 campaign. Of all the fantastic actors in Loudoun County who appeared on the stage of this campaign, Larry Roeder was extraordinary. He had a biography that read like something out of the movie *Indiana Jones*, but with one exception—Larry's biography was real.

Larry Roeder was born in the Middle East in Beirut, Lebanon, the son of a State Department diplomat whose assignments took the family around the world to Lebanon, Saudi Arabia, Egypt, Israel, Tunisia, France, Germany, Cuba, and Canada. Larry had wide exposure to different countries and cultures, particularly Muslim oriented cultures. His mother was in the OSS, the Office of Strategic Services, the precursor to the Central Intelligence Agency.

Next for Larry came a tour in the United States Army, not as an infantry soldier, no sir, not for this Indiana Jones. Larry's MOS (Military Occupational Specialty) was an Electronic Morse Code Interceptor. His job was to intercept Morse code signals from terrorists coming out of Africa and identify them. He got help from the NSA (National Security Agency), which does signals intercepts, decoding, cryptanalysis, and cryptography. Larry was like an NSA staffer but one who wore a uniform.

He followed his father's footsteps and went on to a career in the State Department as a Foreign Affairs Officer. His assignments took him all over Europe, France, Germany, Albania, and Belgium and into the Middle East in Egypt, Turkey, Somalia, Sudan, and more. He was almost everywhere and doing phenomenal things. He rode camels to negotiate with gangs of killers in Somalia, rode more camels in Egypt to negotiate with Bedouin tribes, and planned a road system in Albania. He developed knowledge of economic planning and emergency management. Think of a modern day Lawrence of Arabia and you'll get an idea of Larry Roeder.

When he was 12 years old Larry was out knocking doors with his mother for John F. Kennedy in the campaign of 1960. That's where he caught the political bug. In 1990 he worked as an early volunteer in the Bill Clinton for President Campaign. He campaigned in Virginia, Maryland, and New York's Bronx and Brooklyn. Always a volunteer, never a paid staffer, while on the road Larry often slept on mattresses thrown on the floor. In the campaign of 2000, he was attached as a volunteer to the Al Gore national staff as an emergency management expert.

Larry went on to become a Policy Adviser to the US State Department on Disaster Management. Later he was attached to the Bureau of International Organization Affairs. He worked as an International Commodity Economist for the State Department, and was then assigned to the United Nations, where he assisted in providing the first UN disaster relief in the United States after Hurricane Katrina. In 2005, after a long career in the State Department he resigned in disgust over the foreign policies of the Bush administration and the treatment of prisoners of war. He and his family made a special contribution to the Obama campaign from late September through Election Day. We'll save that story for the Big Rumble chapter.

Many volunteers worked on their own with no direct human supervision for all or part of the campaign. My wife, Barbara, and I were primary examples of those who fell into this category for our initial time on the campaign trail. So I'm going to tell you a little more about how I happened to get on this stage. After graduation, I lived in Paris and Caen in France for several years, learning French, cognac, champagne, and wine drinking along the way. My first candidate in the 2008 campaign was Senator Mark Warner; when Warner dropped out, I moved over to Bill Richardson. When Richardson threw in the towel after the New Hampshire primary I listened to a magnetic speaker on satellite radio in January 2008. I initially had no idea who he was, subsequently learned it was Barack

Obama, and immediately became a supporter. Two weeks later I read a Rolling Stone article about his website, my.barackobama.com, signed up, and began phone banking from home. In August 2008 Amanda Millard from the VV08 recruited Barbara and me to canvass door to door. Later Kathryn Grant from CFC recruited us to go door-to-door on Sundays in western Loudoun County for the Obama Campaign.

Barbara Robisheaux was born in Chicago, Illinois, and moved with her family to West Covina, California in 1953. Later she married and moved to Huntington Harbor, California. In 1986 she moved to Texas, married me four years later, and we moved to Philomont, Virginia, in 1996. In the Great Campaign of 2008 Barbara knocked over a thousand doors in Purcellville, Round Hill, Lovettsville, and Leesburg, ran canvass staging centers for the VV08 Campaign, and did data entry at the LCDC headquarters for CFC. She did everything but phone bank. A travel agent for many years, Barbara had spent too much of her life on telephones to do it again in the Obama Campaign. Her instincts for deflecting racist negative responses or appreciating surprising comments from convicted felons modeled a sterling volunteer, even though she had never before worked in a political campaign.

Carolyn Ronis was another independent operator. An attorney with a law degree, she moved to the Lansdowne development in Loudoun County in 2005. Carolyn was a radio talk show host in Dover, Delaware, back in the 80s when she first started volunteering for political campaigns. She became an Obama fan in October, 2006, when Oprah endorsed him on her television show. Never a Hillary fan, Obama was her first candidate. In 2007 the lady couldn't wait for an official campaign to get involved. She got her contact lists from MoveOn.org, the ACLU, and MyBO, the Obama web site. She was on her own; she needed no supervision, no external motivation. She made multiple calls to the Loudoun County Democratic Committee, and none were returned, so she just organized herself. Who needs help if you can do it yourself? It wasn't a campaign office, and the main phone was not always covered. Inexperienced people may have cleared her messages without realizing what they had done. People do fall between the cracks. Volunteers were our lifeblood, and no one purposefully would have ignored a call from a new supporter.

Carolyn's efforts were remarkable because of her personal circumstances. She was pregnant and would soon deliver a new baby into the world. Her twin sister and her father-in-law passed away during the campaign. In spite of these dramatic personal events, Carolyn pressed on. She networked for support with other independents. She and other women formed a group they called "the Obama Mamas" to provide mutual support. It worked.

She often put her kids in strollers to campaign with her, though sometimes her husband kept them in the car while Carolyn worked. She knocked on doors five days a week, a large number for a volunteer. She worked nursing homes, phone-banked at night, and was an ongoing presence in her neighborhood.

One day in Leesburg, Carolyn knocked a door and a man answered the knock. She then experienced what was becoming a frequent unpleasant canvassing event: She made her pitch, the door flew open, and the man came out shouting "baby killer, baby killer" and chased her down the street. The sublime irony to it all was the fact that her husband was waiting for her in their car with two of their children, and Carolyn escaped to canvass another day. It didn't slow her down one bit. Inspired by their candidate, Barack Obama, perseverance was one of the hallmarks of the volunteers of this campaign.

And a Cast of Thousands

> *"And He looked up, and saw the rich men casting their gifts into the treasury. And He saw also a certain poor widow casting in thither two mites. And He said, 'Of a truth I say unto you, that this poor widow hath cast in more than they all; for all these have of their abundance cast in unto the offerings of God, but she of her penury hath cast in all the living that she had.'"*—Luke 21:1-4

No epic drama is complete without its "cast of thousands," and the grassroots campaign in Loudoun was no exception. You know when a movement takes hold and becomes a force for change... it's when no one remembers who is in charge or feels the need to ask for permission. When the soul of America takes to the streets, the young and the old stride hand in hand with the strong and the meek, and become an organic whole. The following pieces form a collage of souls, overflowing with faith that the America they longed for could be attained at last. (Listed alphabetically by first names below, their full interviews in their own voices can be accessed at www.swingcounty.com)

With metaphor and simile, **Aaron Edlow** explains how hope prevailed in the African-American man's heart in 2008. Having grown up in Philly, with a political father and savvy friends, he saw the political process like a person who has taken a role in a good movie. It's hard to believe in the story as you are watching it, because you know that a 10-second shot may have taken all day to make, and the actor fell down on the third try. So, he was convinced Barack Obama might make a good also-ran candidate, but that the insider power would never let him actually become the Democratic nominee. As an African American, he experienced his participation in the American dream with an * —that is, like a football player who is always playing an "away game," he might win, but he never expected to have the energy of a home crowd rooting for him. Was this Obama "for real"? Hearing Michelle Obama on the radio convinced him, "yes." *"A wife is the mirror to the man, and Michelle is definitely 'Real.'"* In the middle of a cold February night, Aaron confronted his doubts and challenged himself to believe. Logging onto BarackObama.com he donated the maximum $2300 and went on to canvass, raise funds, inspire his friends and family and promote GOTV efforts. Aaron committed to the game with his heart and soul, and this time the Home Team won. The * is gone for good.

Although **Alan Letzt**'s parents voted with the Democratic party, they were not activists, and Alan's interest in politics intensified based on a sixth grade essay contest and viewing the BBC series, "That was the Week that Was." As his passion for public policy increased, so did his multi-faceted career experience which weaved a network of engineering projects with both Ross Perot and Arthur D. Little's firms, spent some time working on a government contract, and then launched a healthcare technology enterprise of his own. As an entrepreneur, Letzt also excelled in marketing and communications (and later volunteered to develop a coordinated communications post with the Loudoun County Democratic Committee after the campaign). Frustrated with the Bush/Cheney Administration and inspired by Loudoun's own Mike Turner who gave a "gutsy endorsement of the underdog" when Obama was down in the polls by 20 points, Alan provided key media outreach for the Loudoun County for Obama grassroots organization as well as the combined campaign and LCDC. As a result, the Democratic Party got more print in a "red" county than the Republican party did. *"People were swayed by the energy and enthusiasm of the grassroots here who believed in the candidate. They made a huge difference,"* said Alan.

Ali McDermott became known for talking her Republican neighbors in Upstate New York in the 1970s into voting Democratic. Passionately motivated to campaign for Jimmy Carter early in life, and Bill Clinton as an adult, Ali was a natural to fend off racists and hostile Hillary supporters alike and turn the community of South Riding into "Obama blue," in spite of having her yard signs repeatedly burned, her house egged, her car keyed, and her parenting skills questioned. She proved to her children in a cynical world, how one tiny family could make a difference. It should be no surprise that she is also an anthropologist, in the finest tradition of Margaret Mead, who reminded us all to *"Never doubt that a small group of people can change the world. Indeed it is the only thing that ever has."*

With a politically passionate grandmother who described herself as a "Southern Catholic Democrat," **Ann Sallgren** was naturally persuaded to skip class at William and Mary College during the 2000 Florida recount and watch Al Gore supporters shoved aside by more aggressive Republicans. Since then she vowed to make a difference in Loudoun politics, the place of her birth and childhood rearing. During the presidential campaign of 2007, Ann supported

Hillary Clinton, but quickly put on her "district chair hat," as leader of the Blue Ridge district for the Loudoun County Democratic Committee, and gave it her all, organizing the numerous volunteers for the 2008 general election. "*She kept her cool, amid a hectic atmosphere of controlled chaos,*" Rollie Winter remarked, congratulating Ann on a job well done.

Retired Colonel **Anthony 'Tony' Fasolo** supports candidates he believes can manage change well. First at the Leesburg Town Mayor level, he supported B. J. Webb as a better change manager than her opponent. Then, in 2007 Tony worked hard through the LCDC to elect County Supervisors that could do a better job of managing the inevitable change in Loudoun County. He wanted officials that cared about the environment and treated citizens with respect in the process. But before then, Tony was an eye-witness to the attack on the Pentagon of 9-11, as a civilian employee there at the time. Two of his close friends died at the Pentagon that day, the next wing over from where Tony sat. Later he observed from the inside the way the Iraq War was promoted and how shabbily those who cautioned restraint were treated. Barack Obama's intelligence and sincere message of working together to effect change resonated with Fasolo, and he participated in several activities to help with the campaign, including installing a 4'x6' lighted sign on his property. If you have time to listen to only a few of the interviews in their entirety, this is one of the ones you'll want to choose, as it is replete with details about the relationships between the military and the executive branch, for both George W. Bush and President Obama. Tony knows the inside story. His favorite memory of the 2008 election: arriving at the polls at 4:30 a.m. as an election official tasked to open, and seeing a young African-American woman waiting outside the locked door to vote.

The valued quality attributed to being a "self-starter" doesn't even begin to describe the motivated and inspired actions quickly, effectively and repeatedly carried forward by **Barbara Mitchell.** A seasoned traveler through her profession, she once took leave from her job, purchased an airline ticket with her own money, and showed up unannounced to work doing whatever was needed—menial or not—for an Indian reservation that mounted a local political campaign in the Northwest. So it was only natural that she would respond to the MoveOn.org request for house parties in 2007. One of her invitees turned out to be none other than Marcia Carlyn, and they connected in their efforts to get Barack Obama elected. Kicking off her shoes and logging on to "MyBO" at home to unwind at the end of a busy day, Barbara made thousands of phone calls on behalf of the presidential campaign.

Born on the island of Cypress, **Barry Aliriza** spent some time in England as a child, received his education in Ohio, and lived in California 12 years. Moving in the 1990s to the Mid-Atlantic region to accept a job with a multi-national Turkish company, Barry became active with the All Dulles Area Muslim community, eventually moving to Ashburn, Virginia. He brought considerable organizing experience with him from his efforts supporting Democratic candidates in California. Very displeased with George W. Bush's presidency, Aliriza was initially attracted to Barack Obama's "no" vote on the Iraqi War and to his charismatic intelligence. He quickly grasped the importance of a swing county within a swing state. Barry also knew that Independents can be persuaded by an effective, enthusiastic and informative campaign, so he got involved early on with the Loudoun County Obama grassroots effort through events in the Muslim community, phone banks, and canvassing.

"*If I wake up on Wednesday, November 5, and John McCain is president, I'm going to be really mad at myself for not doing all I could to elect Barack Obama,*" **Ben Somberg** realized as he read the polls in October 2008. They were favorable, but you couldn't be too sure. He knew he must not sit this one out, even though he had resonated personally with Paul Krugman's reservations regarding Obama's centrist positions. A recent resident of DC [from Cambridge, Massachusetts, via New York], Ben looked around for a more uncertain location in which to volunteer and heard through a friend, Tracey Loh, that the Leesburg office was the hub of a swing county. Moreover, Leesburg was known as the fun place to be, as well, so that sealed it. He became a part of the around-the-clock "midnight volunteers."

Sometimes the wisdom that comes with purity of thought and motive is best expressed by a child, and when eight-year-old **Bobby McDermott's** mother asked him to choose a presidential candidate in early 2007, he instinctively knew Barack Obama expressed his best hope for a world he wished to live in. "*I didn't want our country to be a racist society,*" said Bobby, "*and when I learned that Obama would work for healthier relationships worldwide, I believed we should vote for him, because he wanted to do the right thing.*" Bobby knocked on over 1,000 doors and gave out individually drawn handmade flyers, so that each person he talked to would feel special. At school he convinced the children of South Riding's Republican community to vote for Obama in the straw poll, even though Bobby's mother told him to obey the rules and even though he spent many days in the "Quiet Corner" as a consequence of his refusal to be quiet in his daily campaigning for Barack Obama on school grounds. Still, he respects his school Principal. *"She was simply trying to keep stress out of the school. She's a good principal."* [How much can we all learn from that simple statement?] *"I learned that I could change a vote to change an election to change our lives. And if Obama can stay in office for seven years, we will begin to see the effect of his leadership. I want to give him that time..."* Bobby explains. *"Don't give up. Use a persistent, reasoned approach. Anger doesn't solve anything. It only makes things worse. Don't let yourself be corrupted or let your views be clouded by threats. Don't let someone silence you."* He also relays his admiration for both Abraham Lincoln and JFK: *"It's almost as if they were angels who came down and knew they were going to die for what they had to do—the right thing. Me...myself, I would give up my life for the right thing."* And now All of us know the meaning of Hope.

"I'm not a political animal," said **Brian Bouton**, *"I'm a therapist, and I try to get a couple together to find common ground so they can get together and work out their problems. I hadn't been involved in political action since the 60s when I walked for racial integration in Baltimore. I felt that Obama had a good soul. He really wants to do the right thing and lead the country in a healing direction."* Bouton was inspired by Obama's message of non-aggressive passion. *"This is our country,"* Brian explains, "We need to find common ground and find solutions." Brian worked at the polls, stuffed envelopes, and made phone calls. He wanted to be sure that Obama won the Virginia primary. When that did happen, he knew the presidency was within his candidate's grasp.

Bonnie Bird grew up being mothered by a woman who had been active with both Democratic campaigns and the National Organization for Women (NOW). And Bonnie cried the night Hillary Clinton gave her concession speech. Soon, however, she began working for the Obama campaign in her home state of Maryland, since she had also shared her childhood with Olivia Plouffe. *"It's time to do something,"* she told a friend. *"You have to stand up for something."* Invited to take part in Kathryn Grant's organization in Purcellville accelerated Bonnie's activities considerably. The excitement in Loudoun, along with the thorough organization, training, and follow-through held Bonnie's allegiance through the end of the campaign. Only one canvassing experience became dangerous—when an angry homeowner threw rocks hitting their car. But even that attack did not slow her down. On the eve of the Inauguration, 63-year-old Bonnie Bird took the Metro at 1:00 a.m. from the Shady Grove Station to camp out in the bitter snowy cold early enough to participate on the D.C. Mall when Barack Obama took the oath of office. "*I feel like I did something truly important,*" Bonnie said. "*I plan to do it again.*"

Being a part of the Jim Lehrer News Hour staff during the '04 campaign, **Charlie Jackson** reveals that the "news junkies" knew from the start that the nominee would be either Barack or Hillary, although he himself was an early Joe Biden supporter. And Charlie understood that Barack would prevail, due to "*his passion and sincerity—lifting the morale of the country.*" Hailing from Minnesota's Paul Wellstone country and with a Dad who was active in the construction and factory labor movement, Charlie's values align with Democratic social values.

His double major in political science and journalism led him through the PBS News Hour internship to local newspaper reporting to a public relations firm with a focus on coordinating candidates' campaigns with the media. Jackson coordinated events for the LCDC and the grassroots campaign, such as the Joe Biden Rally in 2008. He currently serves as the 10th CD Chair.

"He could be dangerous," **Chuck Tellachea** thought to himself after hearing Obama speak at the 2004 Democratic National Convention. "He has *capacity*." Tellachea grew up in Miami in a conservative Cuban family, and considers himself a Republican. But although he worked in Bob Dole's presidential campaign and also strongly supported Congressman Tom Davis, he has moved steadily towards the Center-Left point on the political spectrum and now votes Democratic more often than not. In 2007—2008, Chuck canvassed and blogged for Barack Obama, especially supporting his perspective on geopolitical affairs. He likes the President's agile mind and ability to inspire.

Born in New York to a NYC fireman, **Chuck Visnius** grew up in Orlando, Florida, where the family lived after his father became disabled. The move to a "Right to Work" state altered Chuck's father's politics from that of a Nixon Republican to a McGovern Democrat, and he became active. A working mom impressed on Chuck the importance of Equal Pay for Equal Work, as well; and Chuck carried his Democratic roots into his military career as a helicopter pilot, a career that culminated in his being the Air Mission Commander for the weapons for hostages exchange [unbeknownst to him at the time] that formed the basis of the Iran-Contra Affair. A civilian helicopter and corporate jet pilot at that level, he has since flown powerful and celebrated persons all over the world. (When asked what the most memorable flight he ever had was, he said, "That's easy, it was William Shatner." Chuck went to pick him up in Florida, Shatner boarded the helicopter, looked at Chuck and said, "beam me up.") *"Everyone was ready for change in 2008,"* Chuck said. But nothing prepared him for the excitement he found working as a volunteer for the Obama campaign in Loudoun. The whole family participated in canvassing and phone banking, including his 13-year-old daughter. *"It was ten times better than Disney World, as a family experience."*

When she was 16 years old, **Cindy Emmet** worked as an *"I like Ike"* girl selling bracelets and trinkets to campaign enthusiasts. Shortly afterwards, she landed a spot as a Page at the Republican National Convention. But later when she lived in San Francisco and tried voting for the person, not the party, she shortly realized all the "persons" she voted for were Democrats! To top it all off, her sister served as Delegate to the Democratic National Convention when Geraldine Ferraro was nominated for Vice President. The clincher came with Pat Robertson's hate-filled speech at the GOP Convention in 1992—as Cindy went out the next day to officially register as a Democrat. In 2008 her values coincided with others who felt Obama's thoughts in "Dreams of My Father" comprised the perfect words of leadership, and she with friends organized a lovely garden reception in Rhode Island where she has a summer home. One hundred people came, and they raised approximately $70,000. Her memories of volunteering at the Loudoun County for Obama office on King Street and the rally at Ida Lee still retain their thrill.

Daniel Dennison was born in Athens, Alabama, and lived there until he went off to college at Lipscomb University, where he not only got smart, but he also played hoops for the legendary Don Meyer. Don Meyer was and is the winningest men's basketball coach in the NCAA. He first got involved in political campaigns in 2000 with the Gore campaign. Two years later, he was a volunteer organizer in the John Edwards campaign and sent busloads of volunteers into the battleground states of Iowa and Wisconsin. He was also doing a lot of fundraising. For six years he lived in Chicago where he got to know first-hand the Cook County Democratic machine and learned what a real political campaign looks like. Some organizations may do it better than Chicago's Democratic machine, but not many. He also worked as an organizer in the Iowa caucus. Daniel Dennison knows a thing or two about presidential ground game politics.

Encouraged by a single mom who instilled the value of civic duty, **Darby McDermott** never questioned the fact that he would be working energetically for the presidential candidate of his choice in the 2007-2008 campaign, even though he was only 12 years old. After presenting to his mother and brother his handwritten list of reasons why Barack Obama should be president, Darby started his daily rounds of passing out copies to neighbors and strangers in South Riding. He quickly learned he could entice staunchly conservative Republicans to vote for Obama in the primary on the basis of "*well, he'll be easier to beat in the general election than Hillary will.*" Over time, however, Darby became a force for change in Loudoun, not because of who Obama was, but because of who Darby himself was: friendly, relentless, passionate, polite, tireless. An elderly (white) and very conservative couple voted for a "Black man(!)" for the first time in their lives because they saw Darby repeatedly everywhere they went—and when they saw him at 6 a.m. as precinct captain of their polling place—and again at 7 p.m. when it closed, still there, still asking…well, what else could they do? "I want you to know," the old man said to Darby's mother, "that your son has changed my life. And I am very grateful."

David Weintraub originally moved to Loudoun County in 1998 from St. Louis, without ever having been involved in electoral politics. His intention was to build a house in the woods and be left alone; that did not work out, however, as the local political representation fairly quickly caught his attention. Shocked with the bigotry of County Supervisor Eugene Delgaudio and [then] Virginia Delegate Dick Black whose missions in life appeared to him to be to impose their religious views on David, he was deeply offended by their anti-gay agenda. An inspiring example of what it means to believe in the power of individual involvement in the democratic process, David became an organizing leader of Equality Loudoun, a local group which supports the human rights of gays, lesbians, bi-sexual and transgender citizens. He, along with his spouse Jonathan, were an active part of the founding members of the Progressive Action League (PALS), as well. David is renowned regionally for his writing skills, and during the Obama campaign, he transitioned from being an Edwards supporter in the early days to supporting Barack Obama through the Loudoun County Democratic Committee with his activities as webmaster of the LCDC website and his articulate, insightful blog.

When listening to the astonishing life and the extraordinary intellect that **Dr. Dave [David Williams]** embodies, it's impossible not to think of an intersection where Calvinism and The Tao meet. Maybe it is inevitable that a man born of nuclear scientists who met building the Atom bomb in Los Alamos during WWII and then allowed young Dave to grow up near Boston where he would later study theology and history, at Harvard in Massachusetts—the ground zero for determinism and fate—would say, *"The American dream is to be in control of your own life... to not be kicked around by Fate. But ultimately Fate is in charge. Reality is not 'I could be' or 'I should be'; Reality is 'I AM.'"* Still he plays his part with the same enthusiasm as a person who would hope for a particular result, most especially at the local level. The *"rituals of political activism are like Christmas lights on a tree. It is how we define ourselves."* The experiences relayed in Dr. Dave's interview, of being at the center of the 60s activism in all of its manifestations [inflammatory writing, protests, sit-ins, long treks across a continent, merchant marines, the 1968 Chicago convention, and much much more]—is a history lesson in itself... one that is rich in the meaning of the decade and of the ages combined. When it came time to participate in the "Change" movement of 2008, Dr. Dave first supported Bill Richardson, then Barack Obama, with all the skills at his disposal. Now he watches and observes as Americans attack this president for not being able to control the uncontrollable forces of history. Dr. Dave knows that President Obama is doing the best job that could be done in showing the courage to change the things he can, and the wisdom to accept the things he cannot. He will support Barack Obama again in the Election Year Ritual of 2012.

Born in South Korea and immigrating to America with her father, one of **Debbie Hawk's** earliest memories—that of watching her father become a US citizen—motivated her to always vote. Becoming an active volunteer in political campaigns, however, came much later, after her own children were in school. A school boundary issue in Loudoun County that obviously discriminated against low-income students stunned Debbie, an aerospace engineer and Independent centrist voter, into the realization that office holders sometimes act contrary to rational, professional good sense. After that, she helped organize a Loudoun Women's group to campaign for David Poisson for Virginia Delegate, and went on to be instrumental in turning Sterling Blue in 2008, striding past McCain yard signs to doors where homes housed young adult children, ready to vote for Obama. Debbie's own energetic teens provided invaluable help with literature ("lit") drops, and her 10-year old daughter wrote inspiring lists of things for Mom to do.

Inspired by Adlai Stevenson as early as middle school, **Denis Gordon** went on to be completely transformed by the Kennedy campaign in 1960, choosing a career in public service that included becoming a Civil Rights lawyer and helping to implement the 1965 Voting Rights Act in the Deep South. *"State officials were trying to keep African-Americans from voting, and it required a Federal presence to enforce the law,"* remembers Denis. *"It just amazes me to think of the difference between 1967 in Mississippi and the 2008 presidential campaign."* Barack Obama's intellect and his early opposition to the Iraq invasion convinced Gordon that Obama was the best candidate. *"Eight years of the Bush administration were an absolute calamity of war, economic [mismanagement], and climate change. I have a grandson whose children will see the turn of the next century. I had to do something. I did not anticipate that the institutional Republicans' position in the government would have as its [primary] goal the thwarting of Obama's presidency at all costs and at every turn."*

"Anybody who impressed Rollie Winter was certainly someone my husband Bob and I would be willing to look at, so when Rollie invited us to his initial grassroots meeting at his home in 2007, we showed up," relayed **Denise Pierce**, a politically active local Democrat. They then spent some time gathering information and carefully evaluating two candidates, Barack Obama and Hillary Clinton. In the Virginia primary and at the 10th CD Convention, they supported Clinton, because they felt she had more experience and especially more experience in dealing with "the nastiness" some Republicans could dish out. But after the *"Reverend Wright speech"* given by candidate Obama which confronted head-on the issue of race relations in the United States, they became committed supporters, along with Denise's Republican mother who joined them.

Diane Greene grew up in Western Massachusetts, one of seven children born into a Catholic family who, though of modest means, constantly gave to others. Not only that, but her Dad voted Democratic, while her Mother supported Republicans. They could joke about it, claiming they canceled each other's vote, but went to the polls nonetheless. As an adult she studied law, as well as marketing. Her personal philosophy remained, *"We are all humans. What can we do to take care of other humans?"* Hillary Clinton became Diane's first choice in the run-up to the presidential nomination, and after campaigning for her all day one day, Diane decided to go to an Obama rally near Boston to see what all the excitement was about. It was while standing in line that she decided to vote for Barack Obama. The bi-partisan, waiting crowd was so positive, so engaged in sincere conversation regarding issues and how to solve problems, she experienced the hope of change before she heard the speech. When Diane and her husband moved to Loudoun County in August 2008, she immediately went to work at the campaign office, cleaning toilets, scrubbing moldy refrigerators, vacuuming floors—anything she could find to do, until Sophia Chitlik discovered her talent for persuasion and put her on the phones calling Undecided voters. Special memory: hearing her seven-year-old son at the bus stop talking to a friend who said, "*If McCain wins, we'll get more Christmas presents.*" Her son answered, "*So what? We have enough, and people need our help.*"

"He's too new." "He can never get elected." "I'm afraid for his life." "How can you, as a woman, not be for Hillary?" These comments were just some of the negative responses **Doris Kidder** heard when she told her many Loudoun colleagues that she supported Obama in 2007. Truthfully, she and her daughter KD had been hoping he would announce for president ever since she heard his speech at the Democratic National Convention in 2004. Doris had not only been the initial organizer of what became the tradition of a yearly Leesburg Martin Luther King, Jr., march in January of 1992, but had also been secretary, vice-chair and president of the Loudoun County Branch of the NAACP, so she knew quite a few voters. Nevertheless, almost all of her friends were either Edwards or Clinton supporters for most of 2007. In spite of having been one of Gloria Steinem's peers in the women's movement, and contrary to the stereotype of the older white woman, Doris never considered Hillary over Obama, and throughout his campaign did what she could, spending time on phone banks and in person, encouraging others to believe what their hearts were telling them.

As Treasurer of the Loudoun County Democratic Committee, **Ed Burrell** felt compelled to remain publicly neutral in the primary season of 2007. In his heart of hearts, though, he followed the Iowa caucus with growing satisfaction, talking to friends and family who lived there about the gathering support of Barack Obama. Ed felt it was time—"time for the African-American heritage to present a president, time for an intellectual to be a president, and time for someone other than the traditional politician to be president." A veteran of political campaigns, Ed had campaigned for Howard Dean in 2004 in Iowa, and also understood things like the mistake Jimmy Carter made by conceding too soon in his re-election bid in 1979. Not only did Ed participate in canvassing for VV08, but he also organized and brought a bus load of supporters from Leisure World to the Ida Lee rally on October 22, 2008. Several colleagues from his Democratic club in Leisure World volunteered in the county for three campaigns in 2008. Ed has specific campaign advice that future managers need to hear.

A strategic thinker, **Elizabeth "Liz" Miller**, fondly known as the "Doorbell Queen," understands that campaigns are won by boots on the ground. So even though her mother, step-mother and grandmother in New York were all avid Hillary Clinton fans, Liz went searching on the George Mason University campus for signs of energized supporters. Discovering the students to be excited about Obama and no one else, she knew they would work and vote for him, but were likely to stay home if any other candidate received the Democratic nomination. The women in New York, however, would not only volunteer, but also give money for whoever won the Democratic nomination. The logically obvious choice had to be Barack Obama. He could win with this combination. She knocked over a thousand doors and performed countless other tasks, phone banking, and recruiting volunteers. (And she can tell you–strategically–why Loudoun County voted in Barack Obama and Mark Warner—but also voted 70% for a Republican congressman.) Loudoun voters reject the straight-ticket option. You have to win these Independents. Listen to her full interview—and Liz will tell you how.

Raised in Connecticut, but inspired by a Southern grandmother who considered Election Day a religious event, **Emma Ancrum** enthusiastically answered the early 2007 phone calls for Obama volunteers. Responding to Marcia Carlyn's open invitation to "do what feels right...this is your campaign," Emma started with phone banking and data entry, then naturally gravitated to initiating and coordinating a sustained voter registration drive in the Loudoun County African American faith communities. Invited to speak at churches and special events, Emma enjoyed sharing childhood stories she heard from her Grandparents about their voting experiences in the Deep South. Today, the story is more poignant than ever before. One grandparent, the late Virginia Beaton White, born and raised in Ridgeland, SC lived to see the first African American elected

President of the United States of America. For Emma, the 2008 campaign was more than just learning about grassroots organizing. It was the fulfillment of a hope and dream that her grandparents never could have imagined.

"I was excited about the idea that the Capital of the Confederacy could hand the Presidency to an African-American. You get up in the mornings for things like that!" **Evan Macbeth,** knowing that Virginia is a swing state, understood that it would take passionate energy to turn it Blue for Barack. Shortly before the Virginia primary, he found that passion and that energy at the February 2008 Jefferson-Jackson Dinner in Richmond. Although Hillary Clinton gave an outstanding presentation to the dinner guests, after Obama's speech the crowd *"went nuts!"* Two additional significant communications affected Macbeth in a profound way and sent him into the streets for almost nonstop door canvassing: the Emmy-award-winning video *"Yes we can,"* and the Obama speech on race relations. Evan is all about a better world for his children—both in its larger ideals and in its smallest details. Taking his adorable daughter with him door-to-door to bring about that better world was only natural. In 2012, Macbeth leads the Loudoun County Democratic Committee as the county prepares again to be a deciding factor in selecting the President of the United States of America.

Franco Luz was another one of those improbable stories in an improbable campaign. Born in the Philippines, Franco in 1968 participated in the Mexico City Olympic Games. He was a track and field runner who competed in the 1500-meter competition. He was fast; he broke the four-minute mile back in the Philippines. He didn't win in Mexico City, but he did see the world beyond the Philippines. He then took an engineering degree at Berkeley, or as he termed it at the time, "Bezerk-ley." Tandem Computers, Franco's subsequent employer, transferred him to Reston, Virginia in 1980 and a few years later, he moved to Loudoun County and got involved in Democratic politics. He became an LCDC district chair and favored Hillary Clinton in the 2008 presidential election. Disappointed and surprised by her campaign's absence in Loudoun, he realized she may not win and began to lean to Obama.

Descended from the Genghis Khan movement, the "Hazaras" who immigrated to Afghanistan, **Fred Hussein'**s parents in turn immigrated to the United States in 1980. Fred grew up and attended Virginia colleges, culminating in a degree from Virginia Tech in Electrical Engineering. He regretted voting for George W.

Bush in the first decade of the 21st century, and focused his change of heart on Barack Obama in January 2008, impressed with Obama's ability to connect with American voters of all ages. An active canvasser, Fred is proud of his first effort at grassroots action—knowing he helped to turn Loudoun blue.

Gladys Burke, business owner, mother, community leader in her church and in the NAACP, had a reservation about Barack Obama at first: would he come out strongly opposed to drug use? She needed to hear him say it, or she was fully prepared to put all of her considerable energy behind Hillary Clinton, whom she also admired and respected. Obama did give a public denunciation of drug use, and Gladys became an avid supporter—working phone banks for the grassroots Loudoun for Obama group and even attending the Leesburg rally at Ida Lee with a broken foot! She has experienced several levels of race relations in the South, due to her childhood in South Carolina and then as a business woman negotiating bank loans in Loudoun. Her interview gives a perceptive and calm account of the progression of opportunity for minorities here and their decisions regarding civic participation. Gladys' business, ADJ Enterprises, serves a large number of local candidates from all political stripes, as well as businesses, with promotion and advertising materials.

After serving in the US Marine Corps, **Horace "Mutt" Lassiter** settled down in Loudoun to be a family man and a barber. His success at both commitments is unchallenged. Since 1962, he has been cutting hair and talking politics (in addition to relationship counseling) at Robinson's Barber Shop, one of Leesburg's oldest businesses, established in 1888. After being told he couldn't serve African-American customers at the shop, Mr. Lassiter bought the business himself in 1968 and has served all races, cultures, and genders ever since. For a primer in Loudoun politics, settle yourself in his "chair," listen to his interview, and find out who won when and why, plus even how you can win the next one yourself—as well as discover the shop-talk reason Hillary lost the primary and why some African-Americans are unhappy with Obama in 2011. Mutt's favorite president was Truman, until now. President Obama plays well at Robinson's Barber Shop.

"*The Progressive Democratic Party is not as liberal in Virginia as it is in other parts of the country*," explained **Jan Hyland**. "*We focus on economic rather than 'hot button' issues.*" Jan responded early in 2007 to Don Beyer's call for $1,000 towards the Obama campaign for president because she had worked with both Don Beyer and Rollie Winter in an earlier attempt in 1995 to form a grassroots movement in Loudoun. *"Even then [1995] the thought was 'if you can win Loudoun, you can win Virginia,' but back then the Internet was new and not everyone had email, much less social media."* Jan's interview gives a practical account of how old school politics joined with new technology and a diversity of Obama supporters led by those who gave them enough options to maintain energetic involvement. Her interview is filled with unique observations about the candidate, the ingredients of a successful grassroots campaign, and why the experience in the 90s fulfilled the promise of a "wonky, theatrical, disciplined candidate."

Jane Twitmyer grew up as an "Old-time Liberal Republican," casting her first vote for Rockefeller, and she laughs as she recalls how they became extinct. As a young adult she moved to Connecticut and met many "wonderful Democrats" who had moved from New York to Stamford. Writers, professors, artists—she found a new political home. Soon she became active in civic life, chairing The League of Women Voters and serving on the School Board until "the Radical Right threw her off." A move to Loudoun for family reasons placed her in touch with Democrats who worked for Kerry, and she became active again. Obama's 2004 speech inspired her, but she didn't expect his rise to power quite so quickly. Then his speech at the Jefferson-Jackson dinner in 2008, brought tears streaming down her face. In clear contrast to Hillary's "I will fight for you," Obama's pledge that *"Together we can change America and change the world,"* created an energy that sent Jane to Pennsylvania more than once for voter registration; then into Leesburg for parades and on to active support with the Arts for Obama and GOTV with Marcia Carlyn and Gail Wise. Jane expressed the world's determination to end posturing brinksmanship. She dreamed, with Barack, that there's a better way.

Jay Robinson, self-described "geek," and globally aware, but politically inactive voter, gave his first-ever political campaign contribution to the Barack Obama website invitation. After that, he and his circle of friends—some of whom were Republicans—followed the campaign like a sports fan club, sharing daily the ups and downs online, in person and by phone; T-shirts, bumper stickers, conversations…honking and waving at other commuters on the way to work if they had an Obama logo visible. Passionate debates were held in the workplace to influence undecided colleagues. Why? *"We so wanted to show the rest of the world that most Americans are not, after all,*

{Jerks}, and that 'We the people' are still in charge of this country."

Tall, easy-going **Joe Pabis** easily brings to mind the popular icon, Jimmy Stewart—soft spoken but firmly committed. He exhibits his passion with a quiet intensity that can be deceiving if one is not attentive. A home-grown Northern Virginian, Joe spent a short time in Chicago and has lived in Loudoun County for about 10 years, working in the family business with financial records and administrative details. Initially he became involved in politics because of his growing dislike and distrust of the Republican Party in general and George W. Bush in particular. Still, he spent several months making up his mind whom to support in 2008, even after Rollie Winter first discussed the Loudoun County for Obama efforts with him. "*Now if I had thought Hillary Clinton was the best candidate hands down, well, I would have supported her,*" Joe explains, "*but considering the reality of having a Bush in the White House for four years, followed by Bill Clinton for eight years, then another Bush again—if we had had Hillary for 8 years, then by 2016, no one below the age of 50 would have ever voted for a president whose last name wasn't Bush or Clinton. This type of 'dynastic politics' is not healthy for democracy and can even lead to the possibility or at least the perception of family grudges being carried across generations.*" Joe gradually became excited with the hope for transformative change that Barack Obama offered and spent his best efforts phone banking and canvassing in 2008.

Katie Sheldon Hammler, a two-term Leesburg Town Council representative and one-term Vice Mayor, describes herself as a moderate, centrist Independent who also served in the military after attending Brown University in Rhode Island. "*I value diversity and find I vote more often for the Democratic candidate than not,*" she explains. Hammler's goal is to serve as a fiscal conservative who is socially accepting of all the people she represents. "*I disagree with the polarizing tactics of partisan politics, such as the way the Republicans scapegoat homosexuals for the purpose of arousing a voter base.*" Katie also believes in limited government and does not support the Republican extreme policies on women's health and reproductive issues. At first she hoped that the military hero John McCain would live up to his potential to be a moderate leader, but after McCain chose Sarah Palin as his running mate in order to pander to the extreme fringe of his party, Hammler committed her vote to the candidate who actually did provide a vision of Americans "*working together to solve our nation's complex problems*"—Barack Obama

Traveling the world with a father who was in the Air Force,

as well as growing up in the Viet Nam and Civil Rights era gave **KD Kidder** a vision of the possible, a love for what America might become, if only we believed we could. This vision took root in her peak activism of 1986 when she joined over 2,000 others to walk from California to DC on behalf of nuclear disarmament. The diversity of the people she was with and the people she met, along with those who helped them along the way—the ways they kept faith with each other and governed themselves gave birth to a dream. The dream found expression in the words and iconic embodiment of Barack Obama when he spoke at the 2004 Democratic Convention. KD had organized and led the Progressive Action League (PALS) in Loudoun to protest and raise awareness of the destructive policies of the Bush administration, and she frequently engaged her large email list of progressive and political friends. Marcia mentioned to Rollie that KD Kidder joined LCO on the group's MyBO site, and Rollie knew KD well from earlier campaigns. KD offered a number of important resources throughout the campaign. She, along with her husband, Neil Steinberg, offered their place of business in Leesburg for the occasional meeting, especially in the early days. In fact they hosted an important LCO planning meeting in May, 2007, with about a dozen attendees. Neil also was a big help on Election Day as a 14-hour driver. Along with KD was her mom, Doris Kidder, an extraordinary woman. They continued to work through the Loudoun grassroots for Obama organization, until Thoreau was proved correct: *"If one advances confidently in the direction of one's dreams, and endeavors to live the life [s]he has imagined, [s]he will meet with a success unexpected in common hours."*

She handed out Hillary literature at the polls in the Virginia primary, February 2008, led the Town of Leesburg to secure the region for Barack Obama's unprecedented rally in October 2008, shared the Sarah Palin rally with her ten-year old daughter whose greatest wish is to see a woman become president, celebrated with her many African-American friends, honored John McCain for his heroic sacrifice, respected Barack Obama for the content of his character—not the color of his skin—and thinks it unfortunate that Sarah Palin squandered a chance to be influential and effective when Palin chose not to bother becoming well-informed. Leesburg Mayor **Kristen Umstattd's** thoughtful, even-handed evaluation of the 2007-2008 events in this swing county illuminates the stage and the players. A clear historical account is available online in her own words.

"... soon or late the man who wins is the one who thinks he can."—

Walter D. Wintle

"*What Martin Luther King did for Black people, Barack Obama did for all the people. At first, for those of us who wanted to believe in Obama, it was almost like believing in Santa Claus…then as time went on we would talk, 'oh yeah, maybe!' Then, the negative ads of the other side convinced me that they were worried, and then I knew, he can win.*" **Lou Etta Watkins**, a Loudoun resident since the 50s, not only hoped for an Obama presidency because it affirmed an unconscious dream of her own race, but also because he inspired a positive vision of our country that she and everyone she knew wanted to be a part of. She was pleasantly surprised to see not only a multi-racial support for an African-American, but that "Black people themselves who had been brainwashed to think only White men were 'good enough' to be president," started to shed their own low self-esteem. Mrs. Watkins serves many community organizations: the NAACP, the League of Women Voters, the Balch Library advisory board, the Alliance for the Mentally Ill. Through her many connections, she helped move the discussions toward a belief that Barack Obama could actually win the presidential election of 2008.

At 95 years old, **Lydia Pokrass** could take a long view of history. Born in 1913—seven years before women could even vote—to parents who had emigrated from Norway as small children, she had direct connections to every major change in the U.S. since the Civil War. Her parents were adamantly civic minded and even donated space in their home as a polling place in Minnesota. When she was 17, Lydia went with her father to the local courthouse to bar the door so the judge could not get in to sign foreclosure papers on neighbors' farms during the Great Depression. She has been a staunch Democrat and political activist ever since. The Norwegian culture is very inclusive and abhors racial discrimination, so it was Lydia's distinct pleasure to help put Barack Obama in the White House. She held a petition-signing event at her Ashburn, Virginia, retirement apartment complex, promoted voter registration, disseminated information and hosted a post card writing party for several residents and guests.

"*I didn't think he had a chance,*" **Mary Randolph** confessed, "*but it was a wonderful thing to see so many people talking and paying attention—especially the young Black men. And, of course, I encouraged everyone I knew to vote.*" As a child, Mary had gone with her Sunday school class to DC to hear Martin Luther King, Jr., speak; and although that was an exciting trip, the crowd gathered there did not match the reverential attitude of the throng at Ida Lee on October 22, 2008. Even seeing Jack Kennedy eye to eye one day on the streets of Middleburg did not fill Mary with the same excitement she felt when she saw the caravan of Obama's cars arrive at Ida Lee. Decades of voter suppression in the county prevented her, however, from satisfying an urge to go to the Sarah Palin rally, too. In spite of wanting to see history in the making, she bowed to her daughter's fears that she might be singled out.

Mattie Lassiter lives her life in active and loving service to her faith in God, through community and personal acts—and her volunteer efforts for Barack Obama were no different. But, she did not come to this conclusion and conviction quickly or without research. First, she listened and read and determined thoughtfully that Obama had the intelligence and the character to not only win the election, but to move the country towards a healing of its past and a closer realization of the positive force in the world that America needed to be. Then she volunteered her time and voice to the phone banks that Loudoun County for Obama provided in Leesburg. Her remarkable story of their being visited by *"angels unaware,"* and of the sense of divine intervention on Election Night, November 4, 2008, gives thoughtful pause to the concept of synchronicity. Although Mattie doesn't think politics and religion mix well, she believes that morals and a clear understanding of right and wrong must inform our policy decisions at all levels of government.

Born in Long Branch, New Jersey, to a politically active family, **Mike Turner** had a lot going for him, and he developed into one of those rare human beings who can not only speak and write extremely well, but also puts in the hard work to back up his words. Mike's father was a liberal Democrat who supported John F. Kennedy in 1960 and was the Chair of the Bucks County Democratic Party in Pennsylvania. His stepmother was a rabid right-wing Barry Goldwater Republican. (That must have made their after-dinner conversations interesting.) Mike became a superb speaker, and has been a Democrat his entire life. In high school he was on the debate team and the public speaking team. Later he earned a four-year degree at the Air Force Academy. During his 24 years in the Air Force, Turner was under constant siege from the Republicans who dominated the military branch. He has been published by National Public Radio and *Newsweek* and has regularly been on the major TV networks. During Operation Desert Storm from 1990-1991, he served as Norman Schwarzkopf's Air Operations Officer. The

National Council for Credit Counseling offered Turner a job in 2005, and he moved to Loudoun County. He soon joined the local Democratic committee and Thom Beres, the LCDC Chair at the time, appointed him to head the Precinct Operations Committee for the term 2006- 2007. Mike canvassed and worked hard for local candidates. One day he began reading Barack Obama's book, "The Audacity of Hope," and became an instant believer. Soon he was hard at work again, participating in LCO activities.

No one ever actually named **Mukit Hossain** a "Holy Man," but if it is possible to live on this earth from a center of wholeness, Mukit embodied that spirit. Seen stirring stew and discussing politics in a soup kitchen, carrying petitions for obscure candidates who exhibited worthy ideals, and buying winter coats for a hundred day workers were only a few of Mukit's indefatigable contributions to a better tomorrow. Most people who also come into power by coordinating Political Action Committees and interviewing for national newspapers, or who receive death threats for their compassionate attitude toward immigrants, eventually become angry and combative. But Mukit's smiling sense of humor and earnest dialogue carried a heart of love so big that it finally simply had to rest—though not before he proved the meaning of true personal commitment. After passionately coordinating a Virginia PAC for Hillary Clinton to the tune of a quarter million dollars, Mukit stepped into the voting booth and pulled the lever for Barack Obama in the February 2008 Virginia primary. Why? Well, it was simple really. The few days before had revealed a racist theme in the political contest, and Mukit knew that a win for anyone based on that message was a defeat for everything he held dear.

"*Harris Miller has money. Jim Webb has me!*" A now well-known response by dynamo **Patti Nelson**, who won the 2006 LCDC Special Volunteer award without even being a member of the committee. Patti led a hand full of volunteers to call over 1100 voters and persuade them that Webb was the man to choose as the Democratic nominee for Virginia Senator. Growing up in Michigan, the daughter of middle class Democratic activists, working for campaigns came easily to Patti, who still glows when she describes shaking McGovern's hand decades ago. Once her children were old enough, she engaged at a level that even took her to the IOWA caucuses to canvass for Howard Dean, and it has been "*full speed ahead ever since.*" Out of that grassroots effort the local Progressive Action League was born and has remained involved and instrumental in presidential campaigns, anti-war protests and social justice causes ever since. The last Dean event held by PALS in Leesburg included the 2004 convention speech by Barack Obama. There, Patti remarked, "*I can't wait to campaign for this guy,*" and so she did—every day and night for months, with the full support of her family who kept the home fires burning. After continuing to phone voters right up until the polls closed, Patti retreated to her own car and cried tears of exhaustion and hope. She was tired of making compromises on the right thing to do. Obama had to win. Ten years of constant effort after a youth filled with ideals, was enough. "*However it goes,* she told herself, *"I did all I could, for years and years and years."*

At 6 o'clock on Election Day, "Pink State Politics" came to the Leesburg campaign headquarters to film **Phyllis Randall** working there on behalf of Barack Obama. She knew they had also been to the McCain headquarters, so she asked, "*How busy is it over there?*" And the answer she got back was, "*Well, it's busy, but nothing like THIS!*" Phyllis knew then that Obama would be the next President of the United States, because her considerable political experience gave her an understanding that Loudoun is a swing county in a swing state. She had been following the Senator since his early days in Illinois and had volunteered before the Virginia primary to conduct outreach to all county faith communities. Then, two weeks before the election she began driving early voters to the polls. On Election Day she drove continuously all day—taking some to the polls who had not voted in over 25 years. Randall believes passionately in civic participation and took her two adolescent sons to the headquarters frequently to work, telling them, "*Someday you will tell your grandchildren about this.*"

Rev. Reginald Early—as pastor of a cooperative parish, Willisville Chapel United Methodist Church in Upperville, Virginia, and Mt. Zion United Methodist Church in Hamilton, Virginia, as well as President of the Loudoun County Branch of the NAACP—could not canvass or phone bank on behalf of candidate Barack Obama, but he could give financial support, and so he did. When he heard then-Senator Obama speak at the 2004 Democratic convention he knew that a future in leadership was coming. He just didn't know how soon that would be realized. "*As recently as 1965, some of us [African-Americans] died in the struggle simply for the right to vote, and many of us were afraid the country wasn't yet ready to be led by [even] a brilliant African-American. I'm simply glad I lived long enough to see this—to realize we are better than we thought we were, as a country.*"

Rudy Hilado—handsome son of Philippine immigrants, young father, high-tech (work from home!) professional—chose Loudoun County as his home after he and his wife made an exhaustive tour of East Coast communities and schools. Leesburg, they felt, would be the perfect charming place to raise their children—beautiful surroundings, good schools, nearby international airport. What he didn't know was that his progressive, more liberal viewpoint would be in the minority. And when he found himself surrounded by Republican signs every fall—he quietly began to plant his own, which led to a district chairmanship in the Loudoun County Democratic Committee, months of organizing and canvassing and thousands of personally financed Obama/Biden balloons for parades. Unwavering in friendly assertion, Rudy lives his own ideals of a better world by *"being the change he wants to see."*

"I'm just a skinny kid with a funny name," said Barack Hussein Obama, on July 27, 2004, which ignited a passion in **Ruthi David**, who said to herself, *"I'm just a housewife from Chantilly."* With that, she began to follow the Draft Obama movement. As soon as Obama announced and put up his website, she founded a group called "Families for Obama," and then tracked down the closest Obama campaign space, which turned out to be a Mid-Atlantic fundraising office in DC. She was actually the very first volunteer to call their office, and they told her to come on in. This was so early-on that she and three other paid staffers got to see Barack at least weekly, when he would come in to sign books. After that, both their worlds exploded, and Ruthi became a high-end fund raiser, as well as leader in the Virginia Women for Obama steering committee. It was through this Committee and Loudoun's Leslie Brooks and Theresa that we interacted with Ruthi. To top it all, her photography skills were recognized, and she captured the important events for a year and a half—through the Inauguration. Her nine-year-old son became her fascinated escort to thrilling dinners and exhausting canvasses alike. Everyone "got their hands dirty," said Ruthi, "and my son understands he helped change the world." And so he did—because his mother identified with an audacity to hope that America was still a land that had *"faith in the simple dreams of its people, the insistence on small miracles."*

Ryan Myers describes himself as one of the *"First Free,"* meaning the generation of African-Americans who never experienced segregation or Jim Crow. Originally from North Carolina, he was attracted to politics as an early teen, favored to win a student body election. After earning degrees in Finance and establishing himself in national organizations as a leader, friends of friends led him to a wedding in Chicago also attended by Senator Barack Obama, and so the journey began. He acknowledges that in some cities and states, Democratic Party insiders often block African-American inclusion in the party structure—but that Blacks are fast-tracked in the Republican Party. (Once the Civil Rights generation is gone from power, what will this mean to party allegiance?) The key wisdom in Myers' story, though, is what he learned while trying to become a National Delegate to the Democratic Convention in 2008, after running for local school board and also serving on the Loudoun County Democratic Executive Committee. He knows now what it means to "plant wheat early on for an eventual harvest." Those who know the rules, control the game.

S. Ann Robinson grew up in a small West Texas Disciples of Christ church that taught her *"faith without works is dead."* Coming of age during the decade of John F. Kennedy and Martin Luther King, Jr., meant that teaching was melded with public policy viewpoints. *"I was fortunate to live in an era when a 'rising tide lifted all boats.' There's no reason why it can't be so now; we are all interdependent,"* asserts Ann. Her diverse experiences as a business manager/comptroller, military wife and mother of a son in combat, instructor of adults in workforce development, and grandmother of a child born profoundly deaf all inform her knowledge and views on current events. She has lived in Loudoun for 22 years, and is now a Unitarian-Universalist because of its inclusive philosophy and respect for all religions. Ann supports more than a few local NGO groups, and also works as a freelance writer. Early in 2007, she favored Bill Richardson, but influenced by Rollie Winter and Marcia Carlyn to give Obama a closer look, she helped with petitions, post cards, parades, letters to the editor, and phone banking, as well as serving as an Obama delegate to the 10th Congressional District Convention.

Those who have only one hour in their busy lives to give in researching "what happened here," would be well served by listening to **Thom Beres**' dispassionate interview on the Swing County website. One of those rare individuals who can choose with his heart and then let his head and hands do the work, Thom gathered his strong leadership experience as a Veteran and former military officer engaged in counter-terrorism to serve as Chair of the LCDC during the formative year of Loudoun County for Obama. And at the same time, he organized and led Veterans for Obama. His understanding of the larger dynamics of how political groups fit together (or not), what motivates volunteers, how to focus on the smallest details of management, and how to use conflict resolution all focused on the mission. Thom never lost sight of the goal: to effectively deliver an America that, for three centuries, had been struggling to be born.

A true "Liberal," **Timothy Wyant** worked tirelessly for a sustainable future of peaceful co-existence for man and nature itself, often standing in small anti-war vigils or holding ignored signs with colleagues in the Progressive Action League (a local activist group he helped to found in 2005) at the local farmers' markets. Timothy understood the meaning of the old Navajo commandment to *"stand for what you believe even if it is a tree standing alone."* Producer of the film, "Who Killed the Electric Car," and youthful friend of Don Beyer, he came to the Obama campaign in its earliest moments by attending a social function in the spring of 2007, given by the former Lieutenant Governor of Virginia and current Ambassador to Switzerland. Over the years, Tim found he liked to work for his candidate quite independently of the organized campaigns or local Democrats. Although Tim was not an immediate supporter, as the then Senator Obama was too centrist for Timothy's strong principles, he did vote for Obama in the primary and actively supported him in the general election as well. After all, the world simply could not survive another eight years with someone like George W. Bush in charge.

Tom Bellanca spent his formative years, not only traveling throughout Europe, but absorbing the experiences of a military father who was the congressional liaison for NIH, as well as a submarine officer. The culture shock of returning to the US as a teenager, after a long tour of duty in Italy, sent Tom to the CNN channel as the only media he could bear to watch. The contrast of how Americans viewed the world, compared to what he had personally experienced, filled Tom with dismay. Being a congressional intern for a time allowed him to express his love of politics, but both of the Iraq Wars distressed him in contrast to what he thought foreign policy should be, since part of his family's experience had actually been in countries that exposed them to terrorism. Bill Clinton's approach to foreign policy aligned most closely with Tom's views of the world. Dulles district chair for the Loudoun County Democratic Committee, he became a quiet Hillary Clinton supporter in 2008, but Obama's win pleased both him and his Republican parents, as a change from George W. Bush.

Tom Marshall was born in Washington, DC and grew up in

Alexandria, Virginia, with parents who were strong Democrats. Tom's mother passionately supported Adlai Stevenson and poignantly died while listening to Stevenson speaking on the floor of the Democratic Convention. Tom's core issue is education (Marshall served as an elected member of the Loudoun County School Board 2007 - 2011), and he believes the Democrats are more committed to public education than the Republicans are. Tom began working for campaigns with the Jimmy Carter election cycle in the 70s. A strong supporter of Hillary Clinton, he honestly felt shocked when she lost the Virginia primary. But he quickly moved on, supporting Barack Obama with donations, phone banking and canvassing.

Toni Boyd knew something had to be done after watching the 2004 Kerry results come in, losing to George W. Bush a second time. Astonished that the country would make that choice considering his dreadful mismanagement of virtually everything, Toni decided to make a personal commitment. In 2006, she looked at the field of candidates and picked Barack Obama as the one who could win. "Hillary was too polarizing, but my poll of varied voters, including Republicans, gave me feedback that the moderates would vote for Obama. He was my first choice." After that, Toni worked night and day in every way she could to make a difference: voter registration, canvassing, phone banking, opening her home to staffers who needed a place to sleep, and organizing the Loudoun County Women's Forum, a large town hall meeting held in October 2008 which featured Susan Eisenhower, Megan Beyer and other Women for Obama. Toni starred in a commercial at the website http://www.youtube.com/watch?v=y3PxSiyLOhE. Her poignant interview is full of stories about face to face angry Republicans, McCain canvassers who took her door hangers off and replaced them with theirs. Undaunted, she kept working, understanding that every minute to the last minute would be needed. As precinct captain of an eastern Loudoun district, Toni proudly relays that her precinct voted for the Democratic nominee for the first time since the 60s.

Born in Somalia to a father who worked for the United Nations, **Zahra Abar** grew up as a citizen of the world, spending her formative years in Switzerland, her adolescence in France and Britain, her teens in Egypt and her college years in California. California motivated her to make America her home; and after her brothers were shot and killed in the Somalia civil war, she established residence in South Riding, near the US Capital, with a political asylum status. The 2004 presidential campaign afforded her the first opportunity to vote, and when she heard Barack Obama's speech at the Democratic Convention, she felt so stunned, she didn't move for over half an hour. His was an extraordinary intellect with the experience and knowledge to understand the world in all its complexities. America could lead in the right direction with this man at the helm. Eventually Zahra's home became a campaign hub for other volunteers to spend the night, phone, complete data entry, and launch canvasses. This included overnight stays by single mothers with their children. "*It was a movement, not a campaign.*" Zahra feels that next to her children, her work in the 2008 grassroots movement gave her the most meaningful experience of her life. "*I loved it. I believe in America, and I believe in the Constitution. I wanted to be a part of the democratic process. I would never have had this kind of opportunity in any other country.*"

The Big Rumble

Bad politicians are sent to Washington by good people who don't vote.—William E. Simon, Secretary of the Treasury under the Nixon Administration

Labor Day usually marks the kickoff for campaigns at all levels. The second act was about to begin, and the Big Rumble of 2008 ready to start. Multiple stages were scattered around the county. Conventions over, candidates selected, zookeepers trained, strategy devised, and the audience ready to tune in to the election. The question now was whether the troops and bit-actors would show up to do battle.

Success seemed promising. We were mad as hell and we weren't going to take it anymore. Eight years of the Bush administration had trashed the country, trashed the economy, and had us involved in at least one senseless war. Bill Clinton had run up big federal budget surpluses that Bush threw into the rat-hole of the Iraq War, which many believed did nothing of value for the American people. It did, however, kill more Americans than died in the September 11 attacks, even though Iraq had nothing to do with those attacks. Well, a lot of us were motivated, enough so that we were going to the streets and phones to change all this. And we weren't just settling on the lesser of evils; we had someone we could believe in.

All our key players were poised for action, and the campaign began in earnest. We were ready for volumes of new volunteers, and we were not disappointed. Hundreds arrived in Loudoun County on Labor Day weekend; hundreds more began pouring in the following weekends, joining the hundreds of newly awakened locals. Our zookeepers continued to train the dedicated and talented among them as junior zookeepers who, in turn, supervised the new callers and canvassers in Loudoun County.

Timothy Wyant, the Farmer's Market guy introduced earlier, was ready to roll! He had his team primed to hang out the next eight weekends at the same location in Purcellville they had used the four previous years. In fact, the market operator was expecting him. Tim had the material (signs and stickers) he needed for Warner and Feder, but much to his dismay, there was nothing yet for Obama. The Obama Campaign just wasn't into signs and literature yet. They figured that anyone who really wanted them would just buy them. They were right. Over the next two months Tim personally bought about $3,000 worth of stickers and signs and gave them to his 'market' constituents. How's that for commitment?

When Tim showed up the first day at the market with the morning crew, he was stunned to find people actually looking for him. That was a first. You must understand that although we were a swing county, Purcellville is in the western part of Loudoun County, smack dab in the middle of rural and red Republican Loudoun County. In past years, his team's effort to make significant contact with local voters was a hard slog, the whole long day. Because they displayed signs clearly indicating whom they were supporting, shoppers tended to be reluctant to engage with the Democratic volunteer activists.

But the attitude in 2008 was clearly very different. Immediately upon Tim's arrival, people approached his truck and actually started making conversation. Many wanted Obama yard signs, bumper stickers, and the occasional voter registration form. Some even signed up as supporters or volunteers. Yes, this year it was hugely different.

This story about Tim reminds me about a conversation I had with Rollie about signs. I obviously hit another of his hot buttons.

"Ed, this certainly was one of the most contentious decisions made by the Virginia Obama campaign. They did so much that was right, but I believe they were dead wrong on this decision. They were so obsessed by walking and talking, they didn't give much credence to our past campaign strategies in Virginia. What did we know about campaigning? We had lost for 44 years, right? What they didn't realize was that there were thousands upon thousands of Virginians who wanted to identify with, and be a part of, this campaign. Most of them were never going to make phone calls or canvass; it just wasn't their thing. Basically, putting out a sign or attaching a bumper sticker enabled a supporter to shout out to the world, 'This is my guy! I identify with him! He is worthy of my vote.' This act satisfies a fundamental need humans have to 'belong' to a subset of the community. And this public declaration can open up a dialogue with neighbors, an activity the Obama campaign strongly encouraged. We want our signs and bumper stickers! What happened there in Purcellville makes my point."

Many of our supporters even purchased small batches of expensive bumper stickers and yard signs on their own and most shared them with the LCDC and campaign offices. Later to reduce costs, they linked up with other Obama groups to place large orders with an online vendor. Todd Smyth, a volunteer who lived in Fairfax County, was a big-time Obama supporter, and coordinated material buys for the Northern Virginia localities. His help with obtaining campaign material at a much-reduced cost was very useful. Some of the Obama-Biden bumper stickers ordered by LCDC did arrive in mid-September and were quickly distributed at the Obama and LCDC offices in Leesburg. The LCDC Obama yard sign order unfortunately was delayed due to a hurricane and didn't arrive for another month (only three weeks before the election)!

As it turned out, several of the yard signs were stolen or vandalized throughout the campaign. In response, Marcia sent the Big List supporters LCO's instructions on how to contact the Sheriff's Office and file an incident report with the LCDC if this happened to them. However, we didn't want folks to spend any time on yard sign retaliation—it was much more important for them to "get even" by canvassing, phone banking, entering data, or volunteering in other ways to help Barack Obama take Loudoun County.

The Button Lady, Patti Maslinoff, continued to make hundreds of creative Loudoun County for Obama buttons which became "hot items" and were widely distributed. Sophia Chitlik, the young Obama staffer who was about to set up shop at Larry Roeder's home in South Riding, wasn't particularly keen on Patti's buttons—that is, until one day she had some friends in town to see a Redskins game. Patti made and gave Sophia "Redskins for Obama" buttons which were a huge hit, and Sophia was hooked.

The last few weeks before the election were wild and crazy for LCO! Toni Boyd and the Loudoun Women's group did a great job coordinating a very successful Women's Issues Forum on October 4. The large town hall meeting featured Susan Eisenhower (an expert on U.S.-Russia relations and granddaughter of President Dwight Eisenhower), Melody Barnes (who later served as Director of the Domestic Policy Council for the Obama administration), and other prominent female speakers.

LCO volunteers played important roles helping out at the newly opened Obama campaign offices in Sterling, Ashburn, Purcellville, and South Riding. In addition to canvassing, phoning, and entering data, a handful of Eager Beavers worked long hours coordinating office logistics. Steve Ames, of course, was in the thick of things. Many others who didn't have the time to volunteer brought food and supplies (including gas cards and prepaid cell phones), cleaned the offices on a regular basis, and served as greeters. Greeting volunteers who arrived at each office was a critical role since hundreds of Obama enthusiasts from Virginia, Maryland, DC, and farther away descended on Loudoun County during this final push.

In fact, we learned that the national and state Obama campaign offices were telling most new volunteers to go to Loudoun County. These raw recruits had to sign in and be directed to the trainers. In addition to helping out at the new campaign offices, our LCO team also provided lodging for out-of-state volunteers; created poster signs and handed them out at "honk and wave" events; participated in Faith and Values discussions (organized by LCO's Jan Wilson); joined the Loudoun Democrats in the Leesburg Halloween Parade (as we had the previous year before the primary); and signed up to work on Election Day. A successful environmental fundraiser for Obama (organized by Brennan Van Dyke) was held at beautiful Glen Ora Farm in Middleburg. The event featured several top environmental leaders who discussed the importance of Obama's plan to address global climate change.

In October, Marcia and Rollie agreed to send Scott Safranek (Obama's Data Director for Virginia) the information LCO had collected over the previous 18 months about strong and leaning Obama supporters in Loudoun County, including those who had already volunteered (N=1,175) and those who said they would like to volunteer (N=655). By this time, the grassroots organization had over 4,000 Obama supporters living in Loudoun County on our Big List. We did not include the supporters' email addresses or cell phone numbers since we had agreed to keep that information confidential. Scott said he would update the Virginia and Obama VAN databases with the other new information. Our goal was to increase the efficiency of our GOTV effort to secure an Obama victory in Loudoun County. We also thought that adding this information to the VAN would be very helpful to Democrats in future elections.

Given all the events that were happening during the final weeks, there was a wealth of information that Marcia included in the emails she was sending out to supporters on the Big List. To make her emails even more readable, she decided to reformat them and again reached out to Diane Greene, an Eager Beaver with a lot of PR expertise, who had helped her earlier with the email format. The two of them decided to introduce colors, use tables to list all the canvassing and phone banking events, and divide each email into three sections—ways to volunteer, announcements, and fun events.

Marcia was now sending out emails every 4-5 days to keep people well informed. It took quite a while for her to compose each message and send them out since there were now so many Obama supporters on the Big List (over 2,300 email addresses). Because of the limitations of her email provider, she had to break the list down and send to only 100 supporters at a time. That was a real pain, but it was worth it because the response was unbelievable—similar to what had happened in the weeks before the primary election. Hundreds of supporters who had been getting these updates for months decided it was finally time to volunteer! Scores of them had questions and Marcia did her best to answer each one personally as she had done for the last 18 months.

Our April postcard campaign for the Pennsylvania primary was such a success that LCO decided to do an expanded version of it as an LCO project, a useful project for those who didn't feel comfortable walking or talking. Judy Ross tells us the details:

"Lina Burton and I organized this project. We started it in July 2008, and held the completed postcards for delivery just before the election. Altogether, 30,000 postcards were written—5,000 by people in Maryland, 5,000 by people in Fairfax and Arlington counties, and 20,000 by people in Loudoun. I had a lot of help distributing the postcards and then collecting them from the volunteer writers. Lina concentrated on her friends in the Middleburg area; Eva Marie Suntum, Sterling; Patti Maslinoff, Leesburg; and Toni Rader, Purcellville. Joyce McLaurin regularly pitched in and wrote several hundred from her hospital bed. I worked with the MD and Fairfax organizers, giving out boxes of unwritten cards and to accepting back the finished cards. Obama's Chicago headquarters provided me with the database of names/addresses for registered women voters in the 10 main swing counties in Virginia. I produced labels from that list which were applied to finished postcards at 'labeling parties' held in the last weeks before the election.

"Final labeling was completed at the home of Gail Wise on Saturday October 25. Patti Maslinoff, Lina Burton and I delivered boxes and boxes of postcards to the Leesburg post office on that day. Altogether, nearly a thousand people worked on this project for more than three months. It was quite an effort."

Professionals in the Democratic Party believed that a strong field operation would boost voter turnout by 3-5%, but LCO's grassroots efforts in the primary proved that a well-organized, enthusiastic field operation could improve voter turnout by a much higher percentage. This was especially true in small-turnout elections, as was common in Virginia presidential primaries. If an election would otherwise be close, field operations would definitely make a difference in the outcome. Although Republicans carried Loudoun County in the general election of 2004 by a whopping 12% (56%-44%), George W. Bush was so unpopular in 2008 that the Obama Campaign and the VV08 Campaign believed field operations could make a decisive difference in Loudoun County as well as in Virginia. This turned out to be absolutely true, especially because the Republicans failed to mount an effective field operation of their own. And since the polls were showing a close race in Virginia for the first time in decades, volunteers in Loudoun County and elsewhere started to come out in droves to focus on the campaign.

When the VV08 Campaign arrived in early June 2008, it ran phone-banking operations out of the Ashburn field office and the LCDC office in Leesburg. In Ashburn, VV08 staffers Dan Chavez, Rachel Fulk, Kurt Gonska, and Conrad Chaffee ran phone banking with the help of volunteers whom they had recruited. In Leesburg, Conrad Chaffee set up Deborah Morbeto, who we introduced earlier in this chapter, to run phone banking out of the LCDC office on King Street. Deborah also did canvassing and data entry. She was particularly effective on the phone. A month or two before the election, VV08 and CFC established several more canvassing and calling hubs.

Providing food for the canvassers and those who did the phone banking was another way to help out during the campaign. Volunteers prepared home dishes, desserts, and more. Nobody ever went hungry at the field offices. In Ashburn, Robin Posey Blue was known as the "Cookie Lady" because she brought in home-baked cookies dubbed "Victory Cookies." She used an old family recipe called "On Top of the Stove Cookies." She or her husband, Reggie, would make them, and Robin would take them to the office on Tuesdays. Robin also canvassed, called, did data entry, and even ran errands. She made over 3,000 phone calls for the VV08 office. Quite a trooper!

Carolyn Ronis, who worked quite independently for several months, hooked up with CFC after they opened up the Sterling office. She was known as the "Muffin Lady" because she was always bringing in home-baked muffins. Carolyn also did canvassing, phone banking, and food baking for other volunteers.

Sometimes, there was quite a bit of drama on the canvassing trail. In October, Kathy Mohun, the famous Rock Lady, and her sidekick Bonnie Boyd were on a rural road just north of Purcellville not too far from Lovettsville. They're knocking doors and they go up to one door, knock, knock, knock and nobody answers. They leave Obama literature behind and return to Kathy's car. Then the door opens, a man comes out, and Kathy and Bonnie get out of the car to speak with him. The man picks up the literature, looks at it, and goes ballistic. "Get the f*k off my property," he yells. "I don't want any f*king terrorist as a president, get the f*k off my property!"

This continued for a while and Kathy was thinking, "Oh my God! We gotta get out of here." So they started running down the street and the guy at the door took off after them in hot pursuit. When Kathy and Bonnie made it safely into their car, he continued by pelting Kathy's car with rocks. Kathy called the Loudoun County Sheriff's department to file a complaint. And then they continued canvassing because this kind of thing was just like earning another merit badge. Besides, it gave them a new story to tell.

The next day Kathy filed an official complaint with the Loudoun County Magistrate. A Loudoun County Sheriff went out and arrested the man, booked him, fingerprinted him, and threw him in jail. Meanwhile, there was the little matter of $800 in damages to the car, so Kathy sued him in court. The man settled and paid the full amount of the damage plus court costs. The court gave him a year of probation with a requirement to take anger management classes. There was a bit of a coda at the settlement when his wife stood up in open court and announced that the whole incident had strengthened their marriage.

In another incident, two other canvassers headed to a targeted house in Leesburg and found two cars without tires parked on the grass in the front yard. Motorcyclists sporting gang colors on the backs of their black leather jackets were working on their bikes. There was enough grease and oil on their hands to stock a large Pennzoil distributorship.

"Howdy," the canvassers said, "we're out working for the campaign and wonder if John Doe is available?" I call him John Doe because three years after the event, I can't recall his real name. One guy looks up and says he is John Doe. "Just wonder if you have decided to vote for Mr. McCain or Mr. Obama?" After a few seconds he looks up and says, "I'm voting for Obama." Who would have thunk it? Sometimes in this line of work, things don't go so smooth. On this day, they did!

Mike Turner had a similar experience. He was given a door to canvass and in the front yard was a biker with his bike and his "old lady" with him. Until you've done it, you can't imagine how intimidating this can be. But Mike didn't shy away from anything. If the door was on the walk sheet, Mike went to the door. He asked them if they were Republicans or Democrats. The biker shouted back at him, "We are Democrats." You never know what you'll encounter at the door.

On another canvassing day, when you walk up to a house with 400 cigarette butts on the sidewalk right outside the front door, you know pretty quickly you're in for a bumpy ride. When two canvassers approached this house they encountered a heavyset lady in a Muumuu dress. She was sitting in a vinyl folding chair chain-smoking Chesterfields. The canvassers introduced themselves and made their pitch and the lady responded that her husband had bit the dust the week before. How about that for a start? She said her husband decided the car could use a little cleanup, and while attending to it, just keeled over the hood of the car on the spot. He even had the hose in his hand when he expired, if you can imagine that.

So now she sat in the front yard chain smoking Chesterfields talking to canvassers because that was probably the most positive thing that had happened to her in a long time. Every few minutes she would flick another cigarette butt on the sidewalk or in the flowerbed. When asked whom she was supporting for president she pointed with her left hand to an partially hidden Obama sign in the flowerbed. With that response, she automatically became a '10' in their book!

One of the more remarkable aspects of the Campaign of 2008 was the number of non-US citizens who came to Loudoun County because they believed in Barack Obama. They also believed that the Bush administration was a disaster for the United States and for the world in general. They went home with some of their own canvassing stories to tell their friends and families.

One non-US citizen learned that there was a direct flight from his country to Loudoun County. So he booked a flight at his own expense to Dulles International Airport in October that plopped him right down in Loudoun County within five miles of two Obama campaign hubs. He started phone banking on his first day. Then he prepared canvass packages, did data entry, and canvassed door-to-door. He soon graduated to managing a canvass staging location in eastern Loudoun County with similar responsibilities as those of a paid field organizer. This guy was dedicated, working 12-15 hours a day.

While door knocking, he became the only Obama volunteer in the 2008 campaign to canvass a witch! It happened on Halloween night. The lady of the house came to the door dressed as a witch, complete with costume, white makeup, black lips, and blackened eyes. She had a moving skeleton in the doorway. The witch was utterly astounded that a volunteer would come from overseas to campaign for Barack Obama. He was equally astounded to find a witch greeting him at the door!

One of the high points of this volunteer's campaign experience was attending the final Obama rally in Manassas, Virginia on November 3, 2008, the night before the election. There were over 90,000 people in attendance. He described the rally as an incredible experience, and cheered himself hoarse. And after only three hours of sleep, he was up and at the Obama field office by 5:00 a.m. to work on Election Day. And he couldn't even vote for Obama because he was not a US citizen. He just wanted to bring change to this country and thus change the world! He wasn't the only foreign volunteer to campaign that year; there were several from Europe working in Loudoun County, but his efforts were extraordinary by any measure.

I have already told you about a lot of activity in South Riding emanating from the McDermott residence. This family continued their outreach to the community up to and including Election Day in November. Ali also was responsible for coverage of the several South Riding precincts within the Dulles district, with son Darby still serving (unknown to Rollie) as one of the precinct captains.

In the short history of this fast growing housing development, South Riding was a very Republican area, and the McDermotts early on received cool receptions to their campaigning. After months of hard work and contacts, this began to change. The McDermotts were helping to change the political landscape around them. This is what is known as persuasion canvassing—canvassing where you attempt to change the views of people at the door. They were "Making a Difference", and they saw it on the ground. Much of their success may have stemmed from the inspiration of seeing two young boys so enthusiastic about Barack Obama.

Michael Morbeto, another eight-year-old, canvassed hundreds of doors in Leesburg for Obama with his mother Deborah Morbeto. He was knocking doors faster than Little Richard in "Keep A-Knockin," and wasn't bashful at all about speaking to strangers. Nothing discouraged him; he pounded doors for months and months and dismissed rejection easily.

These young people had four characteristics in common. First, the candidate and their parents' support motivated them. Second, they were not afraid to approach strangers to speak with them. Third, they did not hesitate to try to change the minds of Republicans and influence Independent voters. Fourth, they were not discouraged by rejection, and just went to the next door unfazed by the rebuff. No doubt there were many more young people like these on the campaign trail.

Young people are extremely effective canvassers. Potential voters admire those who are willing to act on their beliefs. There is a certain emotional feeling transmitted in listening to a young person willing to stand up for his or her convictions. For this reason adults should, whenever possible, take a young person with them when door knocking and let the youngster do much of the talking. The results will improve significantly.

A Fairfax political friend of Ali's, who knew of her work in Loudoun, mentioned it to one of the new Obama staffers coming aboard at the Fairfax office. Since staffers are rewarded based on the doors knocked and phone calls made by the people they recruit, this staffer decided to ignore county lines and to take advantage of the McDermott's efforts. The overly ambitious Fairfax field organizer called Ali and told her she should start taking instructions from him and report her numbers of how many doors knocked and phone calls made. As you can imagine, she wasn't buying into that, telling him, "You're cute, but this operation started as grassroots, and it's going to finish grassroots. Do what you have to do, but I am not reporting to you." The McDermotts stayed grassroots and were very effective over a long period of time because they knew their area and their neighbors better than any outside field organizer. But they were cooperating big time with Rollie regarding Election Day coverage.

As Election Day approached, the CFC Obama staff decided to open a field office in South Riding. Enter stage left—Larry Roeder and family. They were willing to provide an extraordinary service to

The Big Rumble

the campaign. In late September, Larry and family actually let CFC occupy their entire first floor and basement of their spacious home in South Riding. Then CFC's super field organizer, Sophia Chitlik, was transferred from the Leesburg office to run the show. Larry's home became more active than most other major hubs! A den was turned into an office for a former senior State Department Official who was responsible for arranging VIP visits (including more than one from Madeleine Albright) to help boost the morale of the volunteers.

Volunteers would come to the house, pick up walk packages prepared by "Captain Data", Aaron Edlow and his cadre of trained turf cutters, and canvass the neighborhoods of South Riding. By the week before the election nearly 500 volunteers were processed through the Roeder hub on Saturday and about the same number on Sunday. So many volunteers worked from that location and slept over, he paid to have maid service clean the house several times a week.

Larry was canvassing as well. He didn't do much phone banking because he preferred one-on-one personal contact. Larry did have one tense moment when a man carrying a rifle confronted him at the door. The rifle was pointed down, but anyone greeting a visitor with a rifle quickly gets your attention, as in very fast. But Larry Roeder had seen much, much worse. He made his pitch and was told, "I don't need your literature." That was the end of that. He left peacefully. He didn't want to damage the Obama Campaign with a splashy news story.

With all of these volunteers visiting Larry's neighborhood these last six weekends, parking spaces for his neighbors were clogged for blocks. One day a neighbor accosted him over volunteers parking in front of his house and said threateningly, "Do you realize I can take you out?" Larry, who had ridden camels in the Arabian Desert to negotiate with Bedouin tribes and negotiated with real armed killers and terrorists in the Sudan and Somalia while working for the State Department, knew the guy would back down. Larry had dealt with real murderers, the real deals, not wussies who lived in South Riding, Virginia. Larry defused the situation by telling the neighbor that he would keep volunteers from parking in front of his house. He knew it was not in the best interest of the Obama Campaign to create an incident and how best to smooth over the situation.

Sophia Chitlik did a great job of managing volunteers out of Larry Roeder's hub. She went out of her way to compliment volunteers who did a good job. Part of that was training and part was natural ability. She motivated volunteers repeatedly by praising their accomplishments. She had learned in a few short months that listening and adapting to local volunteers made her job go much more smoothly. Larry sung her praises both during and after the campaign.

One of the more interesting characteristics of the campaign of 2008 was the nearly complete absence of McCain campaign field operations in Loudoun County. The evidence we have for this is strictly anecdotal, but convincing. Late in the campaign, there were thousands of Obama volunteers on weekends canvassing in Loudoun, but only a handful of them reported seeing McCain doorknockers or literature at the door anywhere in the county.

I only experienced firsthand only one home with McCain material left at the door. It happened late in the campaign when I was with Mary Voskian, a tireless Obama campaigner. We were canvassing the Hirst Farm development in Purcellville. Only one house of about 50 homes in the development that had evidence of a McCain campaign, and was a very Republican neighborhood. Mary also campaigned for Obama at the Purcellville Farmers Market with Tim Wyant on weekends, where a McCain supporter actually spit at her one day. Another day, another circus.

A second instance was in Ashburn, where volunteers encountered a woman canvassing for the McCain Campaign with her two small children. When asked, the lady said she wanted to teach her children civic responsibility. The interesting point here was that the McCain Campaign did not send her out to canvass; she initiated the process on her own to educate her sons.

The third instance occurred when Robin Posey Blue was running a canvass staging operation out of her front yard on a cold afternoon. McCain volunteers wandered by Robin's house and she invited them over for hot cocoa.

One day after a GOTV (Get Out the Vote) meeting in Ashburn, I visited the McCain field headquarters in Sterling to check out the scene. There were nine people in the office. Six of them were men discussing the previous performance of the Washington Redskins football team. One person appeared to be phone banking. The contrast between the Obama field headquarters and the McCain headquarters could not have been starker. During the campaign, Nate Silver wrote extensively on his website FiveThirtyEight about the absence of activity in McCain field offices. Silver had people visit many McCain field offices across the United States and rarely found any significant numbers of volunteers or activity going on. A strong "ground game" by the McCain Campaign would have made Virginia a cliffhanger. Most likely, Republicans had carried the state for so many years they took a victory for granted. They were wrong.

If there were other instances of 95-year-old women registering voters and canvassing potential voters in retirement homes, we have yet to find them. Lydia Pokrass was born of Norwegian immigrants on a farm in Lac qui Parle County near Montevideo, Minnesota three years after the Titanic sank in 1912. Her parents came over from Norway shortly after the American Civil War and bought the farm from people who somehow obtained the land from an Indian tribe. Hard economic conditions had driven her parents out of Norway. There were 11 children, but two of them died very young; surviving were six boys and three girls, including Lydia.

Lydia went to college at a time when it was very rare for women to attend college. Lydia Pokrass was a true woman pioneer; she refused to become a secretary or take another menial job normally given to women. She was trained as a teacher, taught seven years, and then went to nursing school at the University of Minnesota. Then she did the unthinkable—she moved to New York City in 1936, a gigantic cultural shock for a farm girl from Lac qui Parle County. She worked as a nurse in New York City, and then enrolled at Columbia University's Master's program to get a master's degree in nursing. While there she met her future husband Albert Pokrass who was enrolled to obtain a Master's Degree in Foreign Affairs. Albert got a job at the State Department, and they moved to Washington, DC.

Lydia has been an avid Democrat all her life, and during the 2008 campaign she was a solid Obama supporter. At the age of 95, a person doesn't have the mobility of younger people, so she did what she could—she registered voters and canvassed people who lived in her retirement home. It was a remarkable story for someone her age. She plans to be active in the 2012 presidential campaign even though she will be nearly 100 years old!

Gillian Higgins was one of the few folks who lived in Fairfax County but was really connected with the LCO zealots. She came to several of our events and did a lot of early canvassing and phone banking with us—at Franco's and elsewhere. She sent the core LCO group the following email in mid-October describing a car accident she had that showed to her and to us that something very positive was going on in this country:

"Gillian's Car Accident—October 20, 2008

"Sometimes us single people get so used to not sharing our experiences and they get buried with so many of our best moments BUT not this one!

"I had a car accident yesterday...

"While backing out of a parking lot at Target in Fair Lakes, I was halfway out of the spot when I saw another car backing out directly behind me. I frantically scrambled for the button that makes my horn sound but alas! I found it just seconds before the bump in the back.

"I pulled back into the spot, and got out of my car laughing to myself at the situation—not being able to find the horn and wondering why I had to do this now. A woman in her early fifties exited the BMW that hit me and asked 'Did I get you?' 'Yes you did,' I replied. 'Let's take a look', I said.

"We both stooped behind my car looking for damage on my old dirty bumper. I said, 'You know what, I don't see anything here that might not have been there before.' She said, 'Are you sure?' 'Oh yes,' I said. Then she said, 'Can I have a hug?' Being one that loves hugs, I was not about to turn one down and so I gladly obliged, and as I hugged her I whispered: 'Now take 12 people to vote with you on the 4th.' She looked at me puzzled, looked back at her bumper with its OBAMA sticker and looked back at my car with its rear windows wearing my OBAMA yard signs (and other Obama items inside), and said 'I love you'. I returned the endearment but wished I had remembered to say 'I love you back!'

"That experience was just great—the best car accident I have ever had. I have Caucasian friends who are very dear to me, but a stranger in a parking lot who just hit my car—who would have thought it in America? Not me! Canada perhaps, but not here. Whilst this may have happened in a non-election year, I tell you...this is the America I once thought would never be. And as a foreign born citizen, this is why I got involved with this campaign—because I saw that America can change with the right leader, and in January 08 I became hopeful. There are some things that MUST be top down. Call it the OBAMA effect; whatever you call it, it's been a great experience."

Another October story and this one is personal: On the south side of Leesburg, less than a month before the election, Barbara and I canvassed a townhouse complex. We were still working for Amanda

Millard, a field organizer for the VV08 Campaign. She was good, very good, very organized. We had about 50 doors to knock on. And at every address we knew with whom to speak.

The Campaign rarely sent us into houses looking for people who were known to be strong Republicans. They were a waste of time to talk to. We were hunting for the undecideds or unknowns. This was where canvassers can make a difference. And we were in the street to make a difference. When people were in the middle, you could tip them to your side.

At this point in the game we had done this enough to know that every few weeks we encounter someone who is so unusual, or has such an atypical story, that we will walk away with something we will never forget. But nothing prepared us for what we encountered at one townhouse on this day. We were looking for a girl named Stephanie (not her real name) about 20 years of age, and I said to Barbara, "Here's another one who will be off to college". These young kids were almost always off at college, but that's who we were to look for and that's what we do.

I knocked on the door and when a man opened it I said, "Hi, my name is Ed, and this is my wife Barbara, and we're neighborhood volunteers canvassing for the election in November. I wonder if Stephanie is available."

Note that we didn't say who we worked for at this point in the conversation. We did this consciously so as to increase the chances that the McCain people would open up with us. We always told them who we worked for if we were asked or if they were Obama supporters or if they wouldn't talk. And we always said we were "neighborhood volunteers". People were much less likely to get ugly with canvassers if they knew you were a person from the neighborhood than if you were some hired gun shipped in from a place like Buffalo Breath, Wyoming. Treat us badly and we might tell your neighbors you acted badly. It worked. Few wanted their neighbors to think they treated others with disrespect.

"Well, Stephanie no longer lives here, but even if she did we couldn't talk to you."

"OK. I'll just write on this form that you can't discuss how she's going to vote."

"Look, this isn't personal. The truth is I am a paid consultant working for one of the campaigns, and I just can't discuss it with you."

So I said, "Hey, that's no problem. That's got to be very

interesting, working for one of the campaigns. You know, if you're a consultant to one of the campaigns you must find it very interesting that McCain is running a base campaign in what is a non-base year."

At this point the guy threw open the door and jumped down the steps, poked me in the chest lightly three times and said,

"OK, I'll tell you. I'm a paid consultant to the John McCain campaign working out of the headquarters office. You two look like you're our kind of people. You know something about elections, don't you?"

And I said, "Not really, but I know enough to get out and canvass. By the way, who do you think is going to win this election?"

"Oh, this election is over. I'm telling you here and now that this election is over. Barack Obama has won this election."

"Really? Why is that"?

"Because McCain is too old, looks awful on television, is running a terrible campaign, and won't listen to a damn thing we tell him."

Then he popped the question. "By the way, who do you guys work for?"

"Oh, we're volunteers for the Obama Campaign," I said.

"Shit, my own daughter's voting for him," the consultant said.

I then marked the canvassing form for Stephanie, "Probably Obama" and we're off to the next townhouse.

If a paid consultant to the John McCain Campaign working out of the national headquarters thought that the campaign was over, then the campaign was probably over. Also, what was a paid consultant to the McCain Campaign doing sitting at home on a Saturday afternoon three weeks before the election? He should have been working in the office and not chatting with Obama volunteers on his porch during halftime of the football game.

When I told this story to Amanda Millard in the parking lot of Heritage High School after canvassing she said, "I can't believe you two can dig up stuff like this." "Neither could we; just lucky, I guess." By this time, though, the circus was becoming more commonplace, in part because we were becoming adept at causing a circus. Once you've knocked enough doors you have enough perspective to make it happen. The middle ring of the three-ring circus had become the new reality. And it wasn't over, either, not by a long shot. The dancing bears and the trained elephants had yet to do their act. And the Fat Lady wasn't going to sing her song until 7:00 p.m. November 4, 2008. Lights out, curtain up: the show continues into the final act of this grand drama. Fade to black.

Some amazing new volunteers streamed into the Leesburg field headquarters on Market Street. One of the most important was Tracy Hadden Loh. Tracy's first candidate in the 2008 race was John Edwards. She was never a Hillary Clinton supporter, though she liked Hillary. Before the South Carolina primary on January 26, 2008 Tracy had switched to supporting Obama.

When the 2008 Campaign began to hit stride, a public school teacher friend named Laura Wells in Fairfax County persuaded Tracy to canvass with her. After doing it Tracy quickly concluded that she loved canvassing. She then began visiting various CFC field offices to find an office she preferred to work out of. She canvassed in Fairfax and Woodbridge, Virginia and went as far as North Carolina. The office in Leesburg made the biggest impression because the atmosphere was energized more than some of the others. She began reporting for duty every day in Leesburg. She canvassed, did phone banking and data entry. It wasn't long before Tracy was training other volunteers to do all of these activities. Three months before Election Day Tracy Hadden Low was a fixture in the Leesburg office. David Cannady, a paid field organizer at the Leesburg office drafted her to become a Deputy Field Organizer. Now Tracy was the major trainer of volunteers in the art of canvassing.

One of the salient characteristics of the Obama Campaign was that it made possible a discussion of values with potential voters, rather than just issues. Tracy Hadden Loh conducted one of the more remarkable phone calls from the Obama field office on the Friday before the election. She spoke with an evangelical Christian who expressed concern about the abortion issue. Tracy, also a born-again Christian, said that she too was concerned about abortion, but stressed that Obama was a Christian man and was committed to reducing the number of abortions. Tracy emphasized that she believed in the power of prayer and that Sunday was coming up. The lady told Tracy she was going to pray on it on Sunday and make her decision then. Tracy believed she made a difference with a swing voter on that phone call.

One of the hubs was out in Purcellville, a friendly, family-oriented town located in western Loudoun County. It was first settled in 1764 by James Dillon and located right off the old Colonial Highway, now Route 7. The village was incorporated as a town in Loudoun County in 1902 and now has about 8,000 inhabitants. Two weeks before the election, Kathryn Grant of the Obama Campaign asked Theresa to find a place to serve as a temporary field office. She found one, and it was perfect.

I got word of this and decided it would be worth a visit on my way to the Leesburg office. The new Purcellville office was just opposite of Nichol's Hardware Store, one of the great treasures of Loudoun County. "Nichols Hardware in Purcellville is a trip back in time. With its uneven wooden floors, tin ceilings and overflowing shelves, this western Loudoun County icon embodies a period of American history when personal service and word-of-mouth advertising were the keys to retail success." (See website: http://www.loudounhistory.org). I parked, whistled into the field office, and was stunned at the scene. One day after it opened the joint was jumping. At least 30 people were inside. The phone bank was jammed. You know something BIG was happening when you opened an office out in the boonies and the next day 30 volunteers were in the office and already making a difference!

There I found the famous "Flying Canvasser," Chuck Visnius, preparing to canvass. Chuck campaigned tirelessly with his son in the Obama Campaign. He is called the "Flying Canvasser" because he is an airplane pilot. He worked as a contract pilot flying people such as Margaret Thatcher, George Bush, Sr., Mikhail Gorbachev, and countless actors and actresses around the country. I asked him, "What was the most memorable flight you ever had?" He responded, "That's easy, it was Captain Kirk." He was referring to William Shatner who played the part of the original Captain Kirk in the Star Trek series. "Why was that memorable?," I said. "Because when he got in the plane he looked at me and said, 'Beam me up, Scottie.'"

Chuck and his son went around western Loudoun County knocking on hundreds of doors for Obama. They phone banked. They were right in the thick of the fight. Chuck Visnius was as good as they come, full of good stories, and a hard campaign worker. I know, I walked the streets knocking doors with him.

Bring back an old scene; dim light, Rollie's basement. He's hunched over his desk, primarily sending and receiving emails. Writing and distributing the occasional informational material needed to get his job done. Receiving and sending lots of calls on his cell phone. If the speculation about cell phones and computer monitors causing cancer is really true, he's a dead man sitting.

Shira called Rollie CFC who told him Scott (not his real name) was the point guy for CFC on Election Day. Scott was from out of state and had previously worked with labor groups and political campaigns. Rollie and Scott hit it off from the beginning, and in less than an hour, came to a quick understanding of each organization's major Election Day responsibilities. LCDC would handle transportation and all poll workers, and CFC would contact all of the identified Obama supporters multiple times by phone and at their doors the week before and on Election Day. VV08 would do the same for their precincts. Some of the drivers recruited by Bob Moses would be assigned to CFC to be used as Runners on Election Day. They would move people and material around on that day between office, hubs and staging areas.

The only unresolved Election Day activity was the check off system inside the polls. CFC was uncertain about implementing this effort, but if they did, they would use a new automated system called 'Houdini.' The major difference between their system and Rollie's was the call list. With Rollie's system, follow-up calls were made directly from the check off lists—calling all voters not checked inside the polls as they voted. Houdini inserted two additional tasks: 1) entering who voted from the check off list into the VAN, and 2) printing call sheets for use at call centers.

Rollie was quite skeptical of their Houdini system. He believed it was much too cumbersome, so he sent an email to the Obama state campaign outlining his concerns. He specifically included a warning about the likely overload on the computer server, as thousands of users were all going to want service at the same time. Anticipating that they would proceed with their plan despite this problem, Rollie strongly suggested they at least schedule an extensive trial run—simulating the expected load and fixing any problems that would be exposed. He received no response to any of his suggestions or concerns.

As Election Day approached, CFC finally made a decision for Loudoun. Scott contacted Rollie and said it was a GO using Houdini in Loudoun. But they were only going to do strong Dem precincts and asked Rollie to provide him an initial estimate of how many precincts would fit their criteria. Rollie's immediate initial response was ZERO, although he knew there may be one or two that met their criteria. Scott was skeptical, and told Rollie they would be running a query against the VAN database in a day or two and would let him know which precincts would be covered with inside checkers.

A couple of days later he came back with the numbers, and found that Rollie was right; there was only one Democratic precinct in Loudoun (which happened to be the second smallest precinct in the county). Two others were close. With that data in hand, they decided to have no checkers in Loudoun County at all. All but one of the district coordinators were happy with that news, since many were having problems filling all their other volunteer needs.

The district coordinator who was upset with this decision was Dave Kirsten of the Leesburg district. He had used Rollie's check off system in several previous elections and was a true believer. He was certain that he could readily find the inside volunteers needed to check off those who voted. Scott was finally able to get approval from the Obama state campaign officials to use Houdini for the six Leesburg precincts, so Dave started recruiting the inside checkers.

As a counterpoint to all of this frenetic activity at the hubs and staging areas, LCDC was quietly and effectively filling up the poll worker slots at each of the 62 precincts. All of the work was done by phone and email. Rollie and Kevin kept in close contact with the district chairs to keep up with their progress with their precinct coordinators in finding openers, closers, and poll workers.

Kevin ran Sunday night conference calls and for the most part, everyone participated. Questions and problems were discussed and addressed. Marcia was a big help in structuring an Excel database for us that was divided by district. That made it possible for the district coordinators to communicate their progress individually without concern for the other district schedules. Rollie maintained the total database and regularly shared it with Kevin so that the two of them could monitor the districts they were managing.

Meanwhile, Kevin Turner had set Sunday night for conference calls and scheduled the first one for October 5. Turned out he had a business trip come up at the last minute, and Rollie handled the meeting. The full notes can be found in the Appendix, but here are Rollie's highlights:

"We agreed on the roles for the LCDC volunteers to be recruited for Election Day, including driver designations and their responsibilities. The essential criteria for Route Drivers were to have a very good knowledge of election law and the duties of the outside workers. What was considered most important about the Rovers was comprehensive knowledge of Loudoun geography—knowing most main roads and how to navigate them efficiently. They should also know in advance where 15 - 20 precincts are located and how to find them most directly from wherever they may be located throughout the day. GPS would be useful (though there were not many drivers using GPS in 2008). They would also need to know in advance where the hubs and Election Day staging areas were located.

"Another major topic discussed in the conference call was how LCO related to CFC and VV08 on Election Day. The latter two organizations and their volunteers would be engaged primarily with GOTV activities—walking and phoning—and will manage those activities through their own teams at the field offices. LCDC would manage the poll work and drivers. Scott, the Obama staffer responsible for their GOTV effort, made it clear to me that CFC would use their volunteers as needed to fill in the for missing outside precinct workers or inside checkers. I was to provide him a list of these shortages needed at least a week before the election. Only LCDC was to be responsible for recruiting all precinct coordinators, openers, closers, route drivers, and rovers.

"We are using the word 'precinct coordinator' to reference LCDC precinct captains. This is because of CFC's insistence on calling 'their' chief precinct worker, 'captain'. Since LCDC was supporting all of the candidates, they could accept the 'coordinator' designation. There was a lot of overlap between the precinct captains and precinct coordinators, with one person often serving both roles.

"We discussed the generation of the GOTV check off/call sheets. If all precincts participated, we estimated that we would have about 15,000 calls to make starting at 2:00 p.m., and with 200 callers, could go through them in less than two hours. We could then do a second pull and call again at 5:30. If we were running short of time, we would only call those whom we didn't reach the first time. We also considered calling cell phone numbers on the Big List as a separate effort. Those calls would begin earlier in the day.

"Rollie pointed out that all of those working for Democrats on Election Day can legally vote absentee, and should be advised to do so. They also should sign up with the Board of Elections ahead of time to receive text messaging in the event of an emergency. Furthermore, the Secretary of the Board, Diana Price, reported that there will be 213 'books' prepared for our 62 precincts—approximately 800 registered voters per book. The books are divided alphabetically so voters can use multiple lines when voting. The number of books defined the number of inside checkers needed for each precinct (one per book).

"Jason Bresler announced that the Feder campaign had as many as 60 young persons to help us cover 30 precincts for the entire day. The names of these precincts would be known by the end of the week and this information passed on to the district coordinators by the Feder campaign. This campaign will also have four 15-seat vans available throughout Election Day to rove Loudoun County and taking people to the polls—especially from Senior Living facilities. That was very good news."

Kevin was very pleased with what was covered at this meeting. He asked Rollie to continue coordinating with the other campaigns and to describe the volunteer roles in more detail for the district and precinct coordinators so they would have a better understanding of their duties. This he did, and here is a summary of his work. The complete text is available in the Appendix.

"*DISTRICT COORDINATORS (DC):*
- *Recruit and manage Precinct Coordinators*
- *Recruit one kit assembler for November 1, 2008*
- *Confirm the names of the precinct openers and closers*
- *Obtain and report worker schedules of all precincts*

"*PRECINCT COORDINATORS (PC):*
- *Recruit and arrange training for all workers*
- *Create and maintain worker schedule*
- *Assure opener on the job by 5:30 a.m. on Election Day*
- *Either call or visit the precinct throughout the day*

"*OUTSIDE POLL WORKERS:*
- *Show up and be ready to start work at your scheduled time*
- *Do your voting outside of your scheduled time to work*
- *Greet and meet voters, handing out sample ballots*
- *Obtain contact info from interested future democrats*
- *Do not leave the polling place until your relief has arrived*

"*INSIDE CHECKERS:*
- *Find call sheets at the Democratic table if first shift*
- *Sit closely behind the person checking in voters*
- *Note that there will be multiple checkers*
- *When voter name is called, check it off on alphabetic list*
- *End your checking activity promptly at 2:00 p.m.*

"*OPENER:*
- *Work with PC before Election Day to find best location*
- *Arrive at the poll no later than 5:30 a.m. to set up*
- *Place your table(s) first, and then plant the signs*
- *Do not place your signs in front of the opponent's signs*
- *Wait until at least two first-shift workers arrive before leaving*

"*CLOSER:*

The Big Rumble

- *Remove table, material, and signs from the poll property*
- *Leave no trash behind*
- *Take the material to the designated location that evening*
- *Include the clipboard with names of future volunteers*
- *Do not lose them!*

"TELEPHONERS:
- *Will be trained on-site on Election Day*
- *Will work from 2:00 p.m. until 6:00 p.m.*
- *Call lists and a script will be provided*
- *You are calling Obama supporters who did not vote before 2:00 p.m. to remind them to go to the polls.*

ROUTE DRIVERS:
- *Work from 5:30a.m. to noon, noon to 7:00p.m., or all day*
- *Must have a working cell phone in your assigned area*
- *Verify the route to use in advance of Election Day*
- *Morning shift will start with a drive-by of assigned precincts*
- *Check in regularly with headquarter with status or problems*

Rollie was becoming more and more impressed with Jack's Route Driver plan and its implementation. Since a major part of the effort required Jack to use his home computer on Election Day to track the drivers and any reports of problems, it made sense to move all of the LCDC headquarter activities to his home from the usual location at the Leesburg office. Despite the dire warnings from a few of our old-timers, it turned out to be a very good decision.

On Wednesday, October 22, 2008, Barack Obama came to town. That's right! With three or four days' notice, the national campaign sensed possible victory in Virginia, decided to fit in another rally in Northern Virginia, and selected Leesburg!

One of the most excited of the youngsters who were looking forward to actually seeing Obama in person was Debbie Hawk's daughter, Jocci. When the day of the event arrived, Debbie was greeted in the morning with a check list Jocci had written for her. It had 18 items listed on yellow memo paper of which the first three were already checked:

Mommy-O's to do list
- Sleep
- wake up by 7:00am
- eat breakfast 7:01 – 7:10
- brush teeth 7:11 – 7:14
- Get dressed 7:15 – 7:20
- Get in "Mama Obama" mood 7:20 – 7:21

- Pack your favorite child's lunch 7:21 – 7:25
- Walk your favorite child to school 7:30
- Put Obama pin on jacket 7:45 – 7:46
- relax 7:46 – 11:00
- inhale 11:00 – 11:00 2 sec
- exhale 11:00 – 11:00 3 sec
- Go to Leesburg to volunteer
- volunteer
- Cheer on Obama!
- Help after Obama leaves
- drive home with a smile on your face

This event was the largest extravaganza Leesburg had ever experienced. Estimates of crowd size varied, but Leesburg town officials pegged it as over 30,000. The local Campaign staff had about 400 VIP tickets to pass out to their most ardent volunteers, LCDC leadership, and local government dignitaries. Marcia obtained a 'super' VIP ticket next to the stage, and Rollie was to sit with the average VIPs, ten rows back. But since there were a couple of seats unfilled, his friends encouraged him to come forward and sit with them in the second row. Senator Mark Warner and Governor Tim Kaine gave spirited welcoming speeches and both were welcomed warmly by the huge crowd.

In early October, Joyce McLaurin had moved to long-term hospice care at a facility in Maryland, more than an hour's drive from Loudoun County. But our support team continued to visit and look after her. As Judy Ross tells us, "this rally in October was Joyce's last opportunity to meet with Obama—at a picture-taking 'meet and greet' held in a tent behind the stage when he arrived. I picked her up for her last road trip. Some reporters assisted Joyce out of the car and into her wheelchair at Ida Lee Park. She was scheduled to lead the Pledge of Allegiance at this huge rally, but officials deemed it too unsafe to lift her and her wheelchair up to the makeshift stage. However, she was able to join the small group of people backstage and had a beautiful picture taken with Obama, with his glorious smile, behind her, reaching around and putting his hands on the arms of the wheelchair. After the event, Steve Ames and Tim Buchholz helped to get her back into the car. Steve followed us to her apartment in Ashburn to help get her to bed. She was in a lot of pain from the cold and hours of sitting—but she was such a trooper. That event was Joyce's last outing. Two days later she transferred from her hospice home to the hospital, and did not go home again.

"Joyce McLaurin lived long enough to see Barack Obama elected President of the United States and then to take the oath of office at his inauguration ceremony in January. She passed away from the cancer a few short weeks after he took office. She was the heart and soul of the Loudoun County Obama campaign, and we all still miss her."

As we were getting close to the election, the pieces were coming together nicely. Ted Carvis, Marcia's husband, was in charge of the "Protect the Vote" operation and had successfully recruited many attorneys to be available on Election Day to get involved if voting rights appeared to be violated. However, Rollie had never seen any sign of this kind of obstructionism at any polling place in Loudoun County. Ted also had volunteered his office as a place to assemble the precinct kits on the Saturday before the election, in addition to spearheading the creation of all the documentation and material included in the kits. This was a huge undertaking, especially because so many people had a part in providing the kit contents. All of it had to be apportioned into the precinct kits depending on the number of voters in that precinct—a very time-consuming process.

A couple of weeks before the election, Rollie had an inspiration! Looking over the Big List, he wondered whether all of those identified as volunteers had been contacted about Election Day. He was aware that several of the district coordinators were short in their Election Day volunteer recruiting and needed significant help. He also realized that VV08 and CFC Election Day plans required a large number of workers. And here he was with a Really BIG List of potential Election Day volunteers! He saw a need and a way to fill it. So he got to work, and then the sauce really hit the fan.

The Election Week Brawl

"The boys are ready for a brawl. No doubt of that.... We've got the best damn ground around, and they're hitting me with one brigade."—Brigadier General John Buford, July 1, 1863, Movie "Gettysburg"

By October 28, the campaign of 2008 had entered its final week. And activity in the Obama Campaign headquarters on Market Street in Leesburg exploded, with a several-fold increase in volunteers over any past campaign in Loudoun County. With Election Day scheduled for November 4, several hundred volunteers a day showed up at the various field offices throughout Loudoun County and doubled by Election Day. All the new trainers were swamped and new ones recruited to deal with problems. In the final weeks, as many as 10,000-15,000 volunteers showed up to work in the Loudoun County campaign, most of them multiple times.

CFC was responsible for half of the 62 precincts, and VV08 was managed the other half. Six hubs and offices were in operation, and several other were getting ready for the last weekend through Election Day. The staff and many of the key volunteers were working sixteen or more hours a day. Most were tired, stressed out, and felt overwhelmed with what yet had to be done. This environment can lead to short tempers and a misreading of motives.

For example, Rollie began implementing his idea to contact the volunteers on the Big List for Election Day duty to be sure no one was overlooked. First he contacted Marcia, who agreed to go through the Big List and send him the names of those who looked promising for working on Election Day and who may not already be lined up. About 300 names fit this criteria. Rollie went through them and struck another 50 names who he knew had been already scheduled, leaving about 250 to contact. He divided them up into three call lists and recruited three excellent, committed callers, Barbara Cunningham, Tina Shukert, and Jean (not her real name). He asked them to complete the calls by Friday, October 31.

It worked perfectly—for one day! Then, one of the callers, Jean, a good political and personal friend of his, called Rollie and questioned him about the list and the instructions. She was one of the long-time key volunteers who had worked on several earlier LCO projects, but had become one of the deputy field managers working in the CFC Sterling field office. She told Rollie that she thought this assignment was not consistent with what the CFC wanted done at this time. Rollie told her not to worry about it as this was not a CFC project, but that the results would benefit them. So she reluctantly agreed to do it. As it turned out, instead of finishing up the job, she took her concerns to the CFC staffer running the Sterling field office, and the sauce hit the fan.

The staffer was convinced that Rollie somehow had copied the names and their contact information from CFC lists, and that he was now was using them for his own purpose. This staffer, in turn, contacted Shira and Scott, the CFC GOTV staffer. Scott went ballistic and confronted Marcia at the Leesburg office, yelling and screaming at her in front of everyone in the office at the time. He accused her and Rollie of stealing their volunteer names. Marcia later told Rollie she had never experienced such a vehement verbal assault. Furthermore, Scott had another verbal scuffle with another staffer and was summarily transferred out of Loudoun County to another location before the current issue about the names had been resolved.

Rollie contacted Shira immediately, and told her he was very perturbed that anyone would think he and Marcia stole names from the campaign. He reminded her that Marcia and he had actually shared over 3,000 names with the CFC campaign on their arrival in Loudoun County in the first place. Furthermore, this effort had already succeeded in finding several volunteers to help them on Election Day. Rollie then took the time to create and send her a detailed report of the results from another of his callers. Shira agreed that what Rollie was doing was valuable, and after retrieving the uncompleted list from Jean, Rollie reassigned it to another caller. The final results showed that out of the 250 potential Election Day workers, nearly 90 additional volunteers were found who had not yet volunteered to help CFC or VV08 on Election Day. Results clearly showed this was a worthwhile project.

With Scott's abrupt departure, LCO coordination with CFC became a problem. Shira attempted to fill the role, but she was already overwhelmed with her own responsibilities; contacting her and getting issues resolved slowed to a crawl. She was able to connect Dave Kirsten in the Leesburg district with the right people to keep the Houdini (voter check off) project in place.

By the last week of the campaign the field organizers for CFC and VV08 had recruited leaders to manage what was known as "canvass staging centers." These leaders would train and dispense canvassing packages to the newer volunteers in their neighborhood, deal with any problems arising from their activities, gather up the completed packages, and turn them in to the CFC or VV08 paid field organizers to which they were assigned. Field organizers would check them over and assign them to volunteers in charge of the nightly data entry. All field-collected data had to be entered into the database every night by experienced volunteers who could manage the process. For example, Aaron Edlow managed this effort in South Riding, working non-stop to be sure all the data was entered for the 300-500 volunteers working daily out of that office. That was a lot of data entry!

It worked the same way with phone banking. By the late stages of the campaign there were many experienced volunteer phone bankers, some of whom had made as many as 5,000 phone calls for the campaign. These volunteers became volunteer managers of other, less experienced phone bankers. They taught the newer ones how to do it, how to handle special situations, and how get out of difficulties if they arose. One of the best was Deborah Morbeto who continued to run phone-banking operations for Conrad Chaffee out of the LCDC office on King Street in Leesburg.

Up to this point canvassers and phone bankers had focused entirely on identifying voters who were going to vote for Obama and other Democrats. Now the push was to implement the GOTV effort to make sure previously identified supporters would get to the polls and actually vote. Materials were ordered, printed, and delivered to the hubs and staging areas. Training was extended to all of the Election Day leaders. The time spent on persuading voters to vote Democratic had ended, though occasionally there would be conversations with voters who indicated they were still undecided. The process also included pushing early voting and the use of absentee ballots by mail. This early voting was not by right; one of several specific conditions had to be met, such as being on vacation, working hours that would not permit voting, or other reasons that impaired voter access to the polls.

The entire staff would stay up almost all night cutting turf (preparing and printing canvassing packages from the VAN database). David Cannady from the Obama Campaign and Amanda Millard from the VV08 campaign stayed up so late they often slept in their respective offices.

Tracy Loh was also "cutting turf" on the computer late into the night on weekends and training new volunteers in the daytime.

Tracy was not the only volunteer cutting turf out this office, but she cut a whole lot of it. Daytimes Tracy was usually sitting on the rail of the porch outside the office training circles of canvassers and distributing turf. She would train one group and then another would come forward for similar training. Let me tell you, this lady was hell on wheels. She was like Moses coming down from the mountain bearing the two tablets to the children of Israel.

A friend of Tracy's, Ben Somberg, joined the Leesburg office effort and excelled in phoning. In the last few days of the campaign he was training new phone bankers, which freed up David Cannady to manage the other volunteer leaders rather than do direct field operations. It was a classic example of leveraging the power of a field organizer by creating multiple deputy volunteer field organizers.

Four days before election at about 10:00 p.m., the "Teamster Brothers" came to Leesburg. Let me tell you something. There was no fake gun for these two; they were ready for business, and their appearance in the office was electric. Tracy nicknamed them The Teamster Brothers because they walked in the door of the CFC office wearing identical black tee shirts inscribed "Teamsters for Obama."

The Teamster Brothers were Matt Kaiser and Varner Seaman. Matt lived in Takoma Park, Maryland. Varner flew in from Portland, Oregon at his own expense to join the campaign. The two are brothers, even though they have different last names. Matt opted to assume his wife's last name.

They Teamster Brothers had researched what areas of the country were important in deciding the election and where they could make a difference. They settled on Virginia because they concluded it was a Swing State. They had done this in past presidential elections but never before in Virginia.

Their personalities were outgoing and exuberant which considerably contributed to the excitement at the Leesburg office. They needed no training—they knew how to do it all. They could canvass, phone bank, do data entry and always demonstrated a positive attitude. They hit the deck running. They were what you would call "low to no maintenance" volunteers. They never complained about anything and never sat around drinking sodas, gossiping, or wasting time. They would do anything asked of them. Tracy Hadden Loh once gave them a canvassing package with 200 doors on it, four times the usual number. They went out and did it. When the office needed someone to take out the trash, the Teamster Brothers did it.

Their first day on the job the brothers saw Tracy robo-calling. That was the technology our callers were using where software on a computer makes the call to pre-selected voters. The value of the technology is that it saves the volunteer time spent finding and dialing a phone number; the computer does it all. The Teamster Brothers asked Tracy to train them how to robo-call so they could do that while their canvassing packages were being prepared. They did not come to the Leesburg office to sit around and waste time. They wanted to make a difference. These boys were all business all the time.

One of the many unsung heroes of the campaign was Tish Murray. Tish provided temporary housing for many volunteers like Tracy Hadden Loh, Ben Somberg, Ziba Cranmer, and the Teamster Brothers.

But sometimes volunteer housing didn't go so well. Occasionally, things got bumpy out there. A husband in Leesburg kicked a male volunteer out of the house one morning. Apparently, things got a little bouncy the night before. Well, not all these volunteers acted like people collecting money for UNICEF. The CFC got him new housing.

Meanwhile the crazy stuff continued to pop up here and there. A German citizen flew over from Germany to help the Obama Campaign, and showed up at the Leesburg office. Tracy trained him to canvass, and gave him a canvassing package—for a trailer park. Now let me tell you, when you canvass a trailer park you are almost always headed for a circus. If you want to have an adventure in this world, canvass a trailer park. You will almost certainly get all you can handle. This poor German had nothing in his history to prepare him for what was to come.

At one home the door opened, the German made his pitch, and the person at the door sicked a dog on him. Clearly the canvass had gone circus. The canvasser took off running like a scalded cat with a dog in hot pursuit. I mean this boy ran faster than Ezekiel fleeing Ahab's chariot in the Sinai Desert. He managed to escape, returned to the Leesburg campaign office, and told Tracy the story. Another day, another circus; it came with the territory. Listen to the oral history interview, and you can hear Tracy tell this amazing yarn.

In the bigger picture, a thoroughly positive and uplifting atmosphere permeated the Leesburg campaign office. The field organizers and volunteers were totally focused on what they were supporting: Obama and his message. The standard canvassing training provided to new volunteers emphasized that the Campaign for Change was not focusing on scaring people or talking down the opposition, but on stressing how promising Barack Obama was.

The "Midnight Volunteers" became a part of the culture of the Leesburg office in the last weeks of the campaign. The Midnight Volunteers were those staffers and volunteers who were still in the field office at midnight. Among them were Tracy Hadden Loh, Ben Somberg, Ziba Cranmer (from the Netherlands), Jordan Schultz, Topher Velava, and, of course, the Teamster Brothers.

All data collected from the field based on voter contacts had to be entered into the VAN before the office closed in the wee hours of every morning. David Cannady also reported additional data to the higher-ups describing other activities of the office operation, which was primarily related to volunteer participation. On occasion Gail Wise filled in for him. David reported numbers nightly until the last week when he began reporting his numbers every two hours because of the huge increase in GOTV activities.

Jordan Schultz volunteered to work out of the Leesburg Obama office on Market Street at the end of September, 2008. His first job was data entry. After one day, David Cannady asked him to become an Obama Intern. Interns did the normal volunteer activity but were treated as staffers—working long hours, but without pay. They often took on special assignments. The Intern program was really a way to give a young person a title and turn him or her into a super volunteer.

Jordan Schultz rarely left the Leesburg office because near the end of the campaign he filled in for David Cannady, who started supervising the new canvass-staging centers. Jordan's primary task was to recruit and train new volunteers. He recruited over 200 new volunteers for the campaign. His source of prospects was the sign-in sheet for people who attended the October 22 Ida Lee Park Obama rally.

One of the funniest phone calls Jordan took was from a McCain supporter. The caller complained bitterly that someone had left "socialist trash" about Obama on his front porch. Jordan asked the man for his address, but he refused to provide it. Then the caller said he was going to call the police if the campaign wouldn't pick up the offending literature. How the campaign would pick up the "socialist trash" without providing an address is a non sequitur apparently not considered by the complaining caller.

On the Sunday before the election a family of four drove up

at 7:00 p.m. to the Rosemeade Road canvass staging area in Leesburg. It was pitch dark and cold. A husband, wife, and two young children had driven from Maryland to canvass. The volunteer in charge of the canvass staging center asked them why they had come so far so late to volunteer in a state that was not their own. They responded, "we want our children to be able to say they helped in this campaign." It was yet another "golly gee moment" in a campaign full of such moments.

On the day before the election, activity at the Leesburg headquarters was especially chaotic. When I arrived, about 200 canvassers, divided into several groups, were assembled in the parking lot. Tracy Hadden Loh sat on the rail training one group after another, with other trainers helping out as well. Gail Wise was still a continuing fixture in the office, directing people and attending to the management of the office. Tables began to fill up with food donated by volunteers. David Cannady was already in the office. Amanda Millard came in just after I arrived. She handed James and me the package for the canvass assignment for the gated community described in Chapter 1 of this book.

After our circus in the gated community, James and I went back to headquarters and partook of the delicious homemade food. Amanda then handed us another canvassing package, this one in Ashburn, and we headed out. James continued to amaze me with his ability to connect with the voters. With these kinds of volunteers, how could we possibly lose this election?

We finished up and went back to the headquarters. We turned in all the canvassing packages to Amanda. It was election eve, and I had finished my last canvass of the campaign. The place was jumping! Soon after we arrived, we had a surprise visit from the ObamaMobile, which had been touring Obama field headquarters all across the country. It created a sensation. Everybody wanted to see it. It had already stopped at the South Riding field office at Larry Roeder's home earlier that day.

A little later in the evening, Sean Quinn dropped in from the online publication 538.com, a political journal with some of the finest journalistic coverage and consolidated polling data of the 2008 campaign available. Sean simply illuminated an already bright place with an ever-brighter light. He entertained the crowd with wild stories and tales of visiting campaign headquarters, both Obama and McCain, across the country. It was a personal window unfiltered by the media on what was happening in campaign offices. The electricity that night in the Obama campaign office was beyond parallel.

On Election Day Tracy Hadden Loh began a "lit drop" at 3:00 a.m. with six others. Some of the group returned to Tish Murray's house where they grabbed a couple of hours of sleep. They all rose early the next morning and continued the lit drop until 9:00 a.m. Lit drops were done throughout the county from all of the field offices.

On Election Day, the number of non-Virginians who came to volunteer was almost overwhelming. Two volunteers flew in the night before from London. Others came from Australia, Germany, Italy, the Netherlands, and other European countries. Most had been told that Loudoun County was the epitome of a swing county in a swing state, and was easy to reach by air. Their motivation was almost universal: the Bush administration had trashed the international reputation of the United States, and they believed Obama could vastly improve the image of the United States throughout the world.

Canvassers visited all of the houses pre-identified as Obama voters and left literature on the door knob or on the front porch reminding them to go out and vote. The literature also told the voters the address of their polling location. They spent no time speaking to them. The priority was to visit as many doors as possible and leave voting information for all of them. After the lit drops were completed, return visits and calls were made to the pool of identified voters. The goal was to "touch" every Obama identified voter several times on Election Day. A "touch" is a visit or call by a volunteer or staffer. When volunteers finished making the required touches, they continued knocking doors and began talking with voters person-to-person until the polls closed.

The phone banks in the Leesburg office were crowded with people. Often, there was no room left for those who came to phone bank because every phone space was taken and others were waiting for one to become vacant. Many of these people began using their own cell phones.

Around noon on Election Day in Leesburg, canvassers blanketed the town. They were everywhere. At one intersection on the southeast side of Leesburg four groups of canvassers simultaneously approached an intersection. Each team consisted of two members. So eight canvassers coincidentally converged at the intersection and did high-fives. The atmosphere was euphoric and in the stratosphere. It was like a party lasting all day and all night.

Rollie was having a party too. But it was a basement party for one! Again he was trying to keep up with the demand of marrying up resources with needs. The last week he was handling a couple of hundred emails and scores of telephone calls every day. Several calls came in from new people who said they had found his name on the Internet when searching for a way to help Obama in Loudoun County on Election Day. During this last week he kept in close contact with most of the district coordinators regarding their recruitment of Election Day volunteers. Since he had access to most of the new volunteers through his Rolodex and the responses to Marcia's Big List blast emails soliciting help, he agreed to assist all of the district coordinators who needed help. Seven of the eight district coordinators were extremely cooperative from the beginning and were thankful for the support. The remaining one finally came around, furnished Rollie with his volunteer schedule, and Rollie helped him at the last minute to fill in a couple of holes.

All of his managers were doing well. Ted Carvis repeatedly followed up with the people who were to provide the contents of the precinct kits. All of it had to be prepared and ready for assembly on the Saturday afternoon before the election. They all came through. The district chairs were responsible for picking up their kits on Sunday and distributing them to those opening up the precincts in their district. Jack Beavers had all of his route drivers assigned and ready to roll. Bob Moses was ready with the rovers. David Kirsten had the checkers scheduled for the Leesburg district.

All the planning and coordinating was paying off. However, that last weekend the number of incoming calls, emails, and problems went up significantly for Rollie. For instance, the Feder campaign ended up with only 30 or 40 young people to work our precincts. They had assigned them to some precincts already well-covered. Rollie's negotiations with them were partially successful, and he was able to switch six of them to lightly covered precincts that really needed the help. In that last few days, he realized the largest precinct in Loudoun County with more than 4,000 voters had no captain and little to no coverage. Earlier in the week, he had been in touch with a woman who lived in Maryland who said she and two friends wanted to work at the polls all day and were willing to go anyplace. She agreed to manage this huge precinct. Then the original precinct captain called Rollie to tell him he was willing and able to run the precinct, especially since we now had three all-day volunteers available. But now we had two precinct captains, so that had to be handled delicately. Several calls were made, and they finally agreed to work together.

By Sunday, Rollie was in meltdown. He really needed some help. There were last minute glitches which required more people at headquarters (Jack's home) by 5:00 a.m. to prepare the packages and then plan how to meet up with the initial dozen Route Drivers with the fix. Knowing that he was in trouble, he called a meeting Sunday afternoon before the election at Ted Carvis's office in Leesburg. There were two people there who immediately volunteered to solve the problem: Scottie Robinson, a personal good friend and Ann Sallgren, the Blue Ridge LCDC district chair. They started immediately and ended up at the headquarters at 5:00 a.m. Election Day—problem solved. This let Rollie get back to the basement and continue with the volunteer processing.

A couple of weeks earlier, Rollie had stumbled into a technique using Microsoft Outlook that made what seemed like an impossible job doable. He found that he could sort emails by 'subject', and that it was possible to insert at the beginning of the subject a coded word that described the volunteer status. A folder was made for the volunteer categories such as 'poll worker', 'caller', 'will do anything', etc. The codes entered in the subject line indicated 'needed processing,' 'contacted,' 'assigned,' etc. When phone calls arrived from new volunteers, he obtained their contact information and together they would make the decision how to use them and where, created an email, sent it to the appropriate manager, and plugged that email into the appropriate folder.

On election eve, Rollie took his computer and cell phone to Jack's home and continued to process last minute changes and new volunteers. A major concern was dealing with the people who had not yet heard back from the manager to which they were assigned. Or they had a change of plans and couldn't do the job they had promised to do. With the several hundred people that he processed, it was bound to happen. Fortunately, it had only happened with about a dozen of them. These Obama people were committed!

Jack had offered the bedroom at the headquarters for Rollie to stay the night. He accepted. Jack and he finished up their work for the evening just after 1:00 a.m. The alarm was set for 4:00 a.m. Rollie was so wired that he ended up with only a couple of hours of sleep.

Election Day was a beautiful clear fall day with temperatures in the low fifties. Being a commuter county, we had stressed to the voters throughout the campaign to vote early to avoid the late afternoon crush. In past elections long lines had developed at the end of the day. And a big turnout was expected. We were not disappointed; it was a huge turnout!

Scottie and Ann showed up at the headquarters first, followed by the drivers. The new material was sorted, bagged and distributed and drivers were on their way. Rollie checked his computer often, but there were few problems to solve. Calls started coming in from the drivers; out of the 62 precincts, only one seemed not to be covered. By the time one of the backups got there by 6:15 a.m. the scheduled poll worker was in place. In fact throughout the day, there were very few no-shows. Crowds of voters were enthusiastic and seemed not to be upset with the long lines.

Jack had his computer set up with a master list of all precincts where he could record problems, causing the background of the precinct field to turn red. It stayed red until the problem was solved. But it was amazing how few problems were reported, and most of them were solved during the reporting. There was no major problem the entire day—none. By 10:00 a.m., Rollie crashed and got in a couple more hours of sleep. Everything was under control.

In the afternoon, we got a report from one of the Western Loudoun precincts regarding Barbara Robisheaux. She was working outside the polling place providing sample ballots. It was a tough conservative area but marginally committed to John McCain All of a sudden one Republican rode up on horseback, let his steed defecate right in front of her at the Democratic table, then trotted away without cleaning up the mess. To Barbara, the action was both funny and symbolic of why she was glad she volunteered. For some time, she was famously known as the 'Poop' Lady.

The volunteers and staffers in Loudoun County had pulled off one of the most improbable and glorious campaigns in a swing county in a swing state. There was no doubt that when the vote was counted, we were going to be a significant factor in making Barack Obama President of the United States. They had done it. All that remained was the celebration. A year and 10 months of hard work was over. It was time to have some fun.

Celebration

"I had a lot of time to think, and that is not good for your mind. And when it actually happened, it was not so much a celebration but the relief. It was an exorcism anxiety. After each race there is a procedure in which you get taken off to the podium and the TV interviews."—Damon Hill

It was finally over—a long day at the office—for thousands of exhausted volunteers and campaign staffers. Barbara and I were bushed (perhaps not the best choice of words) and decided to skip the parties and soak in all the returns on the couch at home. We were optimistic, but not so durable; this campaigning at the polls is hard work!

Over at headquarters at Jack Beavers' home, Scottie Robinson, Tom McKittrick, Rollie, and a few others stayed around for a while after the polls closed. Jack had invited a number of the crew to stick around or come over for food and drink and watch the happenings on his theater-sized screen and take in the returns. I'm talking six by eight feet with perfect resolution. Jack had turned on the tube to see what was going on. No results yet, but it was already known that there was a huge turnout all across the country, which bode well for Obama.

Tom left for home to Fairfax and Rollie headed off to a party at the former Caribou Restaurant sponsored by Arlene Donnelly and others. Arlene was an event planner, a very active LCO member, and helped Joyce plan the unity party at the State Convention. After Rollie arrived, Marcia and Ted arrived, followed soon by Juan and Mo. It was primarily an African American crowd, and they were most welcoming—happy, nervous, and hoping for victory. In their wildest dreams they just couldn't believe that these United States would actually elect an African American president. But they had sensed a possible victory while working at the polls.

Marcia and Rollie had been invited as special guests. They were introduced, gave a short talk to the celebrants, and were given gifts as a token of their appreciation. Rollie had told them he could only stay for a short while, as he was going to the big LCDC sponsored victory bash in Sterling. He had previously convinced Tim Buchholz, LCDC Chair, that if Virginia goes Blue, he wanted to thank his supporters selecting him as a Virginia elector. Although

Tim was initially a little skeptical, he finally acceded to the request, but told him that he could speak only after it was announced that Obama had carried Virginia. Marcia and Ted decided to stay at the Caribou party. I could understand why—the crowd's enthusiasm was palpable and optimistic.

Robin Posey Blue, the "Cookie Lady," was at the Ashburn VV08 headquarters early election night with staffers Dan Chavez, Rachel Fulk, and Conrad Chaffee. The Ashburn office was watching election returns on television when Robin Posey Blue's husband Reggie called. "We've won," Reggie said. "What do you mean, we've won?" Robin said. "Well, they just called Ohio and Pennsylvania for Obama and when you count the western states sure to vote for Obama, there is no way McCain can win." He was referring to California, Oregon and Washington, to say nothing of Denver and New Mexico. Robin told her colleagues about Reggie's math—it was over. The Great Campaign of 2008 was over.

Rollie heard the same news on the radio as he arrived at the LCDC party in Sterling just after 9:00 p.m. It was held at Ned Divine's nightclub, a converted large multi-screen theater. After entering the building, he first ran into Ali McDermott and her posse—just some of her many South Riding friends. They were feeling no pain and bought him a drink. They were in a small billiard room that overlooked the main room, which had a sloping floor, theater style, down to the stage. Two screens flanked the stage—one displaying accumulated Loudoun results using an overhead projector and the other showing CNN live with the national election returns.

Someone was writing down the precinct results on the transparency so everyone could see them on the screen as they came in by phone from the Loudoun Board of Elections. All of a sudden, as the last precinct of the Sterling district was recorded around 10:15 p.m., a loud cheer went up, led by Tony Barney, the Sterling district chair. The last precinct from the Sterling District had gone for Obama! The excitement in the room was building. Then, a few minutes later, the last precinct for Loudoun county came in, and Obama had won Loudoun County by nearly 7,000 votes! Bedlam broke out!

"Looking good for Virginia," Rollie thought, as he circulated through the crowd, being congratulated time and time again by old and new friends. He was the man of the hour—with hugs, handshakes, and high-fives. He was getting a bit apprehensive, wondering when Virginia was going to be called by the television media. We were ahead in the count, and the margin was apparently growing.

Having had little to no sleep the previous evening, he was somewhat nervous about his coming speech. He had scrawled a few notes with no time to practice, and it was a big, rowdy crowd. Pennsylvania had come in early for Obama, and then when Ohio was called, Obama's victory was assured. We soon inched past the 270 electoral mark, but the election was not called. Why not? Because the networks had to wait until the West Coast states had closed their polls.

Time went by, waiting, waiting, waiting—Rollie sidled up to a fellow sitting on the end of a row of seats and asked if he could sit in the empty seat next to him. He seemed a little standoffish at first, but after sitting down, Rollie introduced himself and then a few moments later, the fellow said "I'm sure going to be happy when they say Obama has won". "Me too." "Well," he said, "you're not going to be as happy as I am; I even voted for McCain in February. But today, I voted for Obama, and I'm going to be REALLY happy when he wins!"

Rollie smiled to himself, stopping the little game they were playing, amused that the fellow had a bit of a surprise coming. Just a few moments later, it came: CNN has called Virginia for Obama! The crowd went absolutely wild. Tim Buchholz, the LCDC Chair, went to the podium and called all the elected officials to the stage—about eight or nine of them, and once gathered, said, "We are missing one person who belongs up here. Rollie Winter, come on down!"

Rollie said, "Excuse me, Don. They just called my name," squeezed by him to the aisle and proceeded from the back of the room to the front, with a chant growing 'Rollie, Rollie, Rollie.' Don must have wondered who the heck he was. When he walked up to the podium, he was greeted with more noise, claps, and cheers than he ever received in his entire life. It was a heady experience.

Rollie shook hands with the guests on the stage, and then Tim introduced him as the new elector for the 10th District. He put his notes on the podium, took a deep breath, and started to say, "Well it has been …" when on the big screen next to the stage, CNN made their announcement: Obama had won the presidency! A huge, raucous roar erupted from the crowd, and it wasn't for Rollie. It was 11:00 p.m., November 4, 2008, and CNN had just called the election for Obama.

The crowd went ballistic. It made the earlier outbursts look small by comparison—screams, hugs, laughter, jumping up and down, and just going crazy for several minutes. Over the din, Rollie asked Tim if he should stay and give his little speech now, thinking Tim might want to address the crowd first, but seeing how uncontrolled they were, Tim wisely decided to let Rollie proceed. After several moments Rollie again tried to begin speaking. The crowd was not quite ready; so he waited some more; then finally, they quieted, and his moment had arrived. Sterling had been called, Loudoun had been called, Virginia had been called, and now, the country. BAM, BAM, BAM, BAM! This all happened in about twenty minutes. Because of the excellent microphone, Rollie's amplified voice could be heard easily.

"Now that's a really hard act to follow," as he pointed to the screen. And turning back to the audience, "but you do understand, don't you, that Obama has not yet been elected. I and about 500 other electors were the ones actually elected tonight! And I want to thank all of you for supporting me with your hard work in this campaign."

It stayed pretty quiet for several seconds as my words started to sink in. "And on December 15th, I am driving from Loudoun County to the Electoral College in Richmond to cast my electoral vote for Barack Obama, our next President of the United States of America." And they cheered again! They finally got it.

Rollie continued, "A lot of you already know I started Loudoun County for Obama nearly two years ago. I found Marcia Carlyn, who soon became the most important leader of our effort. We put together a small group who began our planning. At that time I explained to them that Virginia could be an extremely important state in this election, with our primary the very next week after Super Tuesday. If Obama was still in contention, we should be ready for it. And our adventure began, resulting in over 2,000 Loudoun supporters on our local email list by the time of the primary last February and double that number tonight!

"I moved to Virginia in 1963, and in 1964 I voted for LBJ, the last time Virginia was carried by a Democrat—44 years ago! When I arrived, the schools were still segregated in my city. I joined a Human Relations Council and started speaking out. And now, 44 years later, we have elected Barack Obama. It has been a long, long time coming.

"What a night for us here in Loudoun County, in Virginia, the USA, the whole world. What a night!"

He didn't hang around long after he finished. He was exhausted, but still exhilarated. He shook a lot of hands, and thanked everyone for their help. On his way out he encountered a dear old friend of his, Rick Kowalick. He will never forget Rick's words, "I'm real proud of you, Rollie, really proud." That topped off the night for him. Over the years he and Rick had shared many great times campaigning together and attending political events, especially the annual state Democratic Jefferson/Jackson events held in Richmond. But this night had topped them all.

Driving home, Rollie knew he had a lot of odds and ends to finish up before the Electoral College met in December and before the Inauguration in January, but at that moment he was still basking in the events of the evening, finding it the most satisfying, wonderful, and exciting night of his political life.

Phyllis Randall's experience on election night began as she drove her son from the polls to a party in Fairfax being given by her good friend, Mark Warner. On the radio they heard that the polls had closed, and no more than three seconds later, heard the announcement that Senator Mark Warner had won re-election to the US Senate. Barack Obama's results came in later, well after the polls in California had closed, so Senators Jim Webb and Mark Warner were already on stage at the celebration, hands clasped high in the air with Governor Tim Kaine, before CNN's Wolf Blitzer announced "We can confirm that Barack Obama will be the next President of the United States."

"A roar went throughout the hotel," Phyllis told us. "People were hugging and crying and cheering. My son said Momma, why aren't you crying too? And I said, I don't know." Two weeks later, Phyllis drove down Constitution Avenue for the first time since the election, and when the White House came into view, she burst into tears.

Patti Maslinoff, The Button Lady, gave a heartfelt speech to her synagogue the week after the election. Here's how she ended it: *"On the morning of November 4, I thought about making buttons to celebrate an Obama victory. I was a bit concerned that I might jinx the election, but then I recalled that I am a skeptic and an atheist and so I don't believe in jinxing. I made several hundred buttons that day and traveled to various Loudoun celebration sites to hand them out.*

"All told, I made about 4,500 buttons. It was my psychiatrist who convinced me to put my name on the back of the buttons, as I was initially uncomfortable doing so. But I am very glad that I did, as I have been richly

rewarded by the people who thanked me and started calling me the 'Button Lady'.

"As I add this page to my Book of Life, I will include the joy that I felt to have worked together with the most diverse group of people I have ever been fortunate to be a part of. I was moved by an Afghan woman I met who was hoping that her citizenship papers would come through in time for her to cast her vote for Obama.

"A week after the election, the Loudoun volunteers joined together to celebrate. I had never been in a room with people of so many different colors, backgrounds, ages; there was no group that dominated. Was this a one-time event—or might it happen again?"

The six-week period between the election and the meeting of the Electoral College went by in a blur for Rollie. He did a few follow-up calls and wrote up a summary of election night for distribution to his friends and family. He also contacted the Editor of *Leesburg Today*, a terrific local weekly newspaper, and they agreed to publish an article by Rollie as an Op Ed piece, including a picture.

Tons of email arrived with congratulations, many quite heartwarming. This election had meant so much to so many. After any election, it's time for a lot of thank-you's, and Rollie and Marcia sent out scores and scores of them. They also sent apologies to those few who had volunteered or asked to do something for them in the last couple of days before the election, and had apparently dropped through the cracks. Fortunately, that was a small list.

Rollie received an email from Jack Beavers sharing the thanks he sent to all of his Route Drivers. We were so impressed with the organization he had put together and how well it had worked, we've included it here: *"The Route Drivers were awesome yesterday. Every single person did what he or she said they were going to do on all 28 of our planned half-day shifts. And you helped the poll workers in a bunch of creative ways, always with great enthusiasm, and made their work easier and more productive. It's been an honor to work with you. It's also been an honor to work toward the election of a man who, at long last, seems to understand the full measure of what it means to be an American, and who knows how to reawaken this sense of meaning in many of us. My only regret is that I didn't work nearly as hard as many of you toward such a defining historic moment as this. But heck, we're just at the beginning of our new beginning now. Yes we did!"*

Running Precinct Operations for a local Democratic Committee had been a new experience for Kevin Turner. He brought to the table a set of communication skills and techniques for a political campaign that was far superior to anything we have ever seen here in Loudoun County. Kevin sent out this email to the Dems Operations Central (DOC) team, with whom he and Rollie had coordinated for the last several weeks to handle Election Day efforts at the precincts: *"First, I want to echo Tim's comments from last night in thanking Rollie for all of his hard work over the past two years to organize a grassroots organization for Obama and for his leadership in helping us be successful in Loudoun, Virginia, and the US. What a night and a victory for us all! Second, I wanted to thank all of you for your time over the past four months as we ramped up our efforts to plan, recruit and staff canvassers, poll workers, Rovers and Router drivers yesterday—you all played a critical role! Overall, it was a successful day, and I appreciate your hard work, late nights and what seemed at times to be the never-ending conference calls (smile). Again, thank you, and 'Yes We Did'!"*

We are nearing the end of the story. The election was over and most everyone just had his or her memories left of the Great Campaign of 2008. However, Rollie's job was not done. He had the Electoral College (EC) to contend with. I've asked him to write a first-hand account of his experience.

"A couple of weeks after the election, I received an email regarding the EC from Don Mark, the Political Director of the Democratic Party of Virginia (DPVA). He had scheduled a conference call for us on the evening of December 3. The EC was to convene on December 15 in Richmond. He announced in the email that we would be electing a President and Secretary of the EC. I thought that odd. I thought we would meet in person, and that it would be an open competition. But it was not to be. Another surprise was to learn that the State Board of Elections was a significant part of the legal procedures associated with the EC. As a procedure nut, I was concerned with the process. I really had thought that we electors would have more control of, and responsibility for, the process. But all we had to do was show up, which actually turned out for the best. The whole planning process and the implemented procedures were quite satisfactory except for the selection of the officers.

"Norfolk At-Large elector Michael Khandelwal was elected Chair. He had set up a wonderful website for the Virginia electors and their friends and family, and I was pleased he was unanimously elected. Marc Finney was elected Secretary. I had not met or known either of them previously. The only elector I knew was Janet Carver from Fairfax, whom I had met nearly 30 years ago when I was a member of the Fairfax County Democratic Committee.

"One of the more interesting aspects of being an elector was the huge amount of mail I started receiving from the 'birthers,' those folks who believed Obama was not a US citizen. I must have received 50-75 pieces of mail, many sent special delivery or by FedEx. One of the last packages included a petition signed by at least 2,000 names. All of them had essentially the same message: Obama had not been born in Hawaii; he was not a citizen; I would be breaking my constitutional obligation to not demand proof of his citizenship (birth certificate); and if I didn't, I would be subject to prosecution.

"I found these communications to be quite annoying but did read all of them. Most were quite short, had been handwritten, and came from within Virginia. I didn't seek out any advice on the matter until I happened to attend an event in Richmond sponsored by The Center for Politics at the University of Virginia. The conference addressed the political ramifications of the just completed presidential election and was held just before the Electoral College met. I asked Larry Sabato, whom I had known in a previous life (well before he became a national celebrity), if he had heard anything about the 'birther' controversy and if I should have any need for concern. He passed it off as a delusion on their part, but introduced me to a staffer to whom I subsequently sent some of the material. They soon agreed with my assessment of the situation, and I continued to disregard all of these dire warnings. I'm sorry to say I discarded all of that material, especially since the 'Birther' issue has become so prominent.

"For many years, meetings of the Virginia Electoral College had been a fairly subdued affair held in the Senate Chambers at the Capitol in Richmond. This time was quite different. There were so many who wanted to attend the actual event that the Richmond staff of the Democratic Party moved the venue to the House of Delegates Chamber, substantially increasing the number of seats available to onlookers. The 13 electors were each given six tickets, two of which were floor passes. I gave mine to Marcia and to my wife Jill. The other four tickets were in the balcony with a good view and I gave them to Tim Buchholz, Juan Perez, Judy Ross, and Steve Ames.

"On Monday, December 15, Jill and I left for Richmond early in the morning. After a bit of a drizzle, the day turned out to be magnificent—sunny, high 60's—a good sign. The Obama magic continued.

"We got there in time for a planned tour of the Governor's Mansion, and then the 13 Electors met briefly with the Secretary of the Board of Elections at the old House of Delegates Chamber to get our marching orders. Tim Kaine came in, gave us a pep talk, and reminded us to vote right!

"The ceremony was held in the General Assembly Chambers and begun with the 'Procession of electors' exactly at noon. I was the last in line, and as I entered the room, was struck by the throng of people looking at us, wondering who was going to come through the doors next, continuously applauding enthusiastically. As I approached the end of the aisle, I learned I was to sit in the first row, on the aisle, right in front of the podium! What luck. I did have one problem: my microphone didn't work, and I had to share one with Janet Carver, who was seated on my left. That turned out to be quite awkward, and until we got the hang of it, we often spoke into a dead mike—just a minor glitch. Janet was the only elector interviewed and quoted by a Washington Post reporter in an article the following day!

"The Chief Justice of the Virginia Supreme Court took the roll, and we were sworn in. He was an impressive looking fellow. Governor Tim Kaine followed with a welcoming speech that really hit the mark. He is an outstanding speaker, and often speaks without notes—but not this time. After a number of administrative matters were addressed, the electors were polled twice—once for our choice for President, and a second time for Vice President. The specific words I was to use for the Presidential vote were "I, Rolland D. Winter, cast my vote for Barack Obama, of the State of Illinois." I had previously teased Jill that I thought this was much too bland and that I would certainly insert 'Hussein,' his middle name, and say something about the great County of Loudoun as a preamble. Jill was a nervous wreck, certain I was going to make a fool of myself, so to set her fears aside, I promised to behave. But when I stood to speak my piece, I did insert 'proudly' and said: "I, Rolland D. Winter, PROUDLY cast my vote ...." We then did the same for Joe Biden as Vice President. Then, after the roll call voting, we spent 45 minutes signing forms. I'm sure the guests were pretty bored by the time we reached the conclusion of the ceremony.

"The whole process took just over an hour and a half. It was a moment in my life I will never forget. The pomp and circumstance were impressive, Governor Tim Kaine's speech stirring, and my wife and friends very supportive. Later I learned that the entire session was recorded. I'm in nearly every frame—that is, the back of my bald head! Not my best feature. Go to YouTube and search for "2008 Virginia Electoral College" and you can see the whole event for yourself. Tim Kaine's terrific speech was the show stealer.

"But I wasn't through yet! Tim Buchholz and Juan joined us, and we went to the Rotunda room of the Jefferson Hotel for a very nice reception sponsored by the Alexandria Democratic Party. Tim Kaine was one of the dignitaries who attended the reception. Juan was nice enough to take a picture of me with the Governor for my scrapbook. That reception was followed by another at the Science Museum of Virginia, sponsored by the local Democratic Committees in and around Richmond.

"At this latter event, in addition to being introduced, the electors had an opportunity to say a few words. After thanking them for sponsoring the event, I said, 'I'm often asked how one becomes an elector? It's easy! All you have to do is work 45 years in your party through thick and thin, and finally, if you are very lucky, you are selected at a District Convention. But tonight I met Chris.' I then pointed a young good-looking man standing next to me. 'However, it's obvious that there is at least one exception to this rule! This young fellow from Williamsburg hasn't seen his 30th birthday, and yet he is an elector as well. So I made him promise that he will work the next 45 years in the party as hard as I have.'"

Next on the historic calendar was the Inauguration on Tuesday, January 20, 2009. Our Robisheaux Inauguration party had gone circus! And it was a three-ringer! Barbara and I had three great friends and a cousin in town for five days of non-stop celebration. They flew into Dulles Airport on Friday January 16. Two flew in from Florida, my cousin Anne Bennett and her friend Sharon. Two came from Corpus Christi, Texas, David and Mary Carpenter. I've known David for many, many years.

On the morning of the Inauguration, January 20, 2012 it was 12° F. in Philomont. Officials estimated that more than a million people were in Washington DC for Inauguration Day. We went straight over to Pennsylvania Avenue in front of the old Post Office, hoping to hook up with a number of other Loudoun folks who had planned to meet us there. No such luck. But all had a great time. It was a thrill to see our new President and First Lady drive by in the limo, on its way to the White House. It was tough fighting the crowd and traffic to get home, but just being part of this historic event more than made up for it.

Watching Obama at work his first full day, signing executive orders, meeting with the foreign affairs team, and establishing a higher, more ethical tone for the senior White House staff was just a glimpse of what we could expect from this president as he tackled the huge problems facing us—all of this showed us we were right in our assessment of this man. These United States of America were in good hands.

Lou Etta Watkins, former Loudoun NAACP president and influential elder in the Loudoun African-American community, tells of her experience on Inauguration Day:

"We left at 5 a.m. It was the coldest day! We had heard all of this talk about how it was going to be... no bags allowed, so we pinned money to the inside of our clothing. We were concerned that we might not be able to get to a bathroom with the long lines, so we wore "Depends" for the first time in our lives! After riding two buses, we walked almost two miles in the freezing cold, chanting 'Yes we can!' and 'Yes we DID!' We had a great time, even though we didn't have tickets. Those who had tickets stood in the cold, too, just the same."

Here's Rollie's story of his and Jill's Inauguration experience:

"One of the smartest decisions we made was to book early reservations on MARC—a Maryland commuter train—that had special $25 round-trip tickets for Inauguration Day to Union Station and back. A couple of days before the big event, I drove to the train station in Brunswick, MD, to check out the route and parking. It was only a 30 minute drive to reach the station from our home, a piece of cake.

"We also gave a lot of thought to what we would wear. It was certain to be in the teens, and the forecast was cloudy. We put on several layers of clothing (five for the top, four for the bottom!). I also purchased some glove liners, a hat, and toe warmers. We each carried a blanket. We also purchased a disposable camera and borrowed a digital camera. We were all set! We got up at 5:15 a.m., were on the road by 6, and at the station by 6:30. The train was on time, and we started out for DC at 7:07. The crowd on the train was excited, friendly, and jovial. Many were from out of state—Kansas City, Cincinnati, Washington State, Alaska, and others. There were five station stops, and we reached Union Station at 8:15 a.m., as scheduled. It is looking good.

"As we walked to the end of the track just before entering Union Station, we saw two members of a SWAT team, all in black, carrying serious looking guns with their shooting hands at the ready. That was a bit disconcerting. Even though crowds of people were streaming into the station from other platforms, we were moving well. We were told that the front exits were closed and only one side exit was to be used to leave the station. We soon came upon a Metro Station adjacent to our exit route, and their riders joined our throng. For the first time, we could physically feel the crowd around us. But everyone was friendly, not pushing, being careful of one another—talking, laughing, getting into the moment.

"We had to walk to the other side of the Capitol to reach our seats. Because several streets behind the Capitol were closed to cars and pedestrians, we had to walk several additional blocks to reach our assigned area. Up ahead we saw that the crowd was dividing into two lines, one very long line waiting for the 'standing Blue' section, and a much smaller line for the sitting Orange section (ours). There had to be a couple of thousand people in that Blue line, and it wasn't moving fast. (I learned later that it was this line that did not get processed in time for the ceremony, and some really pissed-off people were eventually turned away, even though they were there on time and with tickets.) OK, so Obama is not perfect. And he had picked a lousy day for a party. Oh well, I guess he wasn't God. But wait! As we made our way to our seats, the sun broke through the clouds, and it was sunny all day!

"We easily reached the screening area for the Orange Gate. They must have had 40 stations set up, and when we picked ours, there were only three people ahead of us. We were through there in less than five minutes. We then had about four blocks to go—in a circuitous route—to reach Section 12 of the Orange area. National Guardsmen and other officials were in abundance, helpfully pointing out the way to our destination. We went through three or four checkpoints with yells of 'tickets up—hold your tickets up" as we passed through.

"We ended up at the far end of Section 12, which put us almost directly in front of the podium. We were about two-thirds of the way back in our section from its first row. I estimated the distance to the podium to be about 100 yards. Because the podium was over sized and we were so close to it, we could only see the head and shoulders of the tall people who spoke.

"Two big screens flanked the stage, which would have been a great help, except that there was a tree blocking our view of the one on the right, and National Guardsmen standing in the aisle about six feet apart, effectively blocking our view of the one on the left. The mood was affected, too, by the fact that there were so many people constantly standing on their chairs taking pictures.

"On the plus side, the sound was perfect, and whenever I looked down the mall behind us towards the Washington Monument, I realized how fortunate we were to be sitting where we were. The couple immediately behind us happened to be strong Republicans, and we didn't talk much. The African American lady from Roanoke next to me was quiet, and when I asked if she had worked on the campaign, said simply, 'No'. She had obtained her tickets through Representative Goodblatt, a Virginia Republican Congressman. A short while later she told me that she was the elected Sheriff of Roanoke City and a Democrat! That explained her non-involvement in the campaign, and her clout in obtaining tickets.

"We could hear the wave of cheers behind us from down the Mall. It was amazing to be able to hear one penetrating voice shouting OBAMA on several occasions very clearly! They say there were more than a million on the mall gathered for this historic event. In our immediate area, people were rather quiet and respectful, awed by the historic ceremony. For me, it was a time of fulfillment, thankfulness, and restored hope.

"Soon after the ceremony, a low-flying helicopter suddenly appeared from behind the Capitol. The crowd soon realized who it was and started chanting: "Bye-bye, George, Bye-bye George . . . ."

"We stood to leave, and I caught the eye of a tall, good-looking African American man in the next row and did my first-ever 'fist bump' with him. No words were spoken. It fit the moment perfectly.

"Our return ticket was for the 4:00 MARC train back to Brunswick, so we had about two hours to kill. Most of the crowd seemed to be headed for our destination—back to Union Station. Fortunately the barricades had been removed, but it was slow-moving, and we were tightly wedged in with the huge mass of people. "As we shuffled along, someone remarked that we looked like "The March of the Penguins" although we weren't in a line and we weren't protecting an egg! We did have to get past the street merchants, who had spread their wares on blankets, but everyone respected their space, and no unpleasant instances occurred that we noticed.

We finally got to Union Station and as we reached the food court, a couple left and gave us their seats! What luck. I took off a couple of layers and placed the articles on my seat, told Jill to hold the fort, and went to use the facilities. I saw a couple of long lines in front of both the men's and women's doors. Closer inspection revealed that they were all women—using both restrooms! Lots of laughter inside the men's room, especially when a man yelled, 'I feel VIOLATED'.

"After lunch, we easily reached the departing gate and queued up for our train. We were about 45 minutes early, sat on the concrete floor, and waited. All of a sudden, a deep voice shouted repeatedly, 'POLICE COMING THROUGH, MOVE ASIDE, MAKE A HOLE, POLICE COMING THROUGH!' A contingent of police officers, two in front, two more following, were holding on to a man between them, followed by two more cops. All were big burly officers, striding quickly through the crowd! Later, someone said that the man being escorted was someone who was giving homeland security folks a hassle. The next day, as reported in the papers, the police announced there were no arrests at the inauguration—not one. If that is the case, I can't help wondering why this fellow was being treated that way if he wasn't even arrested. But perhaps it was the Feds, so they don't count as local arrests.

"As we rode back to Brunswick, I reflected on the fact that I was here because of all the people who helped me. Without them, it would not have been possible. They canvassed, called, donated time and money, worked the polls, and wrote postcards. They attended District and State conventions. They supported me in my election for elector. They Voted!

"But I know now that it was only then that the real work began. Our national problems seemed nearly unsolvable. I recently read somewhere that there are time-defining moments in our lives after which we refer to events as occurring 'before' or 'after' the defining moment. This clearly is the case here. We are now in the time of 'after' Obama's first election. We will never forget it."

That's our story, folks. We now await the Great Campaign of 2012. It should be a humdinger.

Ed Robisheaux
Narrator

Where Are They Now

"What in the Wide World of Sports is a-going on here?—Screenplay from the movie Blazing Saddles

So where are they today, the main actors of this Grand Play of 2006-2008 as of June 1, 2012, who gave so much of themselves to make Barack Obama President of the United States?

Rollie Winter, coauthor of this book, is retired and living at Little Oatlands just off the Old Carolina Highway (now Route 15) south of Leesburg, Virginia. He is still active in the Loudoun County Democratic Committee (LCDC).

Marcia Carlyn has been a major consultant on this book. She lives in Leesburg during the winter and in Crystal Beach, Ontario during the summer where she is currently trying to save a beautiful public beach from being taken over by a developer, using many of the grassroots strategies that worked so well in the Great Campaign of 2008. Marcia also provides independent consulting services to organizations seeking expertise in planning and evaluation.

S. Ann Robinson, consulting writer/editor to this book, is a Democratic activist and is involved in numerous community causes in Northern Virginia, especially in Leesburg, as well as continuing to teach accounting and to write for various publications. She recently announced her intention to run for Leesburg Town Council in November 2012.

Ed Robisheaux, coauthor of this book, is battling a serious disease and living in Philomont, Virginia where he pursues his hobby of amateur photography when able. He hopes to be able to soon begin work on a photographic book of Loudoun County historical landmarks. He is "in" for the 2012 campaign and was a Democratic Convention Delegate for the 10th Congressional District in 2012.

Joyce McLaurin, the African American who campaigned with a liver transplant from Leesburg to Chambersburg, passed away from cancer in January 2009. She lived long enough to see the first African American inaugurated as President of the United States on January 20, 2009. She is gone but will never be forgotten among those who volunteered with her.

Bernard Hill, The Great Story Teller, and National Delegate to the Democratic Convention, is retired and living in Ashburn,

Virginia. He lunches from time to time with the authors of this book but has no plans to campaign actively in 2012. The emotional excitement of 2008 was so great Mr. Hill believes a new campaign could only be a let down from 2008.

Steve Ames lives in Ashburn, Virginia where he also works. He campaigned from Leesburg to Harrisburg, Pennsylvania in 2008 and did it all—convention delegation Chair, furniture mover, visibility coordinator, canvassing, phone-banking and data entry. He has been a consultant to the authors of this book and continues to fill in details of the Great Campaign of 2008. He is already very active in the 2012 campaign.

Ali McDermott lives in South Riding, Virginia and works for an agency of the Federal Government. Because of the Hatch Act, her activities in the 2012 campaign may be limited, but she is no less a determined Obama supporter. Ali was a Delegate at the 10th Virginia Congressional Democratic Convention and the Virginia Democratic Convention in 2012 in 2012.

Bobby McDermott, who at the age of 8 told his teacher and school principal that he would not remove his Obama button because it was his civil right to wear them, lives with his mother and stepfather in South Riding, Virginia. He is going to middle school in South Riding. His convictions are as strong as ever and he is eager to hit the streets for Obama in the 2012 campaign.

Darby McDermott, who was acting precinct chair in South Riding at the age of 12, lives with his mother and stepfather in South Riding, Virginia. He is as determined as ever to fight racism and is going out to campaign for Obama in 2012. He told Swing County on May 12, 2012 that he was "fired up and ready to go."

Juan Carlos Perez, who campaigned all the way from Chambersburg, Pennsylvania to Leesburg, is a consultant living in Leesburg. He is still active in Democratic politics and in the campaign of 2012.

Lydia Pokrass, the 95 year old volunteer for the campaign in 2008 still lives in her retirement home in Ashburn, Virginia. She is learning to play pool, belongs to a social group named "The Wild Women," is writing a book to be titled "Under a Postage Stamp," and is preparing to celebrate her 100th birthday while planning to register voters and campaign for Barack Obama in 2012. She is truly one of a kind.

Robin Posey Blue, the famous Cookie Lady, lives in Sterling, Virginia with her family and is still active in Democratic Politics.

Once a week she brought homemade cookies into the VV08 field office in Ashburn, Virginia. She remains a solid Obama supporter.

The Indiana Jones Man, Larry Roeder, who was threatened with death in the 2008 campaign, is retired from the United States State Department, lives in South Riding, Virginia, is active in Democratic politics and pursues outreach to the Islamic and Asian communities of Loudoun County. He hopes to run for local office in 2015. He is an author and is currently writing another book to be published in 2012.

Judy Ross, the Famous Post Card Lady, lives in Taylorstown, Virginia in northern Loudoun County. She didn't just do post cards; she also canvassed, phone-banked and did data entry. Swing County interviewed Judy twice because she had so many experiences. She transported Joyce McLaurin to Obama rallies in Fredericksburg, Virginia and Leesburg when Joyce was confined to a wheel chair and could no longer move on her own. She is on board for the 2012 Obama Campaign.

Patty Maslinoff, the Famous Button Lady, lives in Leesburg, Virginia. She fully intends to make buttons in 2012 for all who want them. She made all the buttons for the 10th Congressional District Democratic Convention held in May, 2012. Once a Button Lady, always a Button Lady. She also attended the state Democratic Convention on June 2, 2012.

Barbara Robisheaux, the Famous Poop Lady, is fully retired and lives in Philomont, Virginia with her husband where she fills her time quilting with the Waterford Quilters' Guild and breakfasting with her lady friends in Purcellville. Barbara knocked nearly a thousand doors in the 2008 campaign. She's "in" for the 2012 campaign and was a Democratic Delegate for the 10th Congressional District and the state Democratic Convention in 2012.

The Famous Shoe Lady, Toni Rader, lives in Purcellville, Virginia, with her husband, is a high school teacher and debate coach for Loudoun County High School. She has a new pair of shoes on special order for the 2012 campaign. The 2008 shoes are headed to the Smithsonian Museum in Washington, DC, who wants them for a future display on the Great Campaign of 2008.

The Famous Rock Lady, Kathy Mohun, is retired and living with her husband near Birmingham, Alabama. She has no more rocks planned for her future.

The Muffin Lady, Carolyn Ronis, called a baby killer during the campaign, is an attorney practicing law and lives in Lansdowne,

Virginia, with her family, including the twins with whom she campaigned in 2008. She and her husband are still active in Democratic politics.

Dan Chavez, the staffer who headed up the Virginia Victory 08 Campaign in Loudoun County, now lives with his wife Rachel Chavez in Harrisonburg, Virginia in the Shenandoah Valley. The Japanese press interviewed Dan in the fall of 2012 about the campaign of 2008.

Rachel Chavez, who was Rachel Fulk during the Great Campaign of 2008 and invented a canvass package tracking system used currently by the Democratic Party nationwide, now lives in Harrisonburg, Virginia, with her husband Dan. They had their first child in the spring of 2012.

Amanda Millard, the Virginia Victory 08 Campaign Staffer who worked 16-hour days 7 days a week, lives in Alexandria, Virginia, and works in the District of Columbia. Work obligations will prevent her from becoming a campaign staffer in 2012.

Conrad Chaffee, the oldest paid staffer for the VV08 campaign in 2008, the man who quit his job with a pregnant wife to help make Barack Obama President, lives near Reston, Virginia. The twins are doing fine. Mom has a third child on the way and the family is relocating to Capitol Hill in the District.

Deborah Morbeto, who ran phone-banking operations for Conrad Chaffee out of the LCDC office in 2008, is a graphic design artist and marketing consultant living with her family in Leesburg. Deborah did the artwork for the marketing materials for the book *Swing County*.

Tracy Hadden Loh, who made the famous Christian phone call in the week before the election, did countless hours of volunteer training, and was in the 3:00 AM lit drop in Leesburg, works in the Federal Government in Washington, DC, and lives in the District with her husband.

The Famous Teamster Brothers, Matt Kaiser and Varney Seamen, who made such a big impact in the last week of the campaign, continue to pursue their careers. Matt lives in Takoma Park, Maryland and has his own law practice in the District. Varney lives in Portland, Oregon. Varney flew over 5,600 miles to make a difference in the campaign.

Mattie Lassiter, one of the great civil rights legends of Loudoun County, lives in Purcellville with her husband Mutt (Horace Lassiter). She continues to be active in Democratic Party causes.

Mutt Lassiter, otherwise known as *Horace Lassiter*, lives in Purcellville, continues to own Robinson's Barbershop in Leesburg, one of the oldest continuing businesses in the town. He continues to be a strong Democratic supporter with the walls of his shop lined with posters of all the current Democratic candidates.

Chuck Visnius, the Famous Flying Canvasser, campaigned with his young son in the streets of Purcellville and to whom Captain Kirk once said, "Beam me up Scottie," remains an airline pilot. He has since 2008 relocated to the Atlanta, Georgia area with his whole family.

Jordan Schultz, a tireless volunteer in the Obama Market street campaign office, is currently living in Blacksburg, Virginia where he is a student at Virginia Tech University.

Toni Bondi Boyd, another great volunteer from the 2008 campaign who housed numerous volunteers, relocated to the state of Washington to accept employment with a national technology firm. Toni worked nearly full time for the election of Barack Obama in the last months of the campaign.

Tim Buchholz lives in Ashburn, Virginia. He relocated to McLean, Virginia from Saint Louis, Missouri, earned a degree in business from Old Dominion University, and then moved on to Loudoun County. Today he works for the Federal Government in Washington, DC.

Joe Montano, who worked for the Democratic Party of the State of Virginia in 2008, and who was attending LCDC meetings in Leesburg, today lives in Northern Virginia.

Barack Obama currently lives at 1600 Pennsylvania Avenue in Washington, DC, and was elected President of the United States on November 4, 2008 because 53,000 Virginia volunteers, thousands of them in Loudoun County, gave up their weekends, their nights, their time and their money to help make it happen in a swing county in a swing state.

Epilogue

*"The wings of Time are Black and white,
Pied with morning and with night.
Mountain tall and ocean deep
Trembling balance duly keep.
In changing moon, in tidal wave,
Glows the feud of Want and Have...
...Fear not, then, thou child infirm,
There's no god dare wrong a worm.
Laurel crowns cleave to deserts,
And power to him who power exerts;
Hast not thy share? On winged feet,
Lo! it rushes thee to meet..."*—excerpts: COMPENSATION by Ralph Waldo Emerson (1841)

Emerson would likely express no surprise at how the next 167 years of racial/class history in the United States evolved, after he wrote his essay *"Compensation"* in 1841.

Slavery and the Abolition Movement
Civil War/Reconstruction and the Ku Klux Klan/Jim Crow laws in the South
The NAACP and Lynching
Civil Rights/Affirmative Action and the Radical Right
Unjust war/Abu Ghraib and Barack Hussein Obama
—viewed through the lens of Emerson's philosophy appear to unfold inevitably.

"If the good is there, so is the evil; if the affinity, so the repulsion; if the force, so the limitation. Thus is the universe alive. All things are moral. That soul, which within us is a sentiment, outside of us is a law. We feel its inspiration; out there in history we can see its fatal strength." [Emerson]

Over 300 years of cruelty and oppression offered the African Americans little choice but to develop, sustain and pass on, deep spiritual connections to the universe and to each other. With family, fortune and fame frequently out of reach, the alternative was annihilation. Then, when America faced itself in a growing despair of shattered self-esteem, after the disarray of an unjust war waged by dishonest leaders who plundered the public Treasury while engaging in torture, the American psyche—the collective soul itself—cried out for redemption. The answer to that cry could come only from the spiritual depths of our dark past—where the soulfulness created and passed on by those who had no other choice, knew how to respond.

Many who heard Barack Obama's 2004 speech given at the Democratic National Convention wept tears of release and joy akin to those of a religious experience—tears which unleashed a Biblical energy: *"...but those who hope...will renew their strength. They will soar on wings like eagles; they will run and not grow weary, they will walk and not be faint."* [Isaiah 40:31] In another era, the movement might have exhibited itself as a spiritual awakening similar to that of Jonathan Edwards' in The Great Awakening of the 1740s; but the evolution of civic life in America created an opening in the political arena embraced by those who knew the intricacies of party politics, as well as those who embodied the technological expertise of a new generation. November 4, 2008, manifested as though ordained by Destiny.

"The world globes itself in a drop of dew...So do we put our life into every act. The true doctrine of omnipresence is, that God reappears with all his parts in every moss and cobweb. The value of the universe contrives to throw itself into every point." [Emerson]

During the Kennedy years—the Martin Luther King, Jr. years—all of the inspiration, all of the sit-ins, all of the songs, came down to a man little talked about today, one-term president Lyndon Johnson, a man some discounted as being a crass politician. "Many believe that Johnson was able to pass the 1964 Civil Rights Act and 1965 Voting Rights Act because of an exceptional set of circumstances. During his 24 years in Congress Johnson had gained unprecedented experience in getting legislation through Congress." [History Learning Site]

Those who know the rules, control the game. Add to that axiom, extraordinary interpersonal skills and technical expertise that complement a spiritual awakening and a rare moment in time that will bear fruit. While Kennedy, King and Johnson were playing their parts in the dramatic changes of the 60s, Rollie Winter "learned the ropes" as he joined with others to challenge the Byrd organization in Virginia. In Wisconsin, Marcia Carlyn steeped herself in studies, perfecting her database management skills; and in D.C., Mary Randolph listened with her Sunday school class as the Reverend King imparted a dream to a new generation. No one suspected that these experiences would merge 45 years later in Loudoun County, least of all Mary, who writes, "*When I gave birth to my children in the hospital downtown, I was assigned to the 'colored ward.' My family was not welcome in the Tally Ho Theater. I had to wait outside the Leesburg restaurants for my order to be taken. Large parties were always planned for Election Day by those in the white community who hired African-American help, so that they did not have time to go to the polls and vote.*"

How amazing a coincidence is it that Rollie Winter lived at Little Oatlands—part of a historic southern plantation—after moving to Loudoun in the 90s, and for a time attended the chapel in Gleedsville that had been built by the descendants of Oatlands slaves—a sanctuary designed and christened their "*Ship of Dreams*"?

And what of the movement for change? For a while that dream of sweeping change seemed to be truly in reach as a moment in time crystalized in the Chicago night air after the election, where thousands wept with joy as millions around the world watched and cried in concert. Truly the key ability mentioned in our Prologue had found its mark. The ability of different Power Groups to set aside their egos and passionately work for something higher and better in unison—which is after all, the only way that "heaven and earth" ever actually meet. Why didn't the rare moment last? The opposition, of course, *was* the opposition—and could be expected to try vigorously to regain power. The supporters, though, what happened to them? The energy and devotion on display in Chicago the night of November 4, 2008, surely should not have been so easily quelled. But, starting with the Creigh Deeds Virginia gubernatorial campaign in 2009 and continuing through the congressional races of 2010 and into the local elections of 2011, the groundswell of energy dissipated, frustrating Democratic Party insiders. Some wanted to blame Obama himself, for not being Franklin D. Roosevelt. Others wanted to blame the media for repeatedly highlighting negative stories, and certainly the severe economic downturn coupled with job losses had their impact. The fuller truth, however, lay in a deeper reality, evidenced by incremental decisions.

Starting as early as the Virginia State Convention, June 14, 2008, we can detect the beginnings of disillusionment. David Kirsten's interview poignantly reveals the seeds of silence being sown. "*The only way we are truly going to change this world is 'bottom up,'*" Kirsten explained, "*and the way that the at-large candidates for National Delegate were chosen at the state convention was terribly handled. Even though there were scores of people who had applied to be a delegate, they should have allowed them to have some time to make their case. In the end, they [the old politics of insiders] worked to shut out the new enthusiasts. Seeing all of the pamphlets of all the people who had worked so hard for the campaign throughout the time—the flyers of all their accomplishments—I wish all of them had been collected to send to Obama. They spoke so much to the true excitement and love that people felt for Barack Obama, which is a tribute to these individuals and the Democratic Party. It is unfortunate it wasn't recognized as such at the State party level."*

Diana Denley relays a further misstep. *"I came back [to Loudoun] from Australia, as an Obama Fellow in June of 2008, to work in the national campaign locally. In June and July, some of the younger Fellows [newly arriving] had no idea of the dynamics of Loudoun County and had no idea of the grassroots. They were not really listening, and local people had a problem with their coming in, and I have a lot of contacts—a lot of older people—who wanted to work with the campaign in the early days of the summer, who were put off by the younger Fellows always texting or working on their computers while they were trying to give help to them."*

Emma Ancrum: *"The way the campaign was run by Rollie and Marcia—'the sky's the limit…you do what you want!' We had a grand time— you could take ownership, with what Marcia brought to those early days, 'this is your campaign…you find something to do and you do it.' Then in the summer, the paid staffers came in from the national campaign who didn't live here and didn't understand the community. The teams needed to mesh, and in the beginning it was difficult. The sense of being on the same team evaporated. Many of the staffers had a personal agenda—'maybe I can get a job with the administration.' Numbers and quotas and personal careers took over"* where passion for a dream had been. Important and influential faith leaders in the area were not given tickets to events; instead the tickets went to insiders. Sometimes pastors were told they would be offering the prayer at an event, and then were dismissed as not needed. Influential local ministers sometimes felt used by the national campaign, instead of included and appreciated. Monica Vickers-Root: *"Local activists' pleas for yard signs were delayed too long. Recommendations to do such things as register voters among public bus riders were ignored."*

The excitement of the historical momentum prevailed, though, and in spite of many being forgotten when tickets to the Inauguration were distributed, the thrill would not be denied—the euphoria of a dream realized.

Afterwards, the hope that a new movement was indeed afoot in the land still held sway, and local meetings were held and facilitated regarding significant issues. Ann Robinson attended one such gathering in Ashburn in the spring of 2009. Sitting beside Rollie Winter in a room of over 50 newly empowered, racially and culturally diverse citizens—all still convinced that they now had a stake in their government, a say in its direction—she confided, *"I'm simply grateful I lived long enough to see this."*

The dramatic and surprising economic news of the collapsing financial system initiated in the Bush years, began to dampen the feelings of empowerment, though; and the ugliness that erupted at the Town Hall debates on health care depressed it. Just as no one celebrates Lyndon Johnson as leader of a movement, none of the impassioned grassroots wanted to be a part of the parking lot screaming matches so favored by the media. The attention given to Town Hall detractors, however, could have been diverted if the moderators had simply said to the audience, *"Who here is in favor of health care reform? Please stand." "Who here would prefer a public option? Please stand."* The majority response would have been visibly overwhelming. The people, who wept for joy at the beginning of the campaign for change in 2004, were not going to be the instruments of face-to-face yelling contests for the media. That is the America they wanted to change.

By the time Creigh Deeds geared up his campaign for Virginia governor in 2009, the staff ignored local community leaders entirely, and afterwards, the local Democratic Party wondered where the grassroots had gone—why they didn't come out to vote.

In 2011, a local candidate for County Supervisor tried to hide his Democratic ties, as well as his contribution to the Obama campaign; then many wondered, *"Why didn't the base show up at the polls?"*

Some cynics say, *"Nothing ever changes. The love of power will always usurp the power of love."* But is that really true? There is no valid reason to believe it unless we choose to. We can find and merge again those who know the rules, control the game and live from their souls at the same time. All we have to do is sustain that leadership—that commitment to the merging of knowledge and soul at every step, lifting the grassroots on our shoulders, as we rise.

And never in the history of our country has it been more important to do that than it is in 2012.

We are proud of our President. He got Osama Bin Laden, he ended the War in Iraq, he prevented another Great Depression, and he is committed to strengthening the Middle Class. *"Under the most horrible of circumstances faced by any president other than Abraham Lincoln, I think President Obama has just been spectacular,"* says Rollie Winter. Debbie Hawk [Independent voter] agrees, *"With all that is going on, thank goodness he is in the White House."*

We the grassroots and campaign staffers are ready to learn from 2008-2009, to create an even more effective and long-lasting union of hope and determination that continues moving America forward.

"This nation is great because we worked as a team. This nation is great because we get each other's backs. And if we hold fast to that truth, in this moment of trial, there is no challenge too great; no mission too hard. As long as we are joined in common purpose, as long as we maintain our common resolve, our journey moves forward, and our future is hopeful, and the state of our Union will always be strong."—President Barack Obama, State of the Union address, Washington, DC, January 2012.

No one said it would be easy.

Ann Robinson

Afterword

"My life has been a tapestry of rich and royal hue
An everlasting vision of the ever changing view
A wondrous woven magic in bits of blue and gold
A tapestry to feel and see, impossible to hold."—Carole King, Tapestry.

Remember the volunteers in the Great Campaign of 2008. There were 10,000 of them in Loudoun County. They gave freely of their time and money because they wanted to change the direction of their country. They were in the streets canvassing, on the phones calling, on the computers entering data, in the kitchens making food and at the house parties writing post cards. Nobody paid them money to do it; they did it to make their country a better place to live for the average citizen. Remember the volunteers.

Remember the dead. Remember Joyce McLaurin, Mukit Hossain, Alice Flemming-Williams, Dan Brigham, Tina Gulland and Judy Coughlin. Joyce McLaurin worked the streets of Loudoun County after having a liver transplant, and then was diagnosed with cancer. From her hospital room she continued to register voters and canvass the hospital staff and other patients. She was African American and lived long enough to see the first African American sworn in as President of the United States. Remember Joyce McLaurin and the others who gave their all to make it happen. Remember the dead.

Remember the staff. They worked brutal 15-18 hour day, seven days a week for months. They gave everything they had to give so that the volunteers could be provided with the tools to be effective in their activities. By the end of the campaign they were exhausted, worn out and finished as an effective campaigning force. However, they did the measure and more than what was expected of them. Remember the staff.

Remember the conventions. There were three of them—the 10th Congressional District Convention, the State Convention in Richmond, and the National Convention in Denver. To all who attended them as Delegates each was a unique experience for them and added to the tapestry of their lives. Many will never attend one again, but the Delegates have the memories etched in their minds forever. Remember the conventions.

Remember the stories. There were many to emerge from the Great Campaign of 2008. Many stories were funny, others were amusing, but all were entertaining. They were unexpected when they happened but that added to the richness of the volunteers' and staff special experiences. The stories enlivened the volunteers and energized them to continue on. Remember the stories.

Remember the comradeship. Within a short period time many of the volunteers were bound at the hip by a common experience of doing something none of them had ever done before. The common experience tied them together. The volunteers and the staff formed thousands of friendships, many of which will last a lifetime. When they get together they continue to share the stories and the adventures of the Great Campaign of 2008. Remember the comradeship.

Remember the buttons and the Button Lady. There were so many—"Dogs for Obama," "Obama-Biden 2008," "Fired Up and Ready to Go!" Many volunteers saved their buttons, stickers and yard signs as mementos of the Great Campaign of 2008. Often the buttons and stickers were so hard to obtain the volunteers purchased them with their own money on the Internet. Remember them all.

Remember the young people. They didn't have to do it but they went into the streets and on the phones to elect Obama President of the United States. They could have stayed at home and played video games or watched television, but many didn't. Some who knocked doors were as young as 8 years old; some 12 years old, others a little older. They threw themselves into the campaign with more energy and verve than most Americans who stayed at home and complained rather than working to change the future. They are the future of the country, our hope that this will be a better place to live. Remember the young people.

Remember the seniors. They were up in age but they worked the campaign like youngsters. Lydia Pokrass was 95 years in 2008 but she registered voters, canvassed her retirement home and held Obama boosting meetings. Barbara Robisheaux canvassed a thousand doors and she was older than 65. Mattie Lassiter was over 65 and she worked the phone bank in the Purcellville Campaign for Change Office. The seniors worked like youngsters and they never complained. They were many; these are only few. They wanted a better America for their children and grandchildren. Remember the seniors.

Remember the understanding. Almost nobody understood what was happening to them during the Great Campaign of 2008 because the events came to them one piece at a time. Only after the whole process was finished could they put all the individual pieces together into a greater understanding. It took time after it was all done to knit all the pieces together into a larger tapestry of what had happened to their lives. Remember the understanding.

Remember the good times. Good to remember the good times—the lunches, the dinners, the parties, the new friends, the adventures in the streets, the post card writing parties and new experiences on the phones. They were all new to us and that made them good because they raised our lives to a new level. Most experiences never compared to this. They were a class unto themselves. Remember the good times.

Remember the Great Campaign of 2008. Great campaigns happen only about every 50 years. Those who came of age in the 1950s say the last one was the John F. Kennedy campaign of 1960. The very young who participated in the Great Campaign of 2008 will probably live to see another one. Most that were older will not. Those who were part of it can never let go of it. It is impossible for them to forget. Remember the Great Campaign of 2008.

Remember the lasting memories. No one knows what will be the final lasting memories from the Great Campaign of 2008. Maybe it will be phone banking out of Franco Luz's office, the Rock Lady running down the streets of Lovettsville; maybe it will be Marianne Bowen and Tim Buchholz in the streets of Ashburn; maybe it will be the Baby Killer Lady in the streets of Leesburg; maybe it will be the Button Lady or the McCain staffer who had given up. More than likely each lasting memory will be different for each person, but everyone will have at least one. This was why it was such a grand experience that will never leave us. Remember the lasting memories.